UNDERSTANDING YOUR ECONOMY: USING ANALYSIS TO GUIDE LOCAL STRATEGIC PLANNING

Mary L. McLean
Kenneth P. Voytek

with

Kevin P. Balfe
Thomas R. Hammer
John F. McDonald

Developed by

NCI Research
The Institute for Urban Economic Development

Planners Press
American Planning Association
Chicago, Illinois   Washington, D.C.

Second Edition
Copyright 1992 by the American Planning Association
122 S. Michigan Ave., Ste. 1600, Chicago, IL 60603

ISBN (paperback edition): 0918286–81–6
ISNB (hardback edition): 0–918286-82-4

Library of Congress Catalog Number: 92–73812

The first edition of this book was published by NCI Research, the Institute for Urban Economic development, in Evanston, Illinois. NCI Research, established in 1986, is a nonprofit research and educational organization affilated with the Kellogg Graduate School of Management at Northwestern University.

CONTENTS

TABLES

FIGURES

vii

FOREWORD

This handbook is a cooperative effort by the Economic Development Administration of the U.S. Department of Commerce, the State of Michigan's Center for Local Economic Competitiveness, and NCI Research of Evanston, Illinois, an organization specializing in economic development research.

Although this handbook is designed to be used in a seminar format, it can also serve as a primer for any person or organization interested in becoming acquainted with widely accepted techniques and data series for analyzing local economies. The success of many of the newer approaches to local and regional economic development—such as industry networking strategies, growth management systems, and small firm incubation—depends on a thorough knowledge of the local economic structure.

Recent innovations in spatially oriented data bases designed to be used on personal computers should facilitate analysis at the local level. The Census Bureau's development of the Topographically Integrated Geographic Encoding and Referencing (TIGER) system for the 1990 census is a prime example of ways the Commerce Department is helping to develop local data base systems. Strategic planning based on such systems and the process outlined in this handbook is bound to improve the competitive posture of local communities.

David H. Geddes
Director
Technical Assistance & Research Division
Economic Development Administration

PREFACE

Because no community is exempt from the forces of economic change, every community sooner or later must wrestle with the unexpected or painful effects of such change on local industries and employers. This handbook is designed to help local planners and policymakers understand and respond to economic changes affecting their community. It presents basic techniques of economic analysis that can be used to 1) analyze changes taking place in the local economy and 2) evaluate their significance for economic development policy. The intent is to build local capacity to undertake economic analysis in support of community "strategic planning," a consensus-building process that involves key segments of a community in joint planning for the area's economic future.

This handbook was developed with the support of the federal Economic Development Administration by NCI Research, the Institute for Urban Economic Development, in cooperation with the State of Michigan Center for Local Economic Competitiveness (CLEC). It distills the experience of NCI Research and CLEC in providing economic analysis services to a variety of communities that have undertaken strategic planning efforts in recent years. The handbook has been developed for individual study or for use in a workshop setting, with sessions corresponding to each handbook chapter (see Appendix D, *Two-Day Training Seminar Format*).

The techniques that are presented in this manual do not require an extensive background in statistics or sophisticated data management skills. They can be accomplished using a personal computer and widely available business planning software. Individuals familiar with basic techniques of social science research or business planning should be able to master them with little difficulty.

Restoring economic health and competitiveness to a community requires commitment, hard work, and a detailed knowledge of the local economy. It also requires the skills and understanding of community leaders. This handbook is a tool to be used in acquiring the knowledge, skills, and understanding necessary for effective economic development decisionmaking. We at NCI Research hope that this handbook will prove a valuable resource for you and for your community.

James E. Peterson
President, NCI Research
Evanston, Illinois

CONTRIBUTORS

KEVIN P. BALFE is a private consultant specializing in labor market policy analysis, employment-training programs and systems analysis and design. Over the past decade, he has performed analyses for organizations including NCI Research, the National Alliance of Business, Fedrau and Associates, and the Office of Technology Assessment of the U.S. Congress, among others. From 1981-83, Mr. Balfe was Director of Policy Development and Evaluation for the National Alliance of Business.

THOMAS R. HAMMER is a consulting economist specializing in economic assessments, feasibility studies, and strategic planning for governmental and corporate clients including, most recently, the General Motors Corporation. As a senior economist at NCI Research, Dr. Hammer concentrated on developing methodologies for local economic analysis and economic development policymaking, including techniques useful in community strategic planning.

JOHN F. MCDONALD is Professor of Economics at the University of Illinois at Chicago. He has taught urban economics and performed research in the field for two decades. As Director of Research at NCI Research from 1988 to 1990, Dr. McDonald developed quantitative applications useful in comparative analysis of local economies and target industry analysis.

MARY L. MCLEAN is an economic development consultant and policy analyst who often writes about development approaches and techniques for a technical audience. She has contributed as a researcher, writer, or editor to publications of organizations including NCI Research, the National Council for Urban Economic Development, the National Task Force on Financing Affordable Housing, the U.S. Conference of Mayors, and the Bureau of Governmental Research at the University of Maryland. Other work has included assignments for corporate, foundation, and governmental clients on issues related to small business development, commercial revitalization, and economically targeted investing.

KENNETH P. VOYTEK is an economist with the Office of Policy Development and Research at the U.S. Department of Housing and Urban Development. Prior to joining HUD, he was an economist with the Center for Local Economic Competitiveness at the Michigan Department of Commerce. His work focuses on economic and community development planning and analysis and on applying policy analysis and evaluation methods to a variety of public policy questions.

1

OVERVIEW OF STRATEGIC PLANNING

The period since the mid-1970s has been marked by fast-paced change in industries, markets, and the nature of competition—change that has been spurred by the globalization of trade, technological advances, and the rise of service and information industries. In the United States, economic restructuring has been accompanied by regional shifts in capital investment, population, and employment. At the local level, some communities have experienced unprecedented growth. Many others have confronted high unemployment and declines in economic activity, brought on by shrinkage in traditional sources of income and employment.

Whether a community finds itself in a strong or weak position in today's economic environment, one thing seems certain—competitive pressures afford little margin for simply maintaining the status quo. To get ahead or stay ahead, a firm or industry needs to be constantly innovating and upgrading—constantly seeking out new markets, better suppliers, improved ways of doing business, more productive uses of human resources—all the things that help maintain a competitive edge. It follows that communities seeking economic growth must look for ways to encourage this type of behavior among the employers and industries that underpin the local economy. This challenge faces areas that have been on the economic upswing in recent years, no less than those wrestling with decline.

In this context, economic development is less and less a matter of offering cost-cutting incentives to lure a firm to a community or induce it to stay there. For one thing, simply reducing a firm's local cost of doing business is unlikely to lead to self-sustaining economic growth. Rather than attempting to influence location decisions on a firm-by-firm basis, forward-looking development agencies are trying to identify and nurture those sectors that can operate at a competitive advantage in the local area. Development strategy then becomes a matter of strengthening important local clusters of related and supporting industries, with explicit emphasis on policies that encourage market leadership and innovation.

This handbook presents techniques that can be used to analyze a local economy, identify industry strengths and weaknesses, and assess local characteristics or "location factors" from the perspective of industry competitive advantage. As outlined below, the various analytical components are designed to support community strategic planning. This is an evaluative decision-making process that involves representatives from various segments of a community in joint planning for an area's economic future.

THE STRATEGIC PLANNING PROCESS

Strategic planning comes to the public and nonprofit sectors via the corporate sector, where it has been employed as a technique for adjusting organizational strategies in response to rapid changes in the external environment. A central issue is how best to deploy resources to maximize the attainment of specified goals. In recent years, strategic planning has become a popular tool for economic development planning in many states and local communities.

As practiced by states and localities, strategic planning is a multi-step decision-making process that relies on data gathering and analysis as a necessary input. Strategic planning is more than analysis, however. It is a way for a community to envision its future and take steps to achieve that future. In addition to identifying strengths and weaknesses of the local economy, strategic planning involves reaching consensus on goals, identifying resources, developing strategies to achieve goals, and agreeing on plans for implementation.

A standard sequence of activities for local strategic planning would include the following analytical and decision-making steps:[1]

1. **Audit the economy**—Evaluate the condition and performance of the local economy; analyze local industrial structure and characteristics of the business base.

2. **Formulate a mission statement**—Identify critical issues and articulate broad goals.

3. **Audit local resources**—Assess labor and non-labor resources; identify locational assets and liabilities in terms of industry competitive advantage and prospects for business investment.

---

[1] See for example Berman (1990), Gregerman (1984), and Swanstrom (1987).

- 2 -

4. **Develop strategy**—Evaluate location characteristics in light of recent trends to identify potential economic opportunities or threats; identify ways to exploit opportunities or minimize threats in order to achieve community economic goals.

5. **Implement action plan**—Develop and pursue a specific plan of action for funding, program operation, etc.

6. **Evaluate results**—Monitor, update, and adjust the plan in response to ongoing change in the economic environment.

The strategic planning process is action-oriented and results should represent a guide for project or program implementation, subject to ongoing monitoring and updating as conditions change. Ideally, the planning process sets the stage for implementation, by involving representatives of key local institutions and interests, both public and private.

ROLE OF ECONOMIC ANALYSIS

Before a community can intelligently develop strategies for economic development, it should understand the nature of the local economy and the area's strengths and weaknesses as a location for economic activity. Analysis, therefore, is an essential element of the strategic planning process. It provides a factual basis for economic development goal setting and strategy development.

It might seem self-evident that economic development policies should reflect a thorough understanding of a community's economy. But data collection and analysis is a demanding process. It is not uncommon for policymakers to feel that they intuitively know how their economy works and what should be done to stimulate economic activity. Alternately, some feel that economic analysis is best left to technically adept experts or "objective" outside consultants, placing little value on community input and insights.

The problem with relying on intuition or outside expertise is that results tend toward superficial explanations and easy rationalizations; there is little motivation to analyze deeply or to reexamine fundamentals. This is unfortunate, because strategic planning is likely to be most effective when it is highly sensitive to the specific needs, resources, and political and institutional environment of a given community. In large part, the usefulness of the analysis depends largely upon the understanding built into it. As author Carl Patton has observed,

> Developing information . . . involves not only collecting data, but also evaluating its relevance and analyzing and communicating its importance . . . . Only when the meaning in a set of data has been discovered and translated into useful concepts does data yield information.[2]

This handbook is designed to encourage community participation in the analytical phase of local strategic planning. It presents a simple, coherent framework for employing data and analytical tools to gain useful insights into the workings of a local economy. The techniques do not require complex statistics or sophisticated data management skills. They can be performed by community development officials or local planners familiar with basic techniques of social science research or business planning.

The focus of the analysis presented here is the so-called "basic" economy, or those activities that generate revenue inflows as a result of sales of goods or services to nonlocal markets. The analysis addresses such critical questions as the following:

- What is the current condition of the local economy?

- Compared to other areas, how has the local economy been performing? Has economic performance strengthened or slackened over time?

- What is the underlying structure of the local economy? Which industries account for the area's economic performance and condition?

- Which local industries appear to be in the strongest competitive position? Which in the weakest?

- What local factors or resources appear to be supporting industry competitive advantage? What factors may be inhibiting it?

- How are larger trends affecting the area's locational assets or liabilities?

The information resulting from this type of analysis can be used to identify steps that a community might take to maximize strengths or minimize weaknesses in order to enhance prospects for economic growth.

---

[2] Carl V. Patton, "Information for Planning," in *The Practice of Local Government Planning*, Ed. Frank S. So and Judith Getzels, Washington, D.C.: International City Management Association, 1988, p.493.

Although economic analysis requires the commitment of staff and resources, it offers significant benefits, among them the following:

- A shared understanding of how a local economy operates and its strengths and weaknesses

- A sound basis for setting realistic goals and objectives and for making effective and intelligent use of limited resources

- Information that can be used to build public awareness and develop consensus on economic development goals and objectives

The role of analysis in strategic planning is not to reveal the ultimate "fix" for a local economy, but to support rational and informed discussion about economic problems and possible solutions in order to reach consensus on preferred policy options.

CHAPTER OVERVIEW

The rest of this handbook introduces readers to analytical techniques that can provide insight into the structure and dynamics of a local economy for purposes of economic development policymaking.

The chapters that follow cover the analytical steps leading up to the implementation phase of community strategic planning (see Figure 1.1). Chapter 2 outlines preliminary considerations that must be addressed in structuring the analysis. The next three chapters cover techniques for conducting an "economic audit," that is, for evaluating the condition, performance, structure, and function of a local economy. Chapter 3 illustrates how to analyze basic population and economic characteristics. The results establish the context for a more in-depth examination of industrial structure, described in Chapter 4. Chapter 5 describes how to flesh out the emerging profile of the local economy by examining industry linkages and organizational characteristics of the local business base.

The information generated by the economic audit should help develop a sense of direction for the planning effort, which can be articulated in a "mission statement." The next phase of strategic planning, the "resource audit," calls for analysis of factors or resources that support local economic activity. People resources have always represented an important local asset and this is especially true today, as the knowledge-intensity of products and services continues to increase. Chapter 6 is devoted to techniques for

Figure 1.1

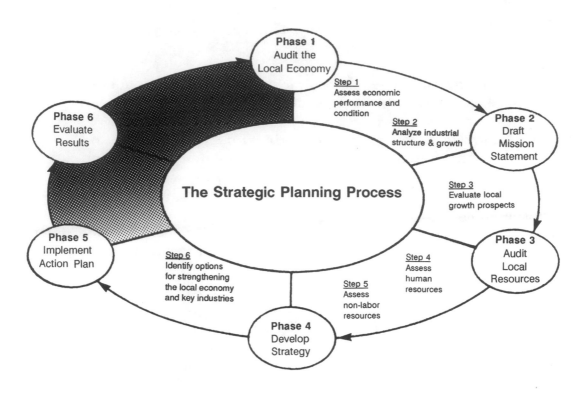

evaluating local human resources, including labor availability, cost, and quality. This is followed in Chapter 7 by an examination of the nonlabor location factors that influence local economic growth prospects and ways they can be assessed. In the final unit, Chapter 8, the focus is on how to bring together the different components of the analysis to identify options for enhancing the competitive advantage of key sectors of the local economy and strengthening the overall environment for business investment.

This manual builds upon technical assistance provided by the Michigan Center for Local Economic Competitiveness and NCI Research to a number of communities that have undertaken strategic planning in recent years. It presents a basic rather than comprehensive treatment of local economic analysis. For those interested in more in-depth coverage or more advanced analytic and quantitative techniques, each chapter is followed by references to additional sources.

Additional Reading

Strategic Planning

For insight on how analysis relates to the larger process of strategic planning, see:

Berman, Norton. *Local Strategic Planning: A Handbook for Community Leaders*. Lansing: Michigan Department of Commerce, 1990.

Gregerman, Alan. *Competitive Advantage: Framing a Strategy to Support High Growth Firms*. Washington, D.C.: National Council for Urban Economic Development, 1984.

Kolzow, David. *Strategic Planning for Economic Development*. Chicago: American Economic Development Council, 1988.

Swanstrom, Todd. "The Limits of Strategic Planning for Cities." *Journal of Urban Affairs* 9 (1987): 139-157.

Methods for Urban and Regional Analysis

For an expanded treatment of urban and regional analysis, including advanced techniques, see:

Isard, Walter. *An Introduction to Regional Science*. Englewood Cliffs, N.J.: Prentice Hall, Inc., 1975.

Krueckberg, Donald A. and Arthur Silvers. *Urban Planning Analysis: Methods and Models*. New York: John Wiley and Sons, 1974.

Richardson, Harry W. *Regional Economics*. Urbana, Ill.: University of Illinois Press, 1979.

STRUCTURING THE ANALYSIS: CONCEPTS AND ISSUES

The objective of local economic analysis is to use data and other empirical information to gain a better understanding of a local economy: its important components, how it has changed and is changing over time, and its strengths and weaknesses as a location for economic activity.

Strategic analysis is as much an art as a science. The analyst will need to exercise careful judgement, beginning with the decisions that establish the framework for the analysis. These preliminary decisions set the parameters for subsequent steps, outlined in the units that follow. There are five broad areas of concern:

- Selecting an appropriate unit of analysis. What constitutes the "local" economy? How is it to be defined for analytical purposes?

- Selecting the time period for analysis. How will trends be established?

- Selecting variables and data elements. What data do you need? What data can you get?

- Establishing a frame of reference for data interpretation.

- Acquiring, updating, and manipulating the data.

Each of these items is discussed in greater detail below.

SELECTING THE UNIT OF ANALYSIS

The first issue in analyzing a local economy is to identify the appropriate geographic unit or area for which the analysis will be conducted. This is one of the most critical yet perplexing questions the analyst will confront. As economist Harry Richardson has observed, "whether one uses economic, administrative, historical, or other criteria, there are no satisfactory methodologies" for defining an economic region.[1]

An inherent challenge for local development policy is the mismatch between economic and political boundaries. The range of impact of economic activity almost never coincides with the jurisdictional boundaries of political units.[2] Spillovers occur in both directions: the policy decisions of one jurisdiction may affect economic activity in adjacent areas, even as economic activity flows easily across jurisdictional lines.

Often the subject of direct interest is the particular city or local jurisdiction that is undertaking the planning effort. Usually it is helpful to assemble as much data as is readily available for the local community conducting the analysis. However, there may be logical as well as pragmatic reasons for focusing on a larger unit of which the subject area is a part.

For example, many residents of small localities find employment outside their town or village lines, just as many city residents find employment in surrounding suburbs and many suburban residents commute to a nearby city. So if the issue is generating employment opportunities for local residents, it is important to analyze the larger area that encompasses the commuting range of residents and reflects their access to employment. The appropriate unit of analysis in such cases is the entire labor market area and not simply the locality where people reside. Similarly, for insights on local industrial structure and economic function, analysis should focus on an economically integrated area rather than an area defined by political boundaries.

Data availability also plays into this question. The federal statistical system provides only limited coverage of geographic areas below the county level. Larger areas, such as economic regions or substate planning districts, can be analyzed by aggregating figures for component counties. However, analysis of municipalities or other units at the sub-county level is often thwarted by the limited frequency and detail of the available data series (see "Selecting Variables and Data Elements," below).

---

[1] Harry W. Richardson, *Regional and Urban Economics*, London: Penguin Books, 1978, p.17.

[2] Though economic boundaries are fluid, political boundaries are typically fixed. In the past, annexation provided a way for municipalities to expand their political boundaries to capture growth in the local economy. Today, few localities have that option, especially in the Northeast and Midwest.

For an initial analysis of a local economy for strategic planning purposes, such as that described here, it is probably appropriate as well as convenient to use counties or county-based economic units as the primary unit of analysis.

Using Counties and County-Based Economic Units (LMAs and MSAs)

The United States is partitioned into some 3,000 counties or administrative equivalents (i.e., towns and villages in New England). Counties have fixed geographic boundaries, reflecting their role as local administrative arms of state government. Their boundary stability, plus the fact that they offer comprehensive coverage of the nation, have made counties the basic local reporting unit of the federal-state data collection system.

For purposes of monitoring economic activity, the federal government has designated counties and county groupings that comprise economically integrated areas. There are two overlapping systems that are especially useful for local area analysis: labor market areas (LMAs) and metropolitan statistical areas (MSAs).

LMAs are designated by the Bureau of Labor Statistics (BLS) of the U.S. Department of Labor for use by states in administering the unemployment insurance program. They are also the unit used by the BLS in reporting key employment and unemployment data. An LMA is defined as "a geographic area consisting of a central community (population or employment center) and contiguous areas which are economically integrated."[3] Economic integration is determined by population density and commuting patterns. Within a labor market area, workers generally can change jobs without changing their place of residence.

LMAs are categorized as "small" or "major." A small LMA is a county or economically integrated group of counties with a central community of at least 5,000 population. Major LMAs are economically integrated counties with a central community of at least 50,000 population. In designating major LMAs, BLS follows the definitions for metropolitan statistical areas (MSAs) used by the Census Bureau and other data collection agencies of the U.S. Department of Commerce (see Appendix A, "Metropolitan Area Definitions").

---

[3] U.S. Department of Labor, Bureau of Labor Statistics, *BLS Handbook of Methods*, Washington, D.C.: U.S. Government Printing Office, 1988.

Unless economic or political issues dictate otherwise, the unit of analysis for strategic planning can be identified as follows:

- If the community has fewer than 2,500 inhabitants or is a township, use the single county containing the subject community.

- If the community is larger than 2,500 inhabitants but not part of an MSA, use the LMA of which it is a part.

- If the community is larger than 2,500 inhabitants and is part of an MSA, use the MSA.

Community-level data can supplement the county-based analysis to the extent that statistics are available and resources permit.

Appendix A provides a list of currently defined MSAs, along with the federal standards that will govern MSA designations in the 1990s.[4] To obtain a current list of LMAs in your state, contact state development agencies or the state agency responsible for administering unemployment insurance.

SELECTING A TIME PERIOD
FOR ANALYZING TRENDS

Analysis of trends helps put data in perspective. Therefore a second issue in beginning the strategic analysis is selecting the time period to examine.

An economy changes over time for two reasons. First, there are cyclical changes related to the national business cycle. These are experienced to some degree by all local economies. Business cycles are thought to be caused by changes or shocks, such as a surge in oil prices, that affect the national economy overall. When the national economy prospers, local economies perform better; when the national economy falters, local economies perform worse. Figure 2.1 displays the historical record of business cycles in the United States, showing a trend toward shorter downswings and more prolonged upswings in the post-WWII period.

---

[4] Since 1980, the federal Office of Management and Budget (OMB) has assumed responsibility for updating the definitions of metropolitan areas including MSAs. The next update, reflecting the results of the 1990 decennial census, is due in autumn 1992. BLS will use the OMB results to update its definitions for small and major LMAs by 1995.

Figure 2.1

200 Years of Booms and Busts

By Geoffrey H. Moore

If all goes well, the U.S. will soon put the finishing touches on its 45th recession. If the current recession, which began in July 1990, ends this summer, as seems likely, its length of about one year will be close to the 11-month average length of the nine recessions during the past 50 years. During the preceding 50 years the average recession took 18 months, while in the two 50-year periods before that, the averages were 25 and 26 months.

The record of business cycles, compiled by the National Bureau of Economic Research, begins in 1790, and shows that the first recession lasted three years, from 1796 to 1799. Many of the early recessions lasted two or three years, but in recent times they have become shorter and less frequent.

This trend can clearly be seen in the chart below. Similarly, there has been a corresponding, and equally dramatic, increase in the length of expansions. The average expansion during the past 50 years lasted 53 months, more than twice the 25-month average for the preceding 50 years. In the two half centuries before that the averages were 31 and 30 months, not much longer than the average recession. The spectacular change was demonstrated by the latest expansion, which ran for 92 months (from November 1982 to July 1990) following a 16-month recession.

Several major developments account for this trend. The economy has become more service-oriented, less dominated by the production of agricultural and manufactured goods, which are subject to wider and more frequent ups and downs. The government plays a bigger role now in maintaining incomes and supporting business and consumer confidence during recessions, by providing unemployment insurance, welfare payments and bank deposit insurance. The Federal Reserve Board, established in 1914, influences interest rates and credit creation in its efforts to stabilize the economy, evidently with some success.

What will the coming expansion look like? The wide variations in the lengths of expansions make forecasting the length of the next one difficult. One thing can be said, however. It will depend to a considerable extent on whether interest rates continue on a downward trend during the recovery, and how long they do so. The record of the prime rate since 1950, for example, shows that if it begins to move up, say, six months after an economic recovery begins, the recovery may last only a couple of years. But if the rise in the prime is postponed for, say, two or three years, the expansion is likely to stretch out to four or five years.

Mr. Moore is director of Columbia University's Center for International Business Cycle Research.

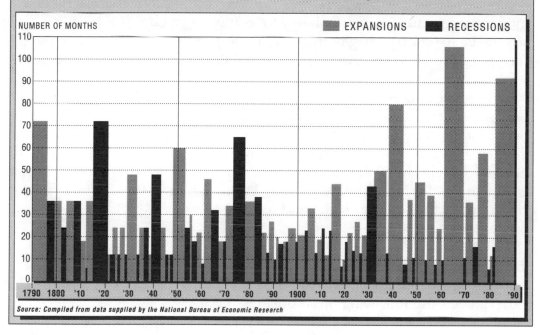

Source: Compiled from data supplied by the National Bureau of Economic Research

Reprinted from Wall Street Journal, August 8, 1991, p. A-12

Local economies also experience long-term (secular) changes in the basic nature and character of local economic activity. Unrelated to national business cycles, secular change is associated with structural shifts affecting industries (such as the shift from manufacturing to service employment) or regions (such as the shift in population from the Midwest to the South and Southwest).

Of course, swings in the national economy can amplify long-term secular change. An example is Michigan's downturn in the late 1970s and early 1980s, when a national recession coincided with the U.S. auto industry's accelerating loss of market share to foreign competition.

Controlling Cyclical Effects

To understand trends in the local economy, the analyst must be able to distinguish between business cycle effects and secular change related to long-term structural shifts. One way to "control" or neutralize business cycle effects is to choose beginning and ending points for the analysis that represent the same relative point in the business cycle (typically the peak).

How can these two time points be identified? One approach is to plot on a graph the area's annual employment totals or unemployment rates over a rather long period of time (10 to 15 years or longer). The analyst can then identify the years when employment was at its highest or the unemployment rate was at its lowest. For example, Figure 2.2 plots employment for the Flint, Michigan, MSA over the 1969-88 time period, clearly depicting cyclical highs and lows.

Alternatively, the U.S. Department of Commerce publishes information on the peaks and troughs of each national business cycle as well as their length. Over the last 21 years the U.S. economy has experienced the following three business cycles:

Peak	Trough	Peak
1969	1970	1973
1973	1975	1979
1979	1982	1989

The analyst can examine how the local economy has performed over each of these three business cycles and can compare performance going into a recession (in 1969-70, 1973-75, 1979-82) and emerging from a recession (in 1970-73, 1975-79, 1982-89).

Figure 2.2
Total Employment, Flint MSA
1968-1986

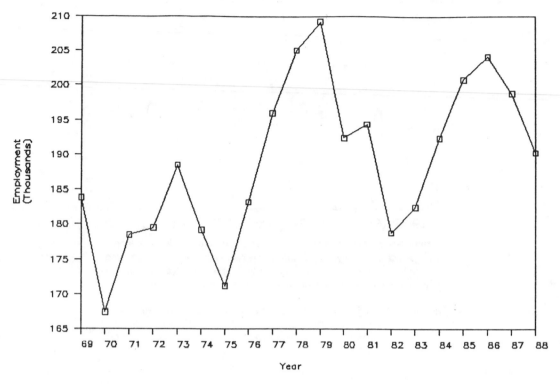

Source: U.S. Department of Commerce, Regional Economic Information System

By examining the entire 1969-89 period, the analyst can also gauge the nature and extent of secular change. In some cases, it may be useful to extend the period of analysis. In the case of Flint, whose highly cyclical economy is tied to the ups and downs of the auto industry, it was necessary to examine local auto industry employment over the entire post-WWII period to discern an overall downward trend since the late 1970s (see Figure 2.3).

To some degree, data availability will dictate the time period or points examined in the analysis, since many data series cover established collection intervals. Differences in the frequency of data collection may mean some variation in the time period of analysis for different types of data. Alternatively, data can be extrapolated to overcome differences in data frequency and obtain a consistent time period.

Figure 2.3
General Motors Employment,
Flint MSA, 1946-1986

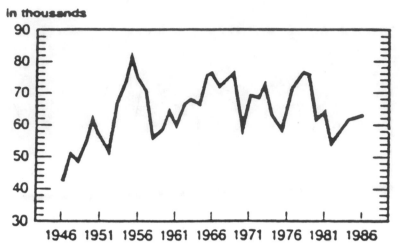

In thousands

Distinguishing cyclical from structural changes takes close observation. In this case, the analyst noted that the 1982-86 auto industry expansion yielded a 1986 employment peak roughly a fifth below typical peaks of the 1960s and 1970s, suggesting long-term (secular) decline.

Source: Michigan Employment Security Commission as reported in Thomas R. Hammer, *Evaluation of Development Potentials for Metropolitan Flint, Michigan*, Evanston, Ill.: NCI Research, 1986, p. 2.

In evaluating the available data from the standpoint of controlling cyclical effects, the analyst must balance other important data considerations such as currency, reliability and level of detail (see below).

SELECTING VARIABLES AND DATA ELEMENTS

The regularly published government data that are most useful for local economic analysis cover the following variables:

- Resident labor force (employment and unemployment)
- Employment (total and by industry)
- Earnings (total and by industry)
- Personal income (total, per capita, major components)
- Population (total and by age group)
- Commuting flows
- Business establishments (distribution by size group)

The chapters that follow illustrate how indicators for these variables may be used in analysis. Also discussed are the types of information that you may need to gather at the local level or from private data sources as the analysis progresses. Here we focus on some of the practical considerations and trade-offs faced in selecting variables. Particularly in local area analysis, variable selection must be tempered by practical considerations of data availability. Much potentially useful data is simply not collected, or at least not collected at the level of detail we would like.

A helpful perspective on this problem was offered by urban analyst and scholar Ann R. Markusen, speaking on the subject of data needs for urban and regional analysis and the limitations of the federal data collection system:

> The ideal database has information along three key dimensions. One is geographic, with possible spatial breakdowns ranging from the nation, to states, to counties or MSAs (which are composed of counties), to cities, to census tracts and census blocks. Another aspect of data is the time dimension, which relates to data frequency and currency as well as the availability of longitudinal data going back in time. The third dimension is the level of detail available for the specific variable under study, such as industry or occupational groupings. . . . The real issue is how highly disaggregated we can get along each dimension. Generally, to get more disaggregation on one dimension you have to give up something on another.[5]

Each of these three aspects of data is considered below.

Spatial Detail

In the earlier discussion about selecting a unit of analysis, we noted limitations on the availability of data for economic analysis at the sub-county level. The only federal source that addresses sub-county areas on a comprehensive basis is the U.S. Census of Population and Housing. Even so, of the data items listed at the beginning of this section, only total population and per capita income are reported for all political jurisdictions, including places of less than 2,500 population and townships. The other items may be obtained on a fragmentary basis if at all, as shown in Table 2.1.

---

[5] Symposium on *Data Needs For Regional Analysis And Economic Development Practice*, October 13-14, 1987, conducted by NCI Research, Evanston, Illinois.

Table 2.1
Data Availability for Sub-County Jurisdictions

	Jobs & Payroll			Commuting		Tot.	Pers.
	Manf.	Trade	Serv.	Out	In	Pop.	Income
Places (City, Town, Village)							
Metropolitan:							
Over 5,000 pop.	X	X	X	X	X	X	X
2,500-5,000 pop.	P	X	X	X	-	X	X
Under 2,500 pop.	-	-	-	-	-	X	X
Nonmetropolitan:							
Over 2,500 pop.	P	X	X	X	-	X	X
Under 2,500 pop.	-	-	-	P	-	X	X
Townships	-	-	-	P	-	X	X

X: Data available
P: Data available for selected jurisdictions
- : Data not available
Source: Thomas R. Hammer, NCI Research, Working paper, 1990.

In contrast, industrially-detailed data on employment and earnings are available on an annual basis for counties from the U.S. Census Bureau (*County Business Patterns*) and the Bureau of Economic Analysis (BEA). Data on employment and unemployment are reported regularly for county-based labor market areas by the Bureau of Labor Statistics (BLS). These circumstances have made counties and county-based aggregates (LMAs and MSAs) the most commonly used geographic unit for local economic studies.

In some cases, such as fiscal or infrastructure issues involving a single local government, there may be an unavoidable need for spatial detail below the county level. Again, the decennial Census of Population and Housing is a basic source of data on population and employment at the municipal or neighborhood level, providing breakdowns to the level of census blocks. However, unlike other data series, the decennial census reports employment on the basis of where workers live rather than where they work (i.e., at-place employment). (See Appendix B for references to 1990 census products.)

In addition, the five-year federal economic censuses provide data on economic activity by industry at the municipal level. The Census of Business provides at-place employment, payroll, and sales data for wholesale and retail trade and selected service establishments in urban places of more than 2,500 population. The Census of Manufactures provides similar information for places with more than 450 manufacturing employees. These statistics are available for every fifth year, with the most recent data available for 1987.

STRATEGIC PLANNING FOR SMALL COMMUNITIES

Economic development studies typically concentrate upon the economic structure of the subject area, with particular attention to its economic strengths and weaknesses relative to other areas. "Strengths" usually mean economic sectors that account for disproportionate shares of the area's employment, or employment growth, or growth potential. "Weaknesses" are industries that are conspicuously lacking in one or more of these respects.

This type of analysis must be approached somewhat differently by smaller communities because of their high levels of economic integration with other areas. For example, small communities are not the best scale for identifying industries that might have high growth potential due to input linkages with other industries. Most input linkages are regional rather than local considerations. For that reason, small communities may need to align themselves with the regional centers of industry growth for industry-specific development initiatives.

The key economic development factors in small communities tend to be site-specific. That is, they involve opportunities for specific types of establishments at specific locations. These opportunities can be influenced by public infrastructure and other potential supportive actions.

To isolate issues for potential action, strategic analysis for small communities can focus on all of the site-specific factors that might cause an establishment to locate or to grow in one place rather than another. If it has not already done so, the community should conduct a land-use and site analysis. This should include a review of policies, regulations, and facilities affecting land use, including zoning ordinances, building and subdivision codes, and transportation systems. Such a survey provides a basis for selecting topics for further consideration, such as industrial development, downtown revitalization, or infrastructure improvements.

Source: Adapted from "Undertaking External and Internal Analyses," by Thomas R. Hammer for NCI Research, in *Local Strategic Planning: A Handbook for Community Leaders*, Norton L. Berman (1990).

Information from the business and manufacturing censuses can be valuable since they cover most of the economic sectors relevant to industrial development, downtown development, and tourism. In the case of manufacturing, industrial detail may be limited due to confidentiality restrictions on disclosure regulations (see discussion of "Industrial Detail" below). Other five-year censuses that are sometimes useful cover government activity, construction, minerals, and agriculture.

From Table 2.1 it is evident that data limitations make it impractical to prepare economic assessments of places under 2,500 population or most townships. In such cases it is necessary to rely on an assessment of the community's home county as an indicator of local conditions (see above, "Strategic Planning for Small Communities").

Timing of Observations

In addition to selecting a time period whose base and terminal years cover roughly similar points in a business cycle, the analyst should make sure that the terminal year is as recent as possible to reflect current conditions (recognizing that even the most current data may be two to three years old).

Frequency affects the currency of the data and their validity as a measure of present conditions. Only a few data series are available on a monthly or annual basis and some are available only on a five- or 10-year basis. For instance, as noted above, the decennial Census of Population contains a wealth of information on population and economic characteristics and is one of the few sources of statistics for sub-county areas. Yet toward the end of each decade, the data are seriously out of date. Clearly, the relevance and reliability of data collected at only five- or 10-year intervals diminishes toward the end of the period, especially if an area has been experiencing rapid change.

However, reliability is affected not only by the frequency of data collection but by coverage. Particularly when working with local-area data, the analyst needs to be aware of the methods used to derive the data. A census is a complete tally of the relevant universe (e.g., population or business establishments). Complete coverage offers the greatest reliability, though results tend to lose currency because it is impractical to conduct a census on a frequent basis. Sample surveys can be undertaken on a more frequent basis and offer more current data; however, their reliability diminishes as the geographic scale gets smaller because the sample size is smaller. Sometimes data are apportioned to smaller geographic areas according to "census share." This method, commonly used in deriving employment and unemployment estimates, bases figures for smaller areas on the share of population each unit comprises of the total. Obviously the analyst must exercise careful judgement as to whether particular data are sufficiently relevant and reliable.

It is often useful to assemble data for a number of points in time (i.e., a time series), rather than relying solely on base-year and terminal-year observations. Intermediate observations provide insight on whether change in a particular economic variable reflects the fortunes of a single firm (i.e., the opening or closing of a major employer) or incremental growth or decline across many firms.

In working with data from prior years, the analyst needs to be aware of how changes in variable definitions or geographic coverage might affect the comparability of the data. For example, metropolitan area boundaries are subject to redefinition; the effects of this type of boundary change (such as the inclusion of additional counties) would need to be taken into consideration when comparing data from before and after the change. Sometimes the data collection agency will update earlier data to conform to revised geography. The analyst should scrutinize the notes to data tables for information on collection or reporting procedures that may affect the geographic comparability of the data from one period to the next. Also problematic are changes in the federal government's industry classification system (see discussion of SIC codes below). Such changes are sometimes required to keep up with changes in the industrial structure of the economy, but they complicate longitudinal analysis—analysis of trends over time. Data reporting agencies may provide methodologies for "cross-walking" the data to ensure comparability.

Industry Detail

The level of detail available for the variables of interest is a third important consideration. Analysis of local economies depends on having detailed data by type of industry. The level of industry detail required will depend on the purpose to be served. If the goal is to examine broad trends in a local economy, highly aggregated data may suffice. On the other hand, a target industry analysis would call for as much industry detail as possible.

The U.S. government has devised a scheme for classifying industries. This scheme is called the Standard Industrial Classification (SIC) code. The coding scheme is based on the primary product or service produced by a business establishment. Figure 2.4 illustrates the SIC coding for a group of industries at progressive levels of detail.

Figure 2.4
The Standard Industrial Classification Scheme

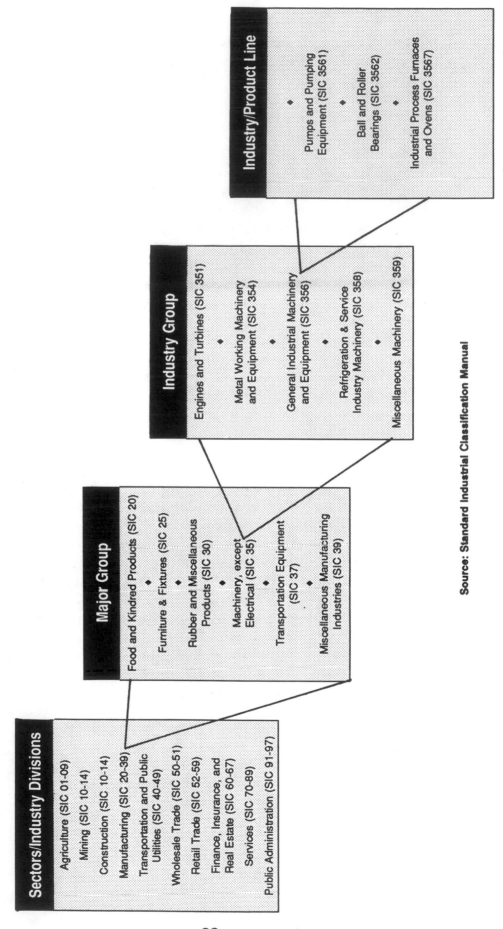

Source: Standard Industrial Classification Manual

The broadest level of industry detail breaks economic activity into ten groupings, commonly referred to as "sectors" or "industry divisions." These are:

- Agriculture
- Mining
- Construction
- Manufacturing
- Transportation, Communication, and Public Utilities (TCU)
- Retail Trade
- Wholesale Trade
- Finance, Insurance, and Real Estate (FIRE)
- Services
- Public Administration (or Governments)

The next level of detail, called "major industry groups," is based on two-digit SIC codes. There are 83 major industry groups currently identified (see "Standard Industrial Classification System," Appendix C). The third level of detail, "industry groups," is based on three-digit SIC codes. The finest level of detail commonly available is based on product lines and is delineated by four-digit SIC codes.

Use of three- and four-digit SIC codes is problematic for examining many local economies due to restrictions on disclosure of data. (Privacy requirements stipulate that data cannot be presented in a way in which an individual firm can be identified.) Sometimes even two-digit industry breakdowns are suppressed. Researchers have devised "gap-filling" estimation procedures that can be used to overcome this problem (see sidebar, "Estimating Undisclosed Data").

Like industries, other variables can be broken down into smaller, more detailed categories for analysis. Income data, occupational data, tax base data, sales data, and wage rate data are often disaggregated. For example, if the taxable value of property in an area has increased by 50 percent over the 1982-89 period, the analyst may want to know the contribution of various property categories—industrial, commercial, residential—to this aggregate change. Clearly, differential rates of change among categories will have different implications for decisionmaking than if growth was uniform.

To summarize, in selecting variables for analysis, the analyst is often pulled in separate directions. On the one hand, there is the desire to be as current as possible so that the analysis reflects present conditions. On the other hand, there is the need to be as accurate and detailed as possible. It

ESTIMATING UNDISCLOSED DATA

The U.S. Census Bureau's *County Business Patterns* (CBP) series is one of the best sources of data on employment by industry at the local level. However, a common problem with the use of CBP data is nondisclosure. Even at the two-digit SIC level, data on employment and payrolls for some industries and some counties are not disclosed to preserve the confidentiality of employers. This problem tends to occur in industries and counties with small employment. But since most MSAs contain at least one small county, some estimate of undisclosed data must be derived before detailed industry analysis can proceed.

Researchers at the Center for Governmental Studies, Northern Illinois University, have devised the following method to estimate nondisclosed CBP data on employment by industry:

1. Create employee-to-establishment ratios for each individual employment-size class for the state for each two-digit SIC code industry.

2. Multiply these state ratios by the establishment count in each employment-size class for the target county.

3. Add the employment counts for each employment-size class across to get an initial estimated employment total for each SIC.

4. Add estimated employment totals in that division (a division is the one-digit SIC code grouping).

5. From the estimated divisional total, subtract the actual employment values in that division (divisional data are always disclosed at the county level) to get the employment residual.

6. Use a proportional adjustment procedure to make the actual and estimated employment values add up to their divisional employment total.

7. Check to make sure that the estimated employment value falls into the employment range given in the original *County Business Patterns* file.

Source: Gardocki, B.C. and Baj, J. *Methodology for Estimating Nondisclosure in County Business Patterns*. DeKalb, Ill: Center for Governmental Studies, Northern Illinois University, 1985.

is often the case that more accurate and detailed data are less current, while more current data are less accurate and detailed. Although there is no hard and fast rule on what to do, it is important for the analyst to recognize these basic conflicts and strike a reasonable balance between conflicting demands.

ESTABLISHING A FRAME OF REFERENCE

Any number generated by the analysis is not absolute—it is only meaningful in a relative sense. As discussed above, comparing values at different points in time is one way to gain perspective. Another is to compare the economy of the local area to that of other areas. Still another is to compare across different data series or variables.

Using Comparison Areas

Comparisons to other areas help identify what is special about a local economy. At a minimum, the analyst should compare the local economy to the state and national economies. When the data are available, comparisons to the economies of other nearby counties are also helpful. Alternatively, a metropolitan area could be compared to other metropolitan economies in the state, or a rural area to other rural areas. For example, an analysis of the economy of Michigan's remote Upper Peninsula examined how that region performed relative to nonmetropolitan areas in lower Michigan, the Great Lakes regions, and the United States.

Comparison areas can also be selected by identifying areas that are comparable to the local area in key respects (e.g., population size, industrial structure, proximity to other metropolitan areas). It is most helpful to select comparison areas on the basis of similarity at an earlier point in time. This type of matching "controls" important explanatory factors. By comparing the performance of similar economies over the same time period, the analyst can often discern distinctive features of the local economy.

This kind of cross-area comparison is more time consuming and requires more data than some of the others, but it may be the most useful type of comparison for understanding a local economy. The criteria used to identify comparison areas for an economic analysis of Flint, Michigan, are shown in the box below.

Comparing Across Variables

Often, insight can be gleaned from a particular data element if it is related to other data elements. For example, it may be useful to examine unemployment rates in the context of changes in population. In one instance, an area had been exhibiting persistently high unemployment rates in recent years, suggesting a stagnant, declining area economy. However, further investigation revealed that the region has experienced significant

IDENTIFYING COMPARISON AREAS
FOR FLINT, MICHIGAN

In a study of the economy of the Flint MSA, which includes surrounding Genesee County, 21 comparable city-county areas were identified based on the following criteria:

1. Location in the northeastern or north central United States
2. MSA status as federally-defined
3. Rough comparability in terms of size (1984 population size between .25 and 1.75 that of Genesee County)
4. Historic dependence on manufacturing (or manufacturing in combination with mining)
5. Proximity to a much larger metropolitan area with a more diverse economy

To meet the fourth criteria, areas were required to have had an manufacturing employment share exceeding 60 percent in 1947. The overall comparison area average of 66 percent was much closer to the Flint figure of 71 percent than to the U.S. average of 46 percent. Thus, the comparison areas—termed "satellite industrial cities"—were cities that generally resembled Flint at the end of World War II.

Characteristics of Flint
Versus Other Satellite Cities

	1947 Manufacturing Share of Private Empl.		1984 Population (thousands)
	Average	Range	
Flint (Genesee)	71%	—	434
Comparison Areas:			
Large	66%	60-72%	500-775
Medium	66%	64-69%	275-500
Small	68%	60-76%	120-275
United States	46%	—	—

In the sample analysis presented in Unit 3, the large and medium satellite industrial cities are used in making economic comparisons. Arrayed by region, they include the following MSAs:

New England MSAs	Pennsylvania MSAs	Midwest MSAs
Springfield-Holyoke-Chicopee	Allentown-Bethlehem-Easton	Youngstown-Warren
Worcester-Fitchburg-Leominster	Scranton-Wilkes Barre	Akron
New Haven-Waterbury	Reading	Gary-Hammond-E. Chicago
Manchester-Nashua	York	Canton
Fall River-New Bedford		Rockford

growth in both employment and population, contradicting the apparent stagnation. The high unemployment rate resulted because people were moving into the area at a rate faster than jobs were being created.

Data from different series can also be combined to produce measures that shed additional light on an issue. For example, data on retail sales, income, and population could be used to develop a series of ratios providing insight into retail sales trends (e.g., per capita retail sales, retail sales as a percent of total income).

The basic message is that data will need to be interpreted in light of other data. Much of the information generated in the analysis must be evaluated in comparison to the same data for other areas and in relation to other variables.

ACQUIRING, UPDATING, AND MANIPULATING DATA

Recent advances in technology have significantly reduced the burden of analyzing local economies. Computers, especially personal computers, allow data to be stored, retrieved, manipulated, and updated with ease. Microcomputers mean you can do this at your desktop almost as soon as new information is available.

A wealth of information is now available in a variety of forms ranging from printed documents, to computer tapes, to floppy diskettes, to new high-density storage disks (CD-ROM). Software packages are available to help the analyst update, organize, and manipulate the data and produce standard reports. Advances in communications technology, such as modems, provide access to a variety of on-line data bases that expand the readily available universe of data and information.

All of the techniques, tabular displays of data, and graphics presented in this handbook can be accomplished by most microcomputers with a minimal level of software. Spreadsheets can be extremely useful for the sometimes tedious calculations associated with economic analysis. The number-crunching software we used primarily was Lotus 1-2-3. Any of the other commonly available spreadsheet programs (e.g., Multiplan, Microsoft Excel) or database software (e.g., dBase) could be used as well. For those who are more daring, Basic programs can be written to perform many of the same procedures. The data used in our studies were entered by hand in most cases.

The use of spreadsheet templates—programs written on existing software—permit development of standardized reports that can be modified as changes occur and data are updated. However, there is considerable risk in using others' programs or templates mechanistically, without an understanding of the underlying concepts, theories, and assumptions.

Finally, it is important to have a good graphics package to help display the data. The old adage—a picture tells a thousand words—applies strongly here, as many among the intended audience may have difficulty interpreting tables of numbers. Visual displays of data are a more effective way to communicate the findings.

Data Sources

The creation of on-line databases by federal data collection agencies as well as by many state units greatly simplifies the task of acquiring data. These sources offer access to a large body of data that can be easily downloaded to a microcomputer at a significant time saving. As a result, they facilitate the comparative analysis that is central to strategic analysis. References to major sources of published data for local economic analysis and descriptions of data offerings are provided in Appendix B.

Other potential sources of information and data include local libraries, local economic development organizations, planning agencies, and state departments. A growing number of universities have units that provide data and information to interested parties. Prior studies performed for an area are also worth consulting.

Additional Reading

Data Sources

For a comprehensive review of data useful for local economic development and a reference to sources, see this excellent compilation:

> Neithercut, Mark E. et al. *Local Economic Development Research: A Guide to Data Sources*. Detroit: Wayne State University, Center for Urban Studies, 1989.

Working With Data

For an overview by experienced analysts of what can and cannot be accomplished with the data presently available for local and regional analysis, see:

> NCI Research. *Data Needs For Regional Analysis And Economic Development Practice: Symposium Proceedings*. Evanston, Ill.: NCI Research, 1988.

For information on the design and use of computer programs applicable to strategic analysis, see:

> Ottensmann, John R. *Basic Microcomputer Programs for Urban Analysis and Planning*. New York: Chapman and Hall, 1986.

> Sawicki, David. "Microcomputer Applications in Planning." *Journal of the American Planning Association*. 50 (Spring 1985): 209-215.

For examples and a discussion of common practices and pitfalls in using graphics for statistical displays, see:

> Simpson, Jeff L. *Visual Display of Statistics*. Applied Community Research Monograph CS-5. Alexandria, Va.: American Chamber of Commerce Researchers Association, 1989.

> Tufte, Edward R. *The Visual Display of Quantitative Information*. Cheshire, Conn.: Graphics Press, 1983.

CHAPTER

3

ASSESSING ECONOMIC PERFORMANCE AND CONDITION

The first step in strategic analysis is to examine the overall economic performance and condition of a local economy. This preliminary assessment provides essential background information and suggests directions for the rest of the analysis.

At this stage the focus is on broad indicators of local economic vitality. Key questions to answer include the following:

- Compared to other areas, how has the local economy performed over time in terms of employment growth?

- How does the current local unemployment rate compare to that of other areas?

- How do earnings per worker in the local economy compare to those elsewhere?

- What do income and population trends indicate about the local economy?

In beginning to examine and evaluate a local economy, the analyst should consider how various broad indicators of economic activity have changed over time and in comparison to other areas. Often overlooked, these types of comparisons are invaluable during the preliminary assessment. Much of the subsequent analysis will focus on understanding the reasons for the local economy's relative performance and condition.

MEASURING ECONOMIC PERFORMANCE AND CONDITION

Before we turn to the variables and indicators useful in assessing local economic performance and condition, it is important to define these two terms more precisely. Economic *performance* measures *changes over time* in important indicators of economic activity within a local economy. It is a dynamic measure of how well or poorly an economy has performed. Economic *condition* measures the *level* of important indicators of economic activity at a particular *point in time*. It is a static measure of how well or poorly an economy is (or was) doing at that time point.

Selecting Variables

What variables should be used to gauge the performance and condition of a local economy? At a minimum, the analysis should employ indicators for the following variables, which are routinely covered by published data sources:

- Employment, which indicates a local economy's ability to retain and create jobs

- Unemployment, which indicates a local economy's ability to use human resources efficiently

- Earnings from employment, which indicates the quality of jobs in a local economy

- Area income, which indicates revenues circulating within the economy from all sources

- Population, which influences local demand for goods and services as well as local labor force characteristics

Other useful data might include tax base value, industry output (e.g., value-added), investment, new business starts, construction permit value, and so forth. However, problems of data availability and reliability may thwart use of such variables. Keep in mind that the objective of this part of the analysis is to assess and gauge the performance and condition of a local economy and not necessarily to judge the well-being of area citizens, although the two are closely related. Thus variables such as welfare dependency or income distribution, while important, are not the focus at this stage.

Developing Indicators

Once variables have been selected, the next step is to collect the relevant data for a local economy and for the comparison areas. To the extent that comparable longitudinal data are available, data should be assembled to measure long-term change (e.g., figures for change over more than one business cycle) as well as change associated with business cycles (e.g., figures for years that represent cyclical highs and lows). The years corresponding to national business cycle peaks and troughs, identified earlier in Unit 2, are used in the analysis below.

The assembled data can be loaded into a spreadsheet and formulas developed to calculate specific indicators (such as percentage changes). For example, to examine the *performance* of a local economy relative to other areas, the following indicators should be derived (at a minimum):

- Percentage change in employment

- Percentage point change in the unemployment rate

- Percentage change in total earnings and earnings per worker

- Percentage changes in personal income, population and per capita income

To assess local economic *condition*, you must know the level of key indicators at specific points in time. Data on employment, unemployment, and earnings per worker for the most current year and past years can be compiled and evaluated with reference to other areas to determine whether the local area's economic condition has become relatively better or worse over time.

Deriving Annual Growth Rates. When comparing time periods of different lengths, it is important to adjust the data accordingly. For instance, assume we find that employment in an area grew by 25 percent from 1973 to 1979 and by 30 percent from 1979 to 1988. At first glance, it might seem that the area experienced stronger performance growth in the later period. However, the two time periods are of different lengths: the 1973-79 period covers six years while the 1979-88 period covers nine years. The growth rates must be adjusted to compensate for this difference.

One way to compensate for differences in the length of time periods is to derive annual rates of growth. "Annualization" converts the percentage change in a variable over a period of time into its equivalent annual rate (see box below, "Deriving Annual Growth Rates"). This procedure, which can be carried out with a spreadsheet program, is essentially a modification of the formula for calculating present value.

DERIVING ANNUAL GROWTH RATES
Annualizing vs. Averaging

Annualized Growth Rate

"Annualization" is a method for deriving the annual growth rate over a given period, so that growth over periods of different length can be compared. It is a more precise method than averaging (see below), because it takes into account the incremental change in the base amount from year to year. The annualized growth rate is always slightly lower than the rate produced by averaging (sometimes considerably lower if growth rates are really high).

The basic formula for deriving annualized growth rates is:

$$Emp_t = Emp_b (1 + r)^n$$

where:

Emp_t = terminal year employment
Emp_b = base year employment
n = number of annual intervals in the time span
r = growth rate over each interval

To take an example, assume that from 1973 to 1979 employment increased 25 percent (from 20,000 to 25,000) and that from 1979 to 1988 it increased 30 percent (from 25,000 to 32,500). To find the compound annual growth rate for each period, one more piece of information is required: the number of years (or other time intervals) covered in each period. The 1973-79 period covers six years of change while the 1979-88 period covers nine years. Solve for r as follows:

1973-79 period

$$Emp_{1979} = Emp_{1973} * (1 + r)^6$$
$$Emp_{1979}/Emp_{1973} = (1 + r)^6$$
$$25,000/20,000 = (1 + r)^6$$
$$\sqrt[6]{1.25} = 1 + r$$
$$1.0379 = 1 + r$$
$$.0379 = r$$

(Note: * means multiply)

Another, more straightforward, approach is to derive a simple average annual rate of growth by dividing the percentage growth over the period by the number of years in the period. Though technically less accurate than compound annual growth rates, it is easier to calculate (see box above).

If we convert to a percentage and round off, the annualized rate of growth over the period was 3.8 percent. Plugging in numbers for the 1979-88 period, we find that the annualized rate of growth was only 3.0 percent:

1979-88 period

$$Emp_{1988} = Emp_{1979} * (1 + r)^9$$
$$Emp_{1989}/Emp_{1979} = (1 + r)^9$$
$$32,500/25,000 = (1 + r)^9$$
$$\sqrt[9]{1.30} = 1 + r$$
$$1.0296 = 1 + r$$
$$.0296 = r$$

The data indicate a slackening of growth in the recent period compared to the 1973-79 period.

In the equation above, the "nth" root can be derived in several ways:

- Spreadsheet programs and some calculators can perform the necessary calculations.

- Published tables give the roots of different numbers.

- It can be estimated by adjusting downward from the *average* annual rate of growth, which is always slightly higher.

Average Annual Growth Rate

A simple, non-compounded annual average can be derived by dividing the growth rate for the period by the number of years in the period. For example, a 25 percent growth rate over a six-year period would average 4.2 percent growth per year (25/6 = 4.2). Employment growth of 30 percent over a nine-year period would result in an annual average growth rate of 3.3 percent (30/9 = 3.3).

Adjusting for Price Changes. For those indicators denominated in dollars, it may be useful to adjust monetary values to "control" price changes. For example, one recent study of a two-county area found that total earnings rose by 152 percent over the 1973-88 time period. After adjusting for inflation, however, it was apparent that total earnings had fallen by six percent in "real" terms. "Real" values refer to inflation-adjusted dollar amounts and "nominal" values refer to dollar amounts that have not been adjusted for inflation.

ADJUSTING FOR INFLATION

This example illustrates how monetary values can be adjusted for inflation to arrive at comparable data for different points in time.

Assume that in the area under study, earnings per worker were $10,000 in 1979, $15,000 in 1982, and $20,000 in 1988. Also assume that the price index we are using states that the price index was 75 in 1979, 100 in 1982, and 160 in 1988. In this case, 1982 is given as the "base" year (the year when the index equals 100). To convert the nominal dollar amounts in each year to constant 1982 dollars, divide as shown in the table below:

(1982 = 100)

Year	Nominal Value	Price Index	Conversion Adjustment	Real Value (Constant $)
1979	$10,000	75	$10,000/0.75	$13,333
1982	15,000	100	15,000/1.0	15,000
1988	20,000	160	20,000/1.6	12,500

In this example, earnings per worker over the 1979–88 period rose by 100 percent in nominal dollars:

$$(\$20,000 - \$10,000)/\$10,000 = 1.0$$

But in real terms, earnings per worker fell by 6.2 percent:

$$(\$12,500 - \$13,333/\$13,333 = -.062$$

There are several price indices available for use in making inflation adjustments, including the Consumer Price Index (CPI), the Personal Consumption Expenditure (PCE) index, and the Gross National Product (GNP) deflator, among others.[1]

---

[1] This discussion addresses changes in price levels but does not address differences in the cost of living among areas, which can have a bearing when interpreting differences in earnings. Unfortunately, there is little reliable information available on cost of living differentials except for the largest metropolitan areas. However, the American Chamber of Commerce Researchers Association (ACCRA) publishes a quarterly report on cost of living indices for participating Chambers of Commerce which may pick up smaller rural and metropolitan counties. Call ACCRA *Cost-of-Living Index* Hotline (703-998-4172) to request information.

The basic process for adjusting monetary variables is relatively straightforward and can be built into the formulas developed for a spreadsheet. It involves converting the nominal dollar amounts for each year to "constant" dollars according to index values for that year (see the box, "Adjusting for Inflation"). The calculation of percentage changes will then be expressed in real terms.

COMPARING ECONOMIC PERFORMANCE AND CONDITION

It is important to remember that numbers must be placed in context; comparisons over time, between reference areas, and between indicators serve as the cornerstone of the analysis.

Differences across indicators should be interpreted with care. Because of the vagaries of data collection, small-area data are best used "for general comparisons and trends but not for precise comparisons."[2] To take an example, slight differences in local unemployment rates (e.g., less than one percentage point) may simply represent measurement imperfections.

Below we illustrate how to examine economic performance and condition in terms of five indicators—total employment, unemployment rates, earnings per worker, area personal income, and population. The study area and comparison areas are the metropolitan areas identified earlier in Unit 2. They are traditional manufacturing centers or "satellite industrial cities" selected for their structural similarity to the study area economy (Flint/Genesee County). Comparisons are also made to the United States as a whole and to the state (Michigan) that includes the study area.

Employment Comparisons

Table 3.1 presents data on total employment for selected years during the 1973-89 period, encompassing the past two business cycles. As shown in the middle panel, the selected years permit comparisons of employment change over the entire period, over the two component business cycles (1973-79 and 1979-88), and over periods leading into and out of the recession of the early 1980s. The bottom panel shows the average annual rate of growth over the entire period and over each of the component business cycles.

---

[2] Lorna Monti, "The Uses and Misuses of Metropolitan Area Employment and Unemployment Numbers," in *Economic and Business Issues of the 1980's*, J.E. Pluta, ed., University of Texas at Austin: Bureau of Business Research, 1980, p.96.

Table 3.1
Analysis of Employment Growth

A. Total Employment, Selected Years

	1973	1979	1982	1989
United States	96,854,200	111,631,900	112,565,400	136,074,700
Michigan	3,813,662	4,204,344	3,773,379	4,666,473
Comparison areas:[a]				
Midwest	208,399	223,361	200,555	224,874
Pennsylvania	205,367	216,060	209,884	242,688
New England	242,582	266,211	263,353	323,516
Study Area	188,492	209,205	178,781	195,835

B. Percentage Change in Total Employment, by Stage in the Business Cycle

	Long-term 1973-89	Prior Cycle 1973-79	Recent Cycle 1979-89	Downturn 1979-82	Recovery 1982-89
United States	40.5	15.3	21.9	0.8	20.9
Michigan	22.4	10.2	11.0	-10.3	23.7
Comparison areas:[b]					
Midwest	7.9	7.2	0.7	-10.2	12.1
Pennsylvania	18.2	5.2	12.3	- 2.9	15.6
New England	33.4	9.7	21.5	- 1.1	22.8
Study Area	3.9	11.0	- 6.4	-14.5	9.5

C. Annualized Rate of Employment Growth, by Period

	Long-term 1973-89	Prior Cycle 1973-79	Recent Cycle 1979-89
United States	2.1	2.4	2.0
Michigan	1.3	1.6	1.0
Comparison areas:[c]			
Midwest	0.5	1.2	0.1
Pennsylvania	1.0	0.8	1.2
New England	1.8	1.6	2.0
Study Area	0.2	1.8	-0.7

[a] Average of totals reported for selected MSAs in each region
[b] Average of employment change computed for selected MSAs in region
[c] Annualized rates based on regional average employment change reported in Part B

Source: U.S. Department of Commerce, Bureau of Economic Analysis, *Regional Economic Information System*.

Over the entire 1973-89 period, employment in the study area increased by only 3.9 percent, substantially lagging employment growth in the nation and state, as well as in the Pennsylvania and New England comparison areas. Only the midwestern comparison areas exhibited a similarly weak long-term performance.

Comparing the study area's performance over the past two business cycles, we see that relatively strong employment growth in the prior 1973-79 period was followed by net decline in the more recent 1979-89 period. No other area experienced a net employment decline in the most recent business cycle. However, the midwestern comparison areas experienced stagnation, while employment growth in both Michigan and the Pennsylvania comparison areas substantially trailed the nation. Only the New England comparison areas kept pace with employment growth in the nation as a whole. An examination of performance going into and coming out of the 1982 recession shows that the study area experienced the strongest downturn of any of the areas, followed by the weakest recovery.

It has been suggested that the most recent business cycle was not as robust as previous cycles. Indeed, the annual growth rates displayed at the bottom of Table 3.1 show that the job-generating performance of the nation and Michigan fell off in the recent period. This pattern, which was especially pronounced in the study area, also held true for the midwestern comparison areas. In contrast, the job-generating performance of the New England and Pennsylvania comparison areas improved in the most recent period.

These data suggest that the recession in 1982 amplified structural changes taking place in economies dominated by heavy industry, such as autos or steel. The auto industry, for example, which has traditionally dominated in Michigan and the study city, has extreme "boom and bust" swings over the course of a business cycle. Areas that are tied to such highly cyclical industries can be expected to suffer more during recessionary downturns, but they should also experience stronger recoveries. Over the last business cycle, Michigan, Flint, and the midwestern comparison areas did experience a much sharper downturn than the nation or the other comparison areas, but not a proportionately stronger recovery—a sign of long-term decline. The comparison areas in Pennsylvania and New England suffered less during the 1979-82 downturn, with the New England areas exceeding national employment growth during the recovery. One possible explanation is that these comparison areas have been more successful in reducing their dependence on highly cyclical heavy industries that have been declining in recent years.

Unemployment Rates

Unemployment data can provide further insights during initial cross-area comparisons. Current unemployment data are available from the U.S. Labor Department's Bureau of Labor Statistics (BLS) and state employment commissions.

Table 3.2 presents data on unemployment rates, changes in unemployment rates, and the average unemployment rate for the study area, comparison areas, the state, and the nation over the 1979-89 business cycle. Also shown is the annual unemployment rate in the most recent year for which data are available (1990).

Current Unemployment Rate. The unemployment rate at a recent point in time provides a measure of economic condition. As shown in the top panel of Table 3.2, the study area's 1990 unemployment rate was higher than that of any of the comparison areas. It also exceeded that of the state, which in turn exceeded the national unemployment rate by more than two percentage points. One issue to explore in subsequent analysis is what aspects of the study area economy (e.g., unusually high wage rates) may contribute to attracting and retaining surplus workers.

Interestingly, although the study area had the highest 1990 unemployment rate among the areas examined, it was the only one to experience a drop in the unemployment rate from 1989. The reasons for this anomalous performance also merit attention in subsequent analysis.

Average Unemployment Rate. A comparison of average unemployment rates (middle panel Table 3.2) shows that unemployment rates in the study area remained higher than those elsewhere throughout the 1979-89 period. Again, a regional dimension is evident in that unemployment rates in Michigan and the midwestern comparison areas are consistently higher than those in the Pennsylvania and New England comparison areas. The study area averaged double-digit unemployment rates throughout the 1979-89 period, which again raises the issue of what might account for its 1990 decline into single digit unemployment for the first time in more than a decade.

Percentage Point Change in Unemployment. The bottom panel of Table 3.2 shows percentage point change in the unemployment rate for the areas under examination.[3] This provides another measure of economic performance that can supplement the analysis of employment change.

---

[3] When a measure is already a percentage—such as unemployment rates—then change can be expressed as the difference between the values for the measure at two different times. This value is called "percentage *point*" change.

Table 3.2
Analysis of Unemployment Rates

A. Annual Unemployment Rate, Selected Years

	1979	1981	1982	1983	1984	1985	1986	1987	1988	1989	1990
United States	5.8	7.5	9.5	9.5	7.4	7.1	6.9	6.1	5.4	5.2	5.4
Michigan	7.8	12.3	15.5	14.2	11.2	9.9	8.8	8.2	7.6	7.1	7.5
Comparison areas:											
Midwest	6.2	10.5	NA	14.7	11.2	9.9	9.8	8.8	6.7	5.9	6.1
Pennsylvania	6.6	8.7	10.9	11.3	8.5	7.9	6.9	5.4	4.8	4.5	5.6
New England	5.0	6.7	8.4	7.3	5.0	4.5	4.2	3.4	3.4	4.2	6.5
Study Area	8.9	15.1	20.8	16.6	11.8	12.3	10.6	12.2	14.2	10.4	9.8

B. Average Unemployment Rate, by Period

	Recent Cycle 1979-89	Downturn 1979-82	Recovery 1983-89
United States	7.7	9.9	6.8
Michigan	10.3	11.9	9.6
Comparison areas:			
Midwest	9.9	10.8	9.6
Pennsylvania	7.5	8.7	7.0
New England	5.2	6.7	4.6
Study Area	13.3	14.9	12.6

C. Percentage Point Change in Unemployment, Selected Periods

	1979-89	1979-82	1982-89
United States	-0.6	3.7	-4.3
Michigan	-0.7	7.7	- 8.4
Comparison areas:			
Midwest	-0.3	NA	NA
Pennsylvania	-2.1	4.3	-6.4
New England	-0.8	3.4	-4.2
Study Area	1.5	11.9	-10.4

Source: Bureau of Labor Statistics, *Employment and Earnings*, May issue, selected years.
Note: BLS began reporting monthly unemployment figures for local areas in 1975; annual averages, reported since 1981, are published in May. The Department of Labor's reporting methodology changed significantly in 1982 and then again to a lesser degree in 1988, affecting the comparability of the data for longitudinal analysis. As a result of the 1982 changes, figures were unavailable for comparison cities in the Midwest. Figures for 1980 were unavailable on an annual basis and are omitted here for simplicity's sake, though they could be calculated from the monthly figures if deemed necessary.

The study area was the only one to experience a net increase in its unemployment rate over the 1979-89 period. The volatility of the study area economy is evident in the large rise in the unemployment rate during the 1979-82 downturn and the relatively large decline in the unemployment rate during the recovery (which was still not large enough to offset the prior rise). In all of the other areas, the unemployment rate declined over the 1979-89 period, with the Pennsylvania comparison areas experiencing the largest percentage point reduction in the unemployment rate and the midwestern comparison areas the least.

Economic performance translates into changes in an area's relative economic condition. Among the comparison areas, the New England areas averaged the lowest unemployment rates in both 1979 and 1989, indicating relatively strong condition. The midwestern areas, however, averaged lower unemployment rates than the Pennsylvania comparison areas in 1979, but higher unemployment rates in 1989. Their economic condition had worsened in relative terms. The relative condition of the study area as measured by unemployment rates also worsened—from measuring 1.3 to 1.75 times the rate for the other comparison areas in 1979, to measuring 1.75 to 2.5 times the others in 1989.

Total Earnings and Earnings Per Worker

Earnings, like employment, are an important measure of local economic activity. Total earnings are one important component of total area personal income and the amount of wealth available for purchases of goods and services. In combination with employment data, earnings data can also provide insight on local wage structure and the relative concentration of employment in high- and low-paying industries. Earnings per worker may also provide insight on equilibrating forces at work in the local economy since earnings levels, like population migration, are one way that labor supply and demand are brought into balance.

Table 3.3 displays data on total earnings and earnings per worker (total earnings divided by total employment) for three points in time—1973, 1979, and 1989. In the study area, earnings per worker have remained considerably higher than elsewhere, despite declining somewhat in the recent 1979-89 period.

The second panel of Table 3.3 shows that Flint, like Michigan and the midwestern comparison areas, has experienced a long-term decline in earnings per worker over the 1973-89 period. In Flint and the midwestern comparison areas, earnings per worker did not begin to decline until the

Table 3.3
Earnings Comparisons
(Constant $ 1982)

A. Total Earnings and Earnings per Worker, Selected Years

	1973		1979		1989	
	Total Earnings	Earnings per Worker	Total Earnings	Earnings Per Worker	Total Earnings	Earnings Per Worker
United States	$1,760,794,879	$18,180	$1,991,168,468	$17,837	$2,638,807,042	$19,392
Michigan	82,872,652	21,730	89,491,014	21,285	98,870,587	21,187
Comparison areas:[a]						
Midwest	4,222,937	20,264	4,586,688	20,535	4,348,118	19,336
Pennsylvania	3,533,707	17,207	3,749,016	17,352	4,540,392	18,709
New England	4,152,443	17,118	4,297,063	16,142	6,335,692	19,584
Study Area	4,630,828	24,568	5,295,852	25,314	4,643,562	23,712

B. Percentage Changes in Earnings, by Period

	Long-Term Change, 1973-89		Prior Cycle, 1973-79		Recent Cycle, 1979-89	
	Total Earnings	Earnings Per Worker	Total Earnings	Earnings Per Worker	Total Earnings	Earnings Per Worker
United States	49.9	6.7	13.1	-1.9	32.5	8.7
Michigan	19.3	-2.5	8.0	-2.0	10.5	-0.5
Comparison areas:[a]						
Midwest	3.0	-4.6	8.6	1.3	-5.2	-5.8
Pennsylvania	28.5	8.7	6.1	0.8	21.1	7.8
New England	52.6	14.4	3.5	-5.7	47.4	21.3
Study Area	0.3	-3.5	14.4	3.0	-12.3	-6.3

[a] Average of totals reported for selected MAs in each region

Source: Bureau of Economic Analysis, Regional Economic Information System. Figures are in constant 1982 dollars, adjusted using the GNP price deflator as reported each year for the prior two years in the April issue of BEA's *Survey of Current Business.*

---

most recent 1979-89 period, coinciding with stagnating or declining employment. In contrast, the comparison areas in New England and Pennsylvania, which experienced earnings decline or stagnation in the prior 1973-79 business cycle, performed somewhat better in terms of growth in earnings per worker in the most recent cycle. Thus the New England comparison areas, which averaged the lowest earnings per worker of any of the three comparison areas in 1973 ($17,118) had the highest in 1989 ($19,584).

Weaving various indicators together reveals patterns that bear further investigation. For instance, if an area is experiencing robust employment growth even while it is experiencing a decline in earnings per worker, as occurred in the U.S. and in Michigan during the 1973-79 period, it is likely that employment gains are occurring primarily in lower-paying industries and occupations.

Income and Population Characteristics

Employment and earnings from employment are important indicators of local economic activity, but employment is not the only source of income in a local economy. Comparisons of income from all sources can highlight features of the local economy that may have a bearing on local development prospects. The personal income statistics available from BEA are reported along with population totals and per capita income figures, making it convenient also to consider these two variables along with income.

Table 3.4 presents breakdowns of total area personal income for the nation, the state (Michigan), the comparison areas (satellite industrial cities), and the study area (Flint). The table shows figures for 1979 and 1989 and 1979-89 percentage changes.

Components of Personal Income. The three major categories of personal income are 1) gross earnings by place of work, 2) adjustments to earnings, and 3) unearned income. The earnings figures reported by BEA include wage and salary payments, self-employment income, and "other labor income" such as gratuities and the cash value of employee benefits.

Adjustments to earnings convert earnings data from a gross, place-of-work basis to a net, place-of-residence basis. Gross earnings become net earnings by subtracting out personal contributions to social security (FICA). This item in an income account is, therefore, always negative. The second adjustment, which recognizes commuting flows, equals the earnings of area residents from working elsewhere minus the earnings of nonresidents who work in the local area. This commuting adjustment can be either positive or negative. It tends to be inconsequential for the U.S. and large regions, but it can be very important for small areas.

The third income category, unearned income, covers personal income derived from all sources other than current participation in the labor force. Unearned income has become very important in the U.S. economy, now accounting for nearly a third of all personal income. The first component is dividends, interest, and rent, covering virtually all unearned income from private sources (including pension plans). This figure provides a crude measure of personal wealth—practically the only

Table 3.4
Analysis of Area Personal Income,
Population, and Per Capita Income

A. Personal Income Profiles 1979
(Constant $1982)

	United States ($000s)	United States (%)	Michigan ($000s)	Michigan (%)	Comp. Areas ($000s)	Comp. Areas (%)	Study Area ($000s)	Study Area (%)
Gross Earnings by Place of Work[1]	1,992,277	(76.9)	89,540	(79.2)	4,246	(71.4)	5,299	(93.3)
Adjustments to Earnings								
Personal Contribution to SSI (subtract)	-103,017	(-4.0)	-4,537	(-4.0)	- 223	(-3.8)	- 273	(-4.8)
Commuting Adjustment	-545	(0.0)	411	(0.0)	157	(2.7)	- 560	(-9.8)
Net Earnings of Residents	1,888,715	(72.9)	85,414	(75.2)	4,179	(70.3)	4,466	(78.7)
Unearned Income								
Dividends, Interest, and Rent	351,487	(13.6)	13,194	(11.7)	666	(11.2)	548	(9.6)
Transfer Payments	350,488	(13.5)	14,487	(12.8)	1,102	(18.5)	664	(11.7)
TOTAL PERSONAL INCOME	2,590,690	(100.0)	113,095	(100.0)	5,948	(100.0)	5,678	(100.0)
POPULATION	224,564,089		9,248,814		488,990		451,082	
PER CAPITA PERSONAL INCOME	$11,536		$12,229		$12,163		$12,587	

B. Personal Income Profiles 1989
(Constant $1982)

	United States ($000s)	United States (%)	Michigan ($000s)	Michigan (%)	Comp. Areas ($000s)	Comp. Areas (%)	Study Area ($000s)	Study Area (%)
Gross Earnings by Place of Work[1]	2,638,807	(72.7)	98,871	(73.2)	5,113	(67.4)	4,644	(79.9)
Adjustments to Earnings								
Personal Contribution to SSI (subtract)	-176,177	(-4.9)	-7,052	(-5.2)	- 353	(-4.7)	- 332	(-5.7)
Commuting Adjustment	-487	(0.0)	696	(.5)	404	(5.3)	- 416	(-7.2)
Net Earnings of Residents	2,462,143	(67.9)	92,515	(68.5)	5,164	(68.0)	3,896	(67.1)
Unearned Income								
Dividends, Interest, and Rent	636,085	(17.5)	21,847	(16.2)	1,252	(16.5)	865	(14.9)
Transfer Payments	529,181	(14.6)	20,696	(15.3)	1,175	(15.5)	1,047	(18.0)
TOTAL PERSONAL INCOME	3,627,409	(100.0)	135,058	(100.0)	7,591	(100.0)	5,808	(100.0)
POPULATION	248,257,800		9,273,400		500,000		428,700	
PER CAPITA PERSONAL INCOME	$14,611		$14,564		$15,136		$13,551	

C. 1979-89 Percentage Change in Personal Income, By Component

	United States	Michigan	Comparison Areas	Study Area
Gross Earnings by Place of Work	32.5	10.4	20.4	-12.4
Adjustments to Earnings				
Personal Contribution to SSI (subtract)	-71.0	-55.4	-58.3	-21.6
Commuting Adjustment (gain if positive)	—	69.3	157.3	negative
Net Earnings by Residents	30.4	8.3	23.5	-12.8
Unearned Income				
Dividends, Interest, and Rent	81.0	65.6	87.9	57.8
Transfer Payments	51.0	42.9	6.6	57.7
TOTAL PERSONAL INCOME	40.0	19.4	27.6	2.3
POPULATION	10.6	0.3	2.2	-5.0
PER CAPITA PERSONAL INCOME	26.7	19.1	24.4	7.7

[1] Slight variations from the earnings figures reported in Table 3.3 are due to rounding off before converting to constant dollars.

Source: U.S. Department of Commerce, Bureau of Economic Analysis, Regional Economic Information System *Local Area Personal Income* series.

measure available for small areas—since most personal wealth is deployed to yield an economic return. Transfer payments are the other component of unearned income. They include social security retirement, survivor, and disability payments; military and government pensions; unemployment compensation; direct and in-kind welfare payments; and miscellaneous government transfers. The dominance of social security makes the transfer payment level for an area quite sensitive to the presence of retired persons (which is also true for dividends, interest, and rent). Unemployment compensation and welfare create an inverse relationship between transfer payments and general economic prosperity.

Analyzing Area Personal Income. The percentage distribution of income among the various components and shifts over time are the main topics of interest. As shown in Part A of the table, in 1979 the study area's income structure was characterized by an unusually large share of personal income attributable to gross earnings—more than 90 percent compared to under 80 percent in the other areas. Also, commuting patterns produced a net outflow of earnings from the metropolitan area equivalent to a loss of about 10 percent of area personal income. The data for individual comparison areas (not shown) reveal that only four other areas (all in the Midwest) experienced net income losses due to commuting. Elsewhere, area residents tended to generate more income for the area as a result of out-commuting than was lost because of nonresidents commuting into the area.

To the extent that local jobs are held by nonresidents, income is apt to leak out of the area because the in-commuters will spend a large share of their earnings elsewhere. It is often worth examining commuting patterns in more detail to see whether patterns of job-holding among residents and nonresidents suggest particular development strategies (see the discussion in Chapter 5, "Assessing Economic Geography").

Flint's 1979 income structure also reveals an unusually low share of unearned income, particularly income from dividends, interest, and rent. As mentioned above, this category is a rough indicator of accumulated personal wealth. Low levels of such income raise two concerns. First, the consumer spending of accumulated wealth can be one of the most stable sources of economic support for a community. The same is true of accumulated transfer entitlements such as social security and government pensions. Second, local wealth can have a supply-side influence on economic development. Studies of economic development at the local, regional, and national levels increasingly have stressed the importance of entrepreneurship and small business activity to economic growth and adjustment. A majority of small business startups are financed at least in part from the personal wealth of business founders and their relatives. In addition, backing for small businesses may be linked to local wealth through the operation of various types of financial institutions.

Deviations from patterns observed elsewhere suggest directions for further investigation. Flint's low levels of unearned income led one analyst to consider the age structure of the local population, because persons in older age groups receive a large share of all dividend, interest, and rental income as well as the bulk of all types of transfer payments.[4] A follow-on analysis investigated whether the area was losing retirement-aged persons—along with their accumulated wealth and entitlements—through net outmigration. (See the section on "Analyzing Economic Geography" in Chapter 5 for a discussion of techniques for demographic analysis.)

Analyzing Shifts in Income Structure. We have already observed that the 1979-89 period was one of structural change for the study area economy. The data in Part B of Table 3.4 show that by 1989, Flint's income structure more nearly resembled that of the other comparison areas. Even so, the distinctive pattern of income losses due to commuting and relatively low shares of unearned income is still evident. Population and per capita income figures suggest a painful transition. The study area's population is lower in 1989 than in 1979 and the level of per capita income—which exceeded that of the nation, state, and comparison areas in 1979—had by 1989 dropped below that of the other areas.

The percentage changes in the components of personal income over the recent business cycle are summarized in Part C of Table 3.4. The study area's earnings decline has been analyzed as part of the earlier earnings comparisons (Table 3.3). Here we see that increases in the social security tax created greater losses of income in other areas (which experienced gains in employment over the period) than in the study area (which lost employment). Although Flint's income losses due to commuting were lower in 1979 than in 1989, this component still represents an outflow from the local area at a time when the state and comparison areas gained income from this source. Also, though Flint's income from dividends, interest, and rent experienced strong growth over the 1979-89 period, growth in this component was even stronger elsewhere. The state also lagged in this segment, perhaps for similar reasons such as retirement-related migration. Flint's growth in transfer payments exceeded that of the other comparison areas but was quite close to the national growth rate. Because this was a period of decline for the local area, it is likely that this increase reflects greater reliance on unemployment and welfare benefits.

---

[4] Thomas R. Hammer, *Evaluation of Development Potentials for Metropolitan Flint, Michigan*, Evanston, Ill.: NCI Research, 1986, pp. 35-38.

Overall, these income changes translate into a negligible increase in total personal income in the study area at a time when other areas were showing strong growth. Population declines appear to have mitigated some of the negative impacts of stagnation, so that per capita personal income increased somewhat. However, a comparison of trends reveals that per capita income growth in the local area substantially lagged growth elsewhere.

The income analysis expands on the analysis of earnings by suggesting topics other than employment that may deserve attention in development planning. Although population factors such as commuting and retiree migration are not a traditional focus of area economic analysis, a recurrent theme in recent literature is that economic development depends on people:

> To an increasing extent, an area's long-term economic prospects depend upon its ability to attract and retain people with the resources necessary to make things happen. Little can be done about the people-attracting capabilities of an area in the short run, but this factor should be considered in formulating any long-term development strategy.[5]

Later chapters of this handbook discuss population factors from two key perspectives: population influences on local and regional markets (Chapter 5) and labor force characteristics (Chapter 6).

SUMMARY

The types of comparisons illustrated above will help identify important aspects of local economic performance and condition. They will also suggest directions for further analysis.

For example, in the foregoing comparative analysis, it is evident that the study area economy has not performed well over the most recent business cycle and that its economic condition has worsened in relative terms. Employment has been declining and unemployment has remained high. Earnings per worker, which remain relatively high in the study area despite recent declines, are one factor that undoubtedly serves to attract and retain surplus workers. A regional dimension to the study area's economic problems is evident in the relatively weak performance of the midwest comparison areas and, to a lesser degree, the state (though the state is

---

[5] Thomas R. Hammer, Ibid., p. 38.

probably buffered by a more diverse economy than either the study city or the midwestern comparison areas). Yet the study area's weak economic performance stands out.

It is the task of the analyst to identify the distinctive features of the local economy that are responsible for its relative performance and condition. This information is needed to identify potential points of influence and to provide a sound basis for economic development policy. The next several chapters illustrate how this can be done.

4

ANALYZING THE STRUCTURE AND DYNAMICS OF A LOCAL ECONOMY

What accounts for differences in local economic performance and condition? A major factor is the underlying structure of the local economy—what it is that a local economy produces or does. This in turn influences the economy's dynamics—its distinctive employment and income-generating patterns.

The objective of the analytical techniques described below is to gain greater insight into factors affecting the level and growth of economic activity within a local economy. This type of analysis is sometimes referred to as an economic base study. Key questions to answer include the following:

- Which sectors or industries are most important to the local economy in terms of employment and earnings?

- Is the structure of the local economy changing? If so, in what ways?

- How diversified is the local economy?

- Which sectors or industries are growing and which stagnating or declining? How do these trends compare to those elsewhere?

EXAMINING INDUSTRIAL STRUCTURE AND PATTERNS OF GROWTH

Local economies differ in the types of activities they engage in. Moreover, an economy dominated by manufacturing will have very different dynamics from one dominated by agriculture or by service or government activity. The analysis can proceed by taking a closer look at the industrial structure of the local economy—the distribution of economic activity by industry.

ANALYZING INDUSTRIAL STRUCTURE: DATA SOURCES

How can the industrial structure of a local economy be determined? There are several sources of data on employment and earnings by industry, each with its advantages and disadvantages. Unfortunately for the analyst, differences in timing and coverage mean that these data series rarely agree completely and sometimes even contradict each other in direction of trend!

The Regional Economic Information System (REIS), a computerized data bank and retrieval system operated by the Bureau of Economic Analysis of the U.S. Department of Commerce, provides data on earnings and employment for broad one- or two-digit SIC industries (*Local Area Personal Income Series*). Though the BEA data lack industry detail, they are in some respects more comprehensive than *County Business Patterns* in that they cover agricultural and government employment and the self-employed. The annual data are available with a two to three year time lag. As of this writing, the latest REIS data available are for 1990.

County Business Patterns, a publication of the U.S. Department of Commerce, provides data by detailed industry category at the county level on employment covered by the unemployment compensation law, total payrolls, and the number of establishments. Although it excludes government, agricultural and railroad employment, as well as self-employed proprietors, the CBP series is the best source for detailed industry data at the local level. Data are collected annually but there is a time lag of approximately three years between data collection and availability. Currently, the most recent data available are for 1989. Because the data on employment and payroll are collected as of mid-March, there may be a downward bias in sectors or industries that are seasonal (e.g., tourism, food processing, and construction).

For the most recent local area statistics on industry employment, the source is the Bureau of Labor Statistics (BLS). In cooperation with the states, BLS produces several data series on local labor markets and employment and unemployment. Monthly employment figures by one-digit SIC industry are reported for major labor market areas as part of the BLS series, *Industry Employment, Hours, and Earnings*. However, like CPB data, these data are collected from a sample of establishment records and exclude agricultural employment and the self-employed.

All of the above data series report employment or earnings on a "place of work" basis; they cover those who work in establishments located in a local economy, regardless of where they live. Employment and earnings data are also available on a "place-of-residence" basis, though less frequently, from the decennial Census of Population. Depending on the extent of work-related commuting into and out of a local area, there may be substantial discrepancies in the totals reported one way versus the other. It is often useful to analyze commuting patterns—also covered by the decennial census—for insights on the economic geography of the local region (see Chapter 5) and local labor market characteristics (see Chapter 6).

Industrial structure encompasses ·the whole range of economic activity, including provision of services as well as production of manufactured goods. As described in Chapter 2, the federal government's SIC coding system exhaustively categorizes economic activity based on a firm's primary product or service. This makes it possible to express industrial structure in terms of the share of total activity that falls into each of the various SIC code categories. The resulting profile of the local economy can be used to identify local industry specializations and to analyze industry growth patterns that may have implications for the community's economic development agenda.

Industrial structure usually is measured either in terms of *employment shares* (the percentage of total employment accounted for by employment in each of the SIC industries) or *earnings shares* (based on payrolls or wages paid to people employed in each SIC industry). The box, "Analyzing Industrial Structure: Data Sources," reviews some of the most important sources of employment and earnings data by industry.

In examining economic structure, keep in mind that establishments are assigned a single SIC code based on their primary product, not the occupations or skills of those involved in producing it. Thus, all workers at a manufacturing establishment are considered to be employed in manufacturing, even if they are nonproduction workers such as accountants, engineers, architects, lawyers, and managers who work at that establishment. Some analysts have argued that what the workers in an economy *do* (i.e., their job function) is at least as important in economic development terms as what they produce. Consequently, it may be helpful to complement the analysis of industry structure with a separate analysis of an area's occupational mix (see Chapter 6, "Profiling Local Human Resources").

Industrial Structure:
Past and Present

A first step in analyzing industrial structure is to break out the distribution of employment or earnings (or both) at the most general level of one-digit SIC sectors. Table 4.1 provides an example, showing the distribution of employment and earnings by industry for the Flint metropolitan area, Michigan, and the United States in 1973, 1979, and 1989. These data allow the analyst to compare industry employment and earnings shares at different time points and to chart percentage point changes.

Table 4.1
Analysis of Industrial Structure,
Study City, State, Nation
1973, 1979, and 1989

A. Percentage of Total Employment by Sector

	1973			1979			1989		
	Flint	Mich	U.S.	Flint	Mich	U.S.	Flint	Mich	U.S.
Farm	0.8	2.7	4.0	0.7	2.3	3.5	6.6	1.7	2.3
Nonfarm									
Agric., Forestry, Fishing	0.2	0.3	0.6	0.2	0.4	0.8	0.4	0.6	1.0
Mining	0.04	0.4	0.7	0.06	0.4	1.0	0.14	0.3	0.7
Construction	3.7	4.4	5.3	3.6	4.3	5.3	3.7	4.2	5.3
Manufacturing	41.8	30.8	21.1	38.9	27.9	19.3	26.3	21.0	14.7
TCU	3.0	4.3	5.2	3.0	4.1	5.0	2.6	3.7	4.7
Wholesale	5.6	4.4	4.7	5.4	4.3	5.1	4.0	4.4	4.9
Retail	14.9	15.7	15.5	15.3	16.4	15.9	21.0	18.1	16.6
FIRE	3.8	5.0	5.9	4.3	5.5	6.5	5.1	6.3	7.6
Services	14.8	17.8	19.5	16.1	19.8	21.2	24.0	26.2	27.0
Government	11.5	14.5	17.6	12.5	14.6	16.6	12.2	13.5	15.2

B. Percentage of Total Earnings by Sector

	1973			1979			1989		
	Flint	Mich	U.S.	Flint	Mich	U.S.	Flint	Mich	U.S.
Farm	0.4	1.6	4.2	0.2	1.1	2.4	0.2	0.8	1.6
Nonfarm									
Agric., Forestry, Fishing	0.1	0.2	0.5	0.1	0.3	0.6	0.2	0.3	0.6
Mining	0.1	0.5	1.1	0.1	0.6	1.7	0.1	0.4	1.0
Construction	3.8	5.5	6.7	3.6	5.5	7.0	3.6	4.9	6.2
Manufacturing	56.9	42.3	25.3	57.8	41.4	24.9	48.8	34.1	19.7
Nondurable	1.9	6.5	9.2	1.7	6.4	8.7	1.8	6.5	7.3
Durable	55.0	35.9	16.2	56.1	35.0	16.2	47.0	27.5	12.4
TCU	3.6	5.5	7.4	3.6	5.6	7.5	2.8	5.1	6.6
Wholesale	5.9	5.3	5.9	6.0	5.2	6.6	4.8	5.9	6.6
Retail	8.2	9.9	10.7	7.3	9.2	10.2	8.8	8.9	9.5
FIRE	2.1	3.7	5.5	2.3	4.1	6.1	2.4	4.4	7.1
Services	9.8	13.0	15.9	10.4	14.7	17.6	17.4	22.1	25.5
Government	9.2	12.6	16.8	8.6	12.5	15.4	10.9	13.1	15.7

Source: Bureau of Economic Analysis, Regional Economic Information System

Comparing Employment Structure. As Table 4.1 makes clear, the industrial structure of the Flint MSA differs from that of Michigan and, to an even greater degree, from that of the nation as a whole. Employment in Flint has been, and remains, relatively more concentrated in the manufacturing sector and correspondingly less concentrated in many non-manufacturing sectors, including government, services, and finance, insurance, and real estate (FIRE).

It is also evident from Table 4.1 that the industrial structure of all three economies changed substantially between 1973 and 1989. Manufacturing became a less important source of employment while services increased in importance. This shift was already well advanced in the nation as a whole by the beginning of the period, when the manufacturing share of employment was only 21 percent. Since then, the share of national employment in manufacturing has fallen 6.4 percentage points, which translates into a decline of 30 percent (0.147/0.211 - 1 = -30.3). Michigan, which began the period with a higher manufacturing employment share than the nation, experienced a more noticeable falling off as its manufacturing employment share dropped 10 percentage points, a decline of 32 percent (0.210/0.308 - 1 = -31.8).[1]

Flint, meanwhile, which had a manufacturing share of employment almost twice that of the nation in 1973, experienced the most dramatic shift over the period. Its manufacturing employment share fell from 41.8 percent in 1973 to 26.3 percent in 1989, a drop of 15.5 percentage points (equivalent to a 37.1 percent decline in employment share). Most of this drop occurred since 1979, a period when—as we saw from the earlier analysis of performance and condition—the Flint economy experienced overall employment declines. By 1989, Flint's employment structure approximated the national employment structure of 16 years earlier, with the service share of employment almost matching the manufacturing share. Nevertheless, its 1989 manufacturing employment share remained almost twice that of the nation as a whole. With the exception of retail employment, all other sectors exhibited a lower employment share in Flint than in the state or the nation.

Comparing Earnings Structure. Data on the distribution of earnings by sector can be assembled and compared in the same manner as data on employment (see Table 4.1, part B). Note that manufacturing often accounts for a higher share of total earnings than of total employment. This is because manufacturing jobs tend to be, on average, higher paying. For example, although manufacturing accounted for 26.3 percent of all *jobs* in the Flint MA in 1989, it accounted for 48.8 percent of all *earnings*.

A decline in manufacturing is often more pronounced in terms of employment than it is in terms of earnings, since improved productivity will bolster wages of remaining workers. Manufacturing output and earnings may thus retain importance in an area's industrial structure, even as manufacturing employment declines. This is apparent from the data for

---

[1] When working with data, it is preferable to perform calculations using ratios and decimals, although percentages are fine for expressing final results.

Flint. Although Flint's manufacturing employment share dropped 15.5 percentage points, the share of total earnings attributable to manufacturing dropped by only 8.1 percentage points or half as much.

Analyzing Industry Growth Patterns

In addition to noting shifts in the distribution of employment and earnings across industries, the analyst can compare industry growth performance as measured by rates of change in employment and earnings. Patterns of industry growth and decline may signal aspects of local competitive advantage or disadvantage, as explained further in the section below on "Shift-Share Analysis."

To facilitate industry growth comparisons, performance can be expressed as a percentage change from the initial base year (see example, Table 4.2). In the 1973-79 period, employment growth in Flint and Michigan trailed national employment growth across most sectors. In the subsequent 1979-89 period, state employment growth continued moderately to lag national employment growth almost across the board. But Flint's relative performance worsened noticeably, with steep declines in manufacturing, transportation-communications-utilities (TCU), and wholesale trade. Analysis of employment totals for each sector (not shown) reveals that these three sectors lost a combined total of 34,616 jobs (with more than 29,000 lost in manufacturing). The 23,376 jobs added in the main growth sectors of retail trade, the FIRE sector, and services were not enough to offset these declines. The bulk of the new jobs were in services, which added more than 19,000 jobs.

The pattern of recent job growth in Flint compared with the nation—with the Flint MSA experiencing steeper manufacturing employment declines and slower growth in most nonmanufacturing sectors—is typical for an industrially-specialized local economy that is lagging the nation in the shift to a more service-oriented economy.

A comparison of earnings performance by industry can amplify the employment growth comparisons. As noted in the earlier comparison of percentage point changes in employment and earnings shares, earnings in Flint's manufacturing sector did not decline as much as employment—perhaps reflecting productivity improvements in combination with union-protected wage levels. Other sectors exhibited a different pattern. For example, employment declines in the TCU sector were accompanied by even steeper declines in earnings, suggesting a shift to lower-paid jobs or perhaps non-unionized employees. Growth in retail jobs was not matched

Table 4.2
Analysis of Industry Growth Patterns
Study City, State, Nation
1973-79 and 1979-89

A. Percentage Change in Employment by Sector

	1973-79			1979-89		
	Flint	Mich	U.S.	Flint	Mich	U.S.
Farm	0.8	-3.5	-1.3	-9.3	-18.6	-17.7
Nonfarm						
Agric., Forestry, Fishing	18.7	35.2	38.2	70.6	74.9	63.0
Mining	65.8	9.7	51.5	104.6	-10.1	-16.0
Construction	8.5	8.8	16.1	-4.6	9.1	22.5
Manufacturing	3.2	-0.1	5.3	-36.8	-16.6	-7.2
TCU	8.1	6.2	10.9	-17.3	-1.1	13.6
Wholesale	8.3	7.3	25.3	-31.9	14.5	18.2
Retail	14.5	15.6	18.5	28.1	22.1	27.2
FIRE	26.6	22.4	27.3	10.7	26.6	41.4
Services	21.0	22.8	25.2	39.7	47.1	55.7
Government	20.1	11.4	9.1	-8.0	2.8	11.8
Total	11.0	10.2	15.3	-6.4	11.0	21.9

B. Percentage Change in Earnings by Sector

	1973-79			1979-89		
	Flint	Mich	U.S.	Flint	Mich	U.S.
Farm	-40.0	-26.1	-34.9	-7.8	-18.9	-12.1
Nonfarm						
Agric., Forestry, Fishing	18.0	18.6	30.3	52.8	40.9	38.4
Mining	78.2	39.5	75.2	-3.8	-25.5	-17.7
Construction	8.3	7.0	17.3	-12.1	-1.5	17.9
Manufacturing	16.2	5.6	11.3	-26.0	-9.1	4.6
Nondurable	0.7	6.5	7.1	-2.1	13.1	11.6
Durable	16.7	5.5	13.7	-26.7	-13.2	0.9
TCU	12.3	10.2	15.4	-30.0	0.0	17.0
Wholesale	16.7	6.6	26.3	-30.5	25.8	31.2
Retail	1.2	0.2	7.6	.4	6.6	23.4
FIRE	27.4	20.1	25.9	10.1	19.2	53.8
Services	21.5	22.3	25.7	47.2	66.6	91.4
Government	8.1	6.8	3.7	10.5	16.3	34.5
Total	14.4	8.0	13.1	-12.4	10.4	32.5
Per capita income	14.8	10.0	10.0	7.7	19.1	26.7

Source: Bureau of Economic Analysis, Regional Economic Information System

by growth in retail earnings, indicating that the retail sector may be benefiting from labor surpluses that exert downward pressure on wages. In contrast, in both Flint and the U.S. overall, earnings in services grew more rapidly than employment. However, the differential was even more pronounced for the nation, indicating a relatively larger national share of employment in the higher-paying services.

Refining the Analysis

The comparison of industrial structure and growth at the one-digit SIC level serves to pinpoint important sectors in the local economy and patterns of growth that bear further investigation. Analysis often proceeds to examine individual sectors of interest more closely, using break-outs at the two-digit or, more rarely, the three-digit level of industry detail. Employment data must be used for analysis beyond the two-digit level since earnings data are not available for such detailed industry analysis at the local level.

In the case of Flint (see Table 4.3), a more detailed analysis of its manufacturing sector revealed a high concentration of employment in fabricated metal products (SIC 34) and transportation equipment (SIC 37). This reflects the dominance of auto manufacturing in the local economy—General Motors operated nine plants in the Flint MSA at the time these data were collected. Employment in manufacturing other than SICs 34 and 37 was found to be extremely limited, providing fewer than 5,000 jobs in the local economy (only 7.5 percent of the manufacturing base). Moreover, data on the number of local establishments by industry, which is reported in *County Business Patterns* along with employment data, revealed that non-GM establishments in Flint have tended to be quite small, averaging fewer than 20 workers (Table 4.3, Part B).

The data in Table 4.3 underscore the lack of diversity of the Flint manufacturing base and the limited options for attempting a transition away from dependence on a single, declining industry. In Flint's case, this part of the sectoral analysis generated few surprises, because General Motors' dominance of the local economy has been a fact of life since the company was founded in Flint at the turn of the century. In cases where employment is more diversified, it may be more difficult to tease out the implications of the detailed industry data.

Two techniques that are often used in this type of detailed follow-on analysis are: 1) *location quotient analysis*, which reveals local industry specializations and provides insights on the nature of the local economic base, and 2) *shift-share analysis*, which is a way to evaluate the significance of industry growth patterns from the standpoint of local competitiveness.

IDENTIFYING THE LOCAL ECONOMIC BASE AND INDUSTRY SPECIALIZATIONS

The industries that account for the largest share of employment or earnings are not necessarily the same as those that underpin growth in the local

Table 4.3
Manufacturing Employment and Establishments by 2-Digit Industry,
Flint MSA (Genesee County)
1969, 1978, and 1984

A. Employment and Employment Change

SIC	Sector	1969	1978	1984	1969-84 Change	1969-84 % Change
20	Food and kindred products	1,259	953	749	-510	-40.5
26	Paper and allied products	440	356	232	-208	-47.3
27	Printing and publishing	835	906	929	94	11.3
28	Chemicals and allied prod.	698	503	382	-307	-45.3
30	Rubber and misc. plastics	191	433	370	179	93.7
32	Stone, clay, glass products	370	373	134	-236	-63.8
34*	Fabricated metals	9,266	9,051	6,885	-2,381	-25.7
35	Machinery except electrical	864	1,438	1,262	398	46.1
36	Electric and electronic equip.	210	130	194	-16	-7.6
37*	Transportation equipment	69,555	65,398	53,553	-16,002	-23.0
39	Misc. manufacturing	**	137	122	**	
--	Administrative & auxiliary					
--	All other manufacturing	1,096	364	380	-428	-65.3
	Total	84,775	80,098	65,358	-19,417	-22.9
	Total excluding SICs 34 & 37	5,954	5,649	4,920	-1,034	- 17.4

B. Establishments and Establishment Change

SIC	Sector	1969	1978	1984	1969-84 Change	1969-84 % Change
20	Food and kindred products	29	20	17	-12	-41.4
26	Paper and allied products	5	4	6	1	20.0
27	Printing and publishing	41	55	56	15	36.6
28	Chemicals and allied prod.	8	15	9	1	12.5
30	Rubber and misc. plastics	4	14	14	10	250.0
32	Stone, clay, glass products	21	16	15	-6	28.6
34*	Fabricated metals	48	40	47	-1	-2.1
35	Machinery except electrical	62	64	65	3	4.8
36	Electric and electronic equip.	3	5	8	5	166.7
37*	Transportation equipment	14	13	17	3	21.4
39	Misc. manufacturing	**	10	13	**	**
--	Administrative & auxiliary	**	4	6	**	**
--	All other manufacturing	43	26	24	0	--
	Total	278	286	297	19	6.8
	Total excluding SICs 34 & 37	269	278	289	20	-7.4

*   Consists overwhelmingly of GM employment
** Included in "all other manufacturing"

Source: Bureau of the Census, County Business Patterns.

economy. The industries that are most crucial to local economic growth are those that produce goods and services sold *outside* the local economy, generating an inflow of income. These industries are known as an area's "economic base" or "export base." They generate the income that sustains the "local-serving" or "non-basic" sector of the economy—firms such as restaurants, grocery stores, automobile repair shops, laundries, and so on.

In addition to exporting, local economies import goods and services that are demanded by local consumers and businesses but produced elsewhere. The extent and nature of a local economy's imports are also of interest for the analysis, since there may be opportunities to substitute locally produced goods and services for those being purchased from outside the area.

How can the economic base of a local economy be identified? Previously it was thought that an area's economic base was synonymous with its manufacturing sector. Analysts divided local economies into their "basic" sectors—manufacturing and extractive industries such as mining or agriculture—and their local or service sector (all the rest). It is now widely recognized that such a division is misleading and inaccurate. For one thing, not all manufacturers export their products; some—such as beverage bottlers and dairies or newspaper publishers—serve primarily local markets. More importantly, the growth and restructuring of service industries in recent years has been accompanied by rising interregional trade in services.

Clearly, service industries that sell their services outside of a local economy also represent part of an area's economic base. To assist in analyzing the role of service industries in an economy, researchers have attempted to categorize services according to their market orientation. The framework shown in the box below, adapted by researchers Stephen Nord and Robert Sheets from the work of Singlemann (1978) and Stanback and Noyelle (1982), illustrates a useful way to categorize services for purposes of economic analysis (see "Service Industry Classification Framework").

Probably the most accurate method of identifying a local economy's base is to conduct an area-wide business survey of all firms asking them to identify the percentage of their goods and services that are sold outside of the area. Those with comparatively large shares of output sold outside the local area would constitute the local area's economic base. However, such a business survey is a major undertaking and results could be unreliable unless the response rate was quite high.

SERVICE INDUSTRY CLASSIFICATION FRAMEWORK

Producer services (Intermediate Demand)

Distributive services:
- Transportation (400-432)
- Communications (330-342)
- Wholesale trade (500-571)

Advanced corporate services:
- Finance, insurance, and real estate (700-712)
- Business services (721-742)
- Legal services (841)
- Membership organizations and professional services (881-892)

Social services (Mixed Demand)

Nonprofit services:
- Health services (812-840)
- Education services (842-861)
- Social services (862-865, 867-871)
- Museums, art galleries, and zoos (872)
- Religious organizations (866)

Government services: Public administration (900-932)

Consumer services (Final Demand)

Personal services
- Repair services (750-760)
- Personal services (761-791)
- Entertainment and recreation services (800-802)

Retail trade:
- Retail trade (580-691)

Note: Numbers in parentheses are census industry codes. See Census documentation for SIC code equivalents.

Source: Previously published in Robert G. Sheets, Stephen Nord, and John J. Phelps, *The Impact of Service Industries on Underemployment in Metropolitan Economies*, Lexington, Mass.: D.C. Heath, 1987. Reprinted by permission of Macmillan, Inc.; all rights reserved.

Location Quotient Analysis

Among the various techniques for analyzing local economic base characteristics, location quotient analysis is readily understandable and easy to perform.[2] The necessary calculations can be done by hand or on a

---

[2] Other approaches for identifying a local economy's economic base are the minimum requirements approach and the K value technique. See, for example, Edward Ullman and Michael Dacey, "The Minimum Requirements Approach to the Urban Economic Base," *Papers and Proceedings of the Regional Science Association*, Vol. 6, pp. 175-199 and Irving Morrissett, "The Economic Structure of American Cities," *Papers and Proceedings of the Regional Science Association*, Vol. 4, pp. 239-258.

spreadsheet. A location quotient for a particular industry is simply a ratio that compares the percentage of employment in a particular industry in a local economy to the percentage of employment the same industry constitutes in a reference economy (i.e., the national economy). Employment is the measure of economic activity most often used in deriving location quotients because it is the one that is generally available in the greatest industrial detail at the local level.

To illustrate, if employment in a particular industry equals 6 percent of total employment in a local economy and employment in the same industry equals 3 percent of total employment nationally, the location quotient for this industry is: $6/3 = 2.0$. The formula for computing location quotients can be written as:

$$LQ_i = (e_i/e) / (E_i/E)$$

where:
e_i = Local employment in industry i
e = Total local employment
E_i = National employment in industry i
E = Total national employment

Location quotient analysis indicates which industries have a comparatively larger (or smaller) presence in the local economy. A location quotient equal to 1.0 means that the share of employment in a particular industry in a local economy is exactly the same as the share of employment in the same industry nationally. If the location quotient is greater than one, the local share of employment in a particular industry exceeds the national share of employment in the same industry. If it is less than one, the local share of employment in an industry is less than the national share.

Because industries with a location quotient greater than one indicate relatively high production of a particular good or service, it is likely that some amount is being exported. Employment in that industry (or the portion of employment that causes the quotient to exceed 1.0) is then assigned to the economic base and is given credit for supporting the economy as a whole. Conversely, industries with a location quotient less than one are assumed to be local-serving or non-basic industries. For economic development purposes, it is often useful to focus on the extremes—industries with location quotients greater than 1.25 (likely export base components) and those with location quotients less than 0.75 (potential import substitution opportunities). The assumption is that industries falling between 0.75 and 1.25 are probably producing amounts sufficient to meet local demand.

Location quotients are sensitive to the level of industry detail used in calculating them. The use of one-digit versus two-digit industrial detail may make the difference between assigning all of a sector's employment to the economic base and assigning almost none of it. Consequently, for economic base analysis, location quotients should be calculated at least at the level of two-digit SIC industries (even finer levels of disaggregation are desirable if they are available for the local area in question).

Caveats in Analyzing Location Quotients. It is important to be aware of several tenuous assumptions underlying the use of location quotients. These are: 1) that demand or consumption patterns are constant across regions and that income levels are also constant; 2) that labor productivity does not vary from region to region; and 3) that each firm in an industry produces an identical product.

Assumptions about demand patterns are especially problematic. For example, the national distribution of employment or earnings by industry provides a reasonable description of national demand patterns. But a local deviation from this distribution need not mean that there is a production excess or shortfall unless the local economy as a whole resembles the national profile. Otherwise, deviations from the national norm in terms of production can be expected to create deviations in demand, thereby obscuring the meaning of location quotients. "Input-output" tables that are calibrated for the inter-industry relationships of a particular state or region may provide more reliable estimates of supply-demand relationships, but they are seldom available (see the discussion in Unit 5 on "Examining Linkages in a Local Economy").

For these reasons, some analysts hesitate to ascribe economic base interpretations to location quotients, preferring to interpret them simply as "coefficients of specialization." The implication is that industries with location quotients greater than 1.0 represent local strengths that merit special attention in economic planning.

Example: Industry Specializations in Cook County. The example that follows in Table 4.4 uses location quotients to compare employment by two-digit industry in Cook County (the central county of the Chicago metropolitan area), the nation, and a reference area called "Super County." The Super County reference area is an aggregate of Cook County plus ten other major central counties in the Northeast and North Central regions. Using a reference area that is similar to the subject economy in terms of key characteristics such as scale, regional location, and urbanization is one way to compensate for the problem of demand variation noted above. Here comparisons to Super County are used to provide additional perspective on the results obtained from comparisons to the nation as a whole.

Table 4.4
Location Quotient Analysis
Cook County, Super County, and United States

	Super County vs. U.S.	Cook County vs. Super County	Cook County vs. U.S.
Total 1987 Employment	1.00	1.00	1.00
Agriculture, Forestry & Fisheries	0.46	0.87	0.39
Mining	0.30	0.31	0.09
Contract Construction	0.75	1.03	0.78
15 General Contractors	0.66	1.01	0.67
16 Heavy Construction	0.57	0.64	0.36
17 Special Trade Contractors	0.82	1.11	0.91
Manufacturing	0.97	1.11	1.07
20 Food & Kindred Products	**0.96**	**1.32**	**1.27**
23 Apparel & Fabricated Textiles	0.47	0.80	0.38
24 Lumber & Wood Products	0.17	1.41	0.24
25 Furniture & Fixtures	0.58	1.56	0.91
26 Paper & Allied Products	**0.85**	**1.48**	**1.25**
***27 Printing & Publishing**	**1.38**	**1.23**	**1.70**
28 Chemicals & Allied Products	1.06	0.96	1.02
29 Petroleum & Coal Products	0.72	0.94	0.68
30 Plastic & Rubber Products	0.58	1.53	0.89
31 Leather & Leather Products	0.57	0.85	0.48
32 Stone, Clay & Glass Products	0.62	1.20	0.74
33 Primary Metal Industries	**1.33**	**0.85**	**1.12**
***34 Fabricated Metal Products**	**1.49**	**1.22**	**1.82**
35 Machinery, ex. Electrical	1.05	0.99	1.04
36 Electrical Machinery	**0.77**	**1.72**	**1.32**
37 Transportation Equipment	.094	0.37	0.35
38 Instruments & Related	**0.77**	**1.53**	**1.18**
39 Misc. Manufacturing	**0.94**	**1.65**	**1.56**
-- Admin., Auxiliary & Miscellaneous	**1.99**	**0.87**	**1.72**
Transportation & Other Utilities	1.16	0.96	1.11
41 Local/Interurban Transit	**1.00**	**1.31**	**1.32**
42 Trucking & Warehousing	1.06	0.95	1.01
***45 Transportation by Air**	**1.84**	**1.31**	**2.40**
***47 Transportation Services**	**1.36**	**1.32**	**1.79**
48 Communications	1.15	0.80	0.92
49 Electric, Gas & Sanitary	1.03	0.64	0.66
-- Admin., Auxiliary & Miscellaneous	0.99	0.87	0.86
Wholesale Trade	1.16	1.16	1.35
***50 Durable Goods**	**1.22**	**1.16**	**1.41**
51 Nondurable Goods	**1.03**	**1.09**	**1.13**
***-- Admin., Auxiliary & Miscellaneous**	**1.44**	**1.57**	**2.27**
Retail Trade	0.90	1.00	0.90
52 Building Materials, Garden	0.67	1.04	0.70
53 General Merchandise Stores	0.92	0.87	0.80
54 Food Stores	0.78	1.04	0.81
55 Auto Sales & Service Stations	0.68	0.93	0.63
56 Apparel & Accessory Stores	**0.97**	**1.23**	**1.19**
57 Furniture Stores	0.88	1.11	0.97
58 Eating, Drinking Places	0.94	0.94	0.88
59 Miscellaneous Retail	0.94	1.05	0.99
***-- Admin., Auxiliary & Miscellaneous**	**1.61**	**1.11**	**1.78**

Table 4.4 (cont'd)

	Super County vs. U.S.	Cook County vs. Super County	Cook County vs. U.S.
Finance, Insurance & Real Estate	1.35	1.10	1.49
60 Banking	1.28	1.08	1.38
61 Nonbank Credit Agencies	1.07	1.17	1.26
*62 Security, Commodity Sales	1.90	1.37	2.60
63 Insurance Carriers	1.71	1.04	1.77
*64 Insurance Agents & Service	1.14	1.19	1.36
*65 Real Estate	1.17	1.17	1.37
67 Holding/Investment	1.35	0.95	1.28
-- Admin., Auxiliary & Miscellaneous	1.41	0.43	0.60
Services	1.19	0.92	1.10
70 Hotels & Other Lodging	0.78	1.05	0.83
72 Personal Services	1.00	0.93	0.93
73 Business Services	1.24	1.02	1.27
75 Auto Repair & Garages	1.09	0.95	1.03
76 Misc. Repair Services	1.00	0.98	0.98
78 Motion Pictures	0.71	1.19	0.84
79 Amusement & Recreation	0.85	0.94	0.79
80 Health Services	1.23	0.83	1.02
81 Legal Services	1.52	1.03	1.56
82 Educational Services	1.60	0.85	1.37
83 Social Services	1.08	0.78	0.84
86 Membership Organizations	1.14	0.92	1.05
89 Miscellaneous Services	1.22	0.90	1.10
* -- Admin., Auxiliary & Miscellaneous	1.28	1.46	1.88
Government Total	0.79	0.90	0.72
Civilian	0.99	0.78	0.77
Military	0.41	0.62	0.25
State & Local	0.82	0.96	0.79

Source: County Business Patterns & Bureau of Economic Analysis
Note: Boldface type indicates Cook County industry specialization relative to the U.S. Asterisk indicates Cook County industry specialization relative to other major central counties in the Northeast and Central regions.

The location quotients displayed in the first and third columns of Table 4.4 reveal broad similarities between Cook County and Super County. Industries with location quotients exceeding 1.0 for both Super County and Cook County relative to the United States are industries that tend to exist in higher concentrations in urbanized central areas than in the nation as a whole. The location quotients reveal central county strengths in many types of non-manufacturing, especially financial services and administrative and auxiliary (A&A) activity (e.g. office functions). They also indicate relatively low concentrations in many types of manufacturing.

Industries with a Cook County location quotient relative to the U.S. of 1.1 or above are identified in the table in boldface type as local industry specializations. The comparisons indicate that Cook County specializes in all of the industries that represent Super County specializations except for communications (SIC 48), health services (SIC 80), and A&A activity in the FIRE sector. In addition, Cook County specializes in the following nine industries, including five manufacturing industries, that are not among the specializations of the comparison area aggregate:

Manufacturing	Nonmanufacturing
SIC 20 Food & Kindred Products	Sic 41 Local/Interurban Transit
SIC 26 Paper & Allied Products	SIC 51 Wholesale Trade-Nondurable
SIC 36 Electrical Machinery	SIC 56 Apparel Stores
SIC 38 Instruments	SIC 61 Nonbank Credit Agencies
SIC 39 Misc. Manufacturing	

The location quotients indicate that Cook County has a larger and more diverse manufacturing base than does Super County, with nine manufacturing specializations compared to Super County's four. Overall, of the 21 industries that represent specializations for both Cook County and Super County relative to the U.S., Cook County has a higher degree of specialization in 11 industries or about half (identified by an asterisk in the table).

In this case, analysis has focused on Cook County's specializations relative to the U.S., selecting a relatively low threshold for identification (a location quotient of 1.1 or above). Setting a higher threshold (e.g., 1.25) would have eliminated several modest Cook County specializations, including three manufacturing industries, from further consideration.

It is interesting to note how results would have varied if Cook County's specializations had been identified on the basis of location quotients relative to other urbanized counties instead of the nation as a whole. Relative to Super County, Cook County has some unusual manufacturing specializations for a central county, including lumber and wood products (SIC 24), furniture and fixtures (SIC 25), and plastics and rubber (SIC 30). Other specializations that emerged strongly in the comparisons to the U.S. are revealed as more modest specializations reflecting common strengths of urban areas (e.g. many types of financial services). The judgement of the analyst is central in location quotient analysis. Here the approach could be characterized as inclusive.

A later section of this handbook shows how information on local industry specializations generated by location quotient analysis can be combined with other information to help focus the strategic planning effort (see Chapter 5, "Evaluating the Local Business Base").

COMPARING INDUSTRY GROWTH PERFORMANCE: SHIFT-SHARE ANALYSIS

So far we have considered ways to assess a number of important attributes of the local economy, including its industrial make-up and how that may be changing; patterns of growth or decline in industry earnings and employment; and local industry specializations that are probable components of the economic base. Now we turn to a technique that can be used to put the growth performance of a local economy, as well as individual local industries, in comparative perspective.

Shift-share analysis is a method of analyzing differences between growth in a local economy and growth in the national (or other reference area) economy. It is a way to isolate the effect of local influences on growth from effects that operate industry-wide or at the national level. Shift-share analysis is especially useful for noting variations in the local effect across industries that may signal strengths and weaknesses of the local economy. It is also used to identify the contribution of an area's underlying industrial structure or "industrial mix" to local economic growth overall.

Shift-Share Components

Shift-share analysis partitions local employment or earnings growth into three components: a *national share* (NS) reflecting trends in the larger economy of which the subject area is a part; a share reflecting industry-specific factors or an economy's overall *industrial mix* (IM); and a share reflecting local influences on industry performance or *local factors* (LF). These three factors sum to equal the observed change in local employment or earnings.

For example, from 1979-1986, employment in the United States as a whole grew by 11.8 percent. During the same period, employment in the Detroit MSA grew by only 3.7 percent. Why did employment grow more slowly in the Detroit area than it did nationally?[3]

National employment growth was not, of course, uniform across all industries. Manufacturing employment, for example, declined by 11.6 percent. The national employment growth rate of 11.8 percent was a composite of the growth rates of the whole range of industries in the

---

[3] This section is adapted from Kenneth P. Voytek and Harold Wolman, "Detroit: An Economy Still Driven By Automobiles," in *The Restructuring of the American Midwest*, Richard D. Bingham and Randall W. Eberts (eds.), Norwell, Mass.: Kluwer Academic Publishers, 1990, pp. 171-207.

national economy. The industrial structure of a local area economy can be expected to differ from that of the broader national economy. If a local economy has a higher share of total employment in slow-growing or declining sectors (e.g., manufacturing) and a lower share of employment in fast-growing sectors (e.g., services), its overall employment growth will be lower than the nation's because of its industrial mix.

This is exactly what occurred in the Detroit MSA. In 1979, manufacturing accounted for 30.7 percent of total national employment but 36.8 percent of employment in the Detroit area. At the same time, services comprised 25.3 percent of national employment, but only 24 percent of Detroit area employment. The Detroit MSA had a higher share of its employment in a sector that was declining nationally from 1979-1986 and a lower share in the fast-growing service sector. Thus Detroit's industry mix effect from 1979-1986 was negative, translating into a loss of 36,189 jobs or 2.6 percent of its 1979 employment level.

The industrial mix effect for an area economy as a whole is simply the sum of the industry mix effects for all the individual industries. To take transportation equipment as an example, in 1979 the Detroit MSA had 175,027 employees in the transportation equipment industry (SIC 37). Had the transportation equipment industry nationally grown at the same rate as the national economy as a whole (11.83 percent) and had Detroit received its proportionate share of growth (i.e., a growth in transportation equipment of 11.83 percent), the area would have gained 20,706 transportation equipment employees:

$$NS = .1183 (175,027) = 20,706$$

But employment in the transportation equipment industry nationally did not grow; rather it declined by 9.6 percent. The difference between the growth rate for the industry nationally (-9.60 percent) and the overall national growth rate (11.83 percent) is the industry mix effect:

$$
\begin{aligned}
IM &= (-.0960 - .1183) (175,027) \\
&= -.2143 (175,027) \\
&= -37,508
\end{aligned}
$$

Of course, there is no reason to expect that the rate of employment growth for a particular industry in a local economy will match the national growth rate for that industry. The difference between an industry's performance in the local economy and what would have been expected based on the same industry's performance nationally is called variously the "competitive," "differential," or "local" effect.

In Detroit's case, the local area would have lost 16,802 employees in the transportation equipment industry if local employment in the industry had changed at the same rate as employment in the industry nationally (-9.6 percent). In fact the Detroit area lost a total of 51,037 jobs in transportation equipment (-29.16 percent). The Detroit area was thus losing market share in transportation equipment; it was losing employment in the industry at a greater rate than other areas in the United States. The local or differential shift works out to 19.56 percent:

$$
\begin{aligned}
LF &= (-.2916 - [-.0960]) \ (175,027) \\
&= (-.1956) \ (175,027) \\
&= -34,235
\end{aligned}
$$

The total local or differential shift for the entire economy is the sum of the individual differential shifts for each industry.

The local shift is sometimes interpreted as a change in an area's competitive advantage, but this oversimplifies. For example, some of the negative local shift in transportation equipment in the Detroit area may reflect increasing productivity relative to other areas due to greater replacement of labor by capital. It is better to conceive of the local effect as resulting from factors that distinguish the local economy from other areas and that bear further investigation. Generally, however, negative local shifts indicate problems in the local economy.

In this example, we see that industry-wide trends and local factors contributed almost equally to the employment decline in Detroit's transportation equipment industry in the 1979-86 period:

$$
\begin{aligned}
NS &= \ \ 11.8\% \ = \ \ \ 20,706 \\
IM &= -21.4\% \ = \ -37,508 \\
LF &= \underline{-19.6\%} \ = \ \underline{-34,235}
\end{aligned}
$$

Total employment shift = -29.2% = -51,037

As with location quotient analysis, shift-share analysis is highly sensitive to the level of industry aggregation at which it is conducted. At the one-digit sectoral level, the local effect will be heavily overestimated. As a consequence, shift-share analysis should be done at the lowest possible level of aggregation—at least at the two-digit level and, if possible, at the three-digit level. The example in the box illustrates the data and procedures for performing the analysis (see "Performing Shift-Share Analysis").

PERFORMING SHIFT-SHARE ANALYSIS

Because of their complexity and tediousness, shift-share calculations are best done using a computer. The formula for each of the components is presented below. The example that follows shows how to perform a shift-share analysis of employment change from 1979–1989.

Shift-Share — Basic Formulae

$$\text{Total Employment Shift} = NS_i + IM_i + LF_i$$

National Share: $NS_i = e_i^{t-1}\,((E^t/E^{t-1}) - 1)\,100$
Industry Mix: $IM_i = e_i^{t-1}\,((E_i^t/E_i^{t-1}) - (E^t/E^{t-1}))$
Local Factors: $ILF_i = e_i^{t-1}\,((e_i^t/e_i^{t-1}) - (E_i^t/E_i^{t-1}))$

Where: e_i and E_i are local and national employment in industry i;
e and E are local and national total employment for all industries, and
$t-1$ and t are beginning and end of the time period, respectively.

STEP 1:   Assemble the data indicated in Table A and calculate absolute and percentage change.

Table A
Total Employment in Selected Industries
1979–89

Industry	Local Emp. 1979	1989	1979–89 Change	Percent Change	U.S. Emp. 1979	1989	1979–89 Change	Percent Change
Computers	800	1000	200	25%	9000	10000	1000	11%
Primary Metals	3000	2000	−1000	−33%	35000	30000	−5000	−14%
Bus. Services	900	1000	100	11%	16000	20000	4000	25%
Health Care	5000	6000	1000	20%	35000	40000	5000	14%
	9700	10000	300	3%	95000	10000	5000	5%

STEP 2:   The data from Table A can be used to derive the three shift-share components: the national share (NS), the share due to industry mix (IM), and the local factors (LF) share. First, from the table we know that the rate of growth for the overall national economy (NS) is 5 percent. Second, the industry mix effect is the difference between the rate of growth for a particular industry in the national economy and the rate of growth of the overall national economy. The local factors effect is the difference between the growth rate for a particular industry in a local economy and its growth rate nationally.

Table B
Shift-Share Components
1979–89

Industry	National Share	Industry Mix		Local Factors	
Computers	5%	6%	(11% −5%)	14%	(25%−11%)
Primary Metals	5%	−19%	(−14%−5%)	−19%	(−33%+14%)
Bus. Services	5%	20%	(25%−5%)	−14%	(11%−25%)
Health Care	5%	9%	(14%−5%)	6%	(20%−14%)

STEP 3:   The percentages shown in Table B can be converted to absolute numbers using the base year totals reported in Table A. The results are shown in Table C.

Table C
Shift-Share Components
Absolute Change
1979-89

Industry	National Share		Industry Mix		Local Factors	
Computers	40	(800*5%)	48	(800*6%)	112	(800*14%)
Primary Metals	150	(3000*5%)	-570	(3000*-19%)	-570	(3000*-19%)
Bus. Services	45	(900*5%)	180	(900*20%)	-126	(900*-14%)
Health Care	250	(5000*5%)	450	(5000*9%)	300	(5000*6%)
	485		108		-284	

To check the accuracy of the basic calculations, remember that the shift-share formula is an identity. The sum of the calculated shift-share components (NS + IM + LF) should equal the change in local employment observed. For instance, in the example above, local employment in computers increased by 200 employees (or 25 percent) from 1979 to 1989 in the local economy. Adding the shift-share components together, we find that they also sum to 200 (40 + 48 +112).*

This analysis shows that primary metals, the industry that suffered the largest percentage employment decline (-33 percent), also suffered the largest decline in its local or competitive share (-19 percent). The computer industry, which experienced the fastest growth in employment (an increase of 25 percent), also experienced the largest percentage increase in competitive share (14 percent). The analysis shows that the local contribution to growth is substantially greater for the computer industry than for the health care industry, despite the fact that the 20 percent growth in local health care employment almost matched the 25 percent growth rate of computer industry employment. This is because much of the growth in the health care industry is attributable to overall industry trends rather than to local factors. Growth in business services, meanwhile, was entirely due to nonlocal factors, especially strong industry-wide growth. The local contribution to growth in this sector was negative, a sign of local weaknesses affecting this industry's performance.

The industry comparisons permit the analyst to identify industries that are relatively strong performers locally (in this case computers and to a lesser extent health care), as well as industries that are weak locally compared to elsewhere (such as primary metals and business services). This sets the stage for efforts to determine the nature of local influences on each industry more precisely, with a view toward enhancing factors that support strong performers or ameliorating factors that may be contributing to an industry's weak performance.

---

*In this example, the totals for all four industries sum to 309 instead of 300 because percentages were rounded off.

SUMMARY

The thrust of the analytical techniques described above is to examine local economic structure and growth patterns by industry to better understand influences on overall economic performance and condition.

Data on industry employment or earnings shares will help differentiate sectors in terms of overall size and reveal potentially significant shifts in the distribution of local economic activity. However, the size of a sector is less important than whether or not a sector is part of an area's "export base." Location quotient analysis will help to identify those industries that represent areas of specialization for the local economy and probable sources of export earnings. Shift-share analysis can be used to assess the local influence on industry growth and whether an industry appears to be thriving or suffering in the local environment.

The next chapter describes how to combine the results of these analyses in evaluating the local business base to identify key issues for the strategic planning effort.

Additional Reading

Economic Base Theory

For early formulations of economic base theory, see:

North, Douglas. "Location Theory and Regional Economic Growth." *Journal of Political Economy* 63 (1955), No. 3:243-258.

Tiebout, Charles M. "Exports and Regional Economic Growth," *Journal of Political Economy* 64 (1956), No. 2:160-169.

On the evolution of service industries, see:

Beyers, William B.; Michael J. Alvine; and Erik G. Johnson. *The Service Economy: Export of Services in the Central Puget Sound Region*. Seattle: Central Puget Sound Economic Development District, 1985.

Erickcek, George. "Growth Potential of Services in West Michigan," *Business Outlook* 6 (1990) No. 4:1-5.

Gillis, William R. "Can Service Producing Industries Provide a Catalyst for Regional Economic Growth," *Economic Development Quarterly* 1 (1987) No. 3:249-256.

Singlemann, Joachim. *From Agriculture to Services*. Beverly Hills, Calif.: Sage Publications, 1978.

Stanback, T. M.; P. Bearse; T. J. Noyelle; and R. Karasek. *Services: the New Economy*. Totowa, N.J.: Allanheld, Osmun and Company, 1981.

On the use of location quotients, see:

Heilbrun, James. *Urban Economics and Public Policy*. New York: St. Martin's Press, 1987.

Watkins, Alfred J. *The Practice of Urban Economics*. Beverly Hills: Sage Publications, 1980.

For more information on shift-share analysis, see:

Galambos, Eva C. and Arthur F. Schreiber. *Economic Analysis for Local Government*. Washington, D.C.: National League of Cities, November 1978.

Ottensmann, John R. *Basic Microcomputer Programs for Urban Analysis and Planning*. New York: Chapman and Hall, 1986.

EVALUATING LOCAL GROWTH PROSPECTS

A primary purpose of local strategic planning is to identify critical issues affecting community prospects for economic growth. Obviously the vitality of the existing industry base has a major influence on local growth prospects. This unit begins by showing how to use the techniques described in Unit 4 to assess the strength and competitiveness of local industries. This type of systematic "targeting" analysis can help establish priorities for examining local industries and employers more closely.

Once priority industries have been identified, attention turns to the specific problems and prospects of local industry operations. The analysis shifts from quantitative to more qualitative approaches, and from a focus on industries to a focus on the firms that comprise key industries in the local area. Business surveys, industry directories, and similar sources can provide insights on characteristics of the local business base that may affect local economic growth.

Information on local firms and industries also needs to be considered in light of an area's "economic geography"—the complex of geographic, population, and market characteristics that define its position in the regional economy. This type of analysis may help identify highly localized or site-specific development opportunities, including those in population-serving or nonbasic sectors.

This phase of the analysis addresses issues such as the following:

•   What do industry growth comparisons reveal about local competitive strengths and weaknesses?

•   How might characteristics of the local business base and business environment support or impede innovation and growth within key industries?

- Are there any site-specific development opportunities or problems confronting local decisionmakers?

The results can be used by strategic planning participants to define critical issues and establish directions for subsequent analysis of local resources and response options.

INDUSTRY TARGETING ANALYSIS:
ASSESSING COMPETITIVENESS

The data and analytical techniques described in the preceding unit can be combined to categorize local industries for strategic planning purposes. So-called "industry targeting" analysis may serve different purposes depending on the criteria used. Here the focus is on categorizing industries according to 1) their relative concentration in the local economy as indicated by location quotients, and 2) their recent growth performance.

Local industry specializations (industries with high location quotients) signal local competitive advantages that have caused these industries to become more concentrated in the local economy than elsewhere. Recent industry growth performance, meanwhile, indicates how competitive advantages may be changing either positively or negatively.

In evaluating growth performance it is important to consider growth in relative as well as absolute terms. For example, an industry may account for 20 percent of employment locally compared to only 10 percent nationally, but if the area has lost 10 percent of its employment in that sector while the nation has gained five percent, the obvious interpretation is that the industry once operated at a competitive advantage in the local area but no longer does. Whether or not an industry is gaining competitive share is probably more indicative of that industry's local growth potential than whether local employment in that industry is increasing or decreasing in absolute terms.

Screening Procedures

The example below illustrates the use of screening criteria to categorize a large number of two- and three-digit SIC industries according to their relative concentration in the local economy and recent growth patterns. The results can be used to identify high-priority "targets" for further investigation. The logic and sequence of the screening are illustrated in Figure 5.1. The screening procedure is outlined below.

Figure 5.1
Industry Targeting Analysis,
Decision Tree

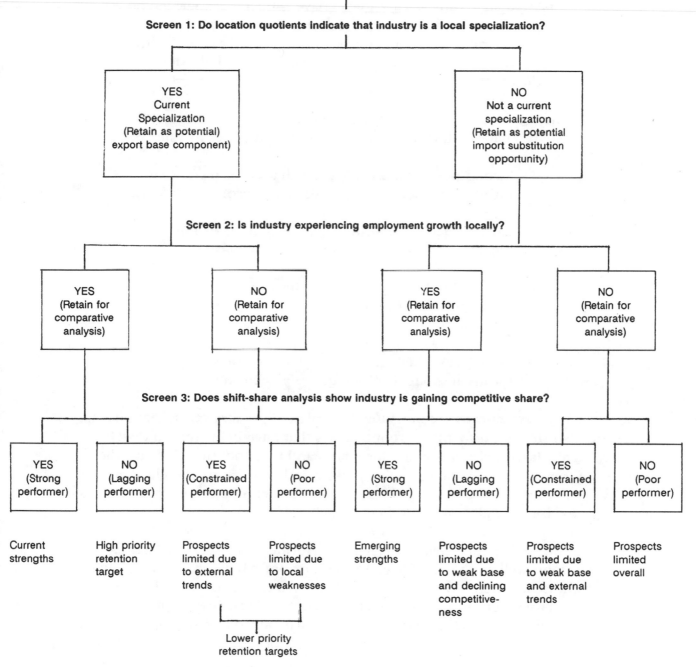

- *Step 1* — Derive location quotients to distinguish current industry specializations from non-specializations. The industry specializations, which presumably include export base components, represent potential *retention targets*. The other industries represent potential import substitution opportunities or *emerging industry targets*.

- *Step 2* — Within each of the groupings identified in Step 1, distinguish industries that have been experiencing employment growth in the local area from those that have been experiencing stagnation or decline. (Employment is the measure of growth most amenable to industrially detailed studies at the local level.)

- *Step 3* — Examine growth in comparative terms using shift-share analysis. Use results to categorize industries as follows:

  - Strong performers (industries that are growing locally and exceeding growth elsewhere)

  - Lagging performers (industries that are growing locally but at a slower rate than elsewhere)

  - Constrained performers (industries that are declining locally but not so rapidly as elsewhere)

  - Poor performers (industries that arc declining locally in both absolute and relative terms)

Analyzing Current Specializations. Local industry specializations that are also strong performers are industries that have been able to develop a relatively large presence in the local area and that continue to thrive there. They represent current strengths. Follow-on investigations might consider ways to enhance factors that contribute to their competitiveness, as well as options for capitalizing upon their presence.

Specializations that are lagging performers are local industries that have done well in the local area in the past but which are now betraying weaknesses. Their loss of competitive share merits attention before problems worsen and lead to employment declines. Investigations might focus on the reasons for their lagging performance in a growth sector. What accounts for their declining competitiveness locally? These industries are prime targets for business retention efforts, especially because early intervention may increase chances for positive results.

Current specializations that have been declining locally, but not so rapidly as elsewhere, exhibit relative strengths that may allow them to retain importance in the local area. However, their local growth performance is apt to be constrained by larger industry or national trends. Follow-on investigations should consider the implications of stagnation or decline in the larger industry of which they are a part. The limited growth prospects of these industries suggests that retention efforts could be better focused elsewhere.

Specializations that have been losing employment in the local area and also losing competitive share exhibit declining competitiveness and diminishing local prospects for growth. Employment losses often draw attention to such industries, but opportunities to reverse decline may be limited. If the larger industry is growing, then investigations need to consider realistically what it would take for the local industry to regain competitiveness in order to capture a share of the growth. If the industry as a whole is declining, the likelihood of reversing local decline seems particularly low. Unless poor performers are of overriding importance to the local economy, it is likely that attention can be better targeted elsewhere.

Analyzing Import Substitution Opportunities. Industries that are not current specializations also merit examination. An industry's strength in a local area reflects not only the extent to which local firms in the industry sell their outputs to customers located elsewhere, but also the extent to which they are fulfilling local demand for the good or service in question. To the degree that an area is not meeting its own demand for consumer goods or production inputs, there will be income "leakages" and fewer dollars circulating within the local economy. Though import substitution is often thought of in terms of building relationships between area manufacturers and local suppliers, it may also be a useful strategy for building the local service sector (see box, "Stimulating Service Sector Development").

As with industry specializations, industries that exhibit an average or below average concentration in the local economy can be categorized in terms of recent growth as strong, lagging, constrained, or poor performers. However, interpretation is somewhat more tentative than in the case of industries with a strong local presence. Analysis should try to distinguish between population-serving industries (which could be expected to have location quotients close to 1.0) and industries that lend themselves to exportation but which are locally weak (or at least not strong enough to show up as local specializations). In the former case, relative growth performance may simply reflect the change in the local population base relative to the reference economy. In the latter case, relative growth performance may signify changing competitive advantage.

STIMULATING SERVICE SECTOR DEVELOPMENT

Importation and exportation typically go on at the same time within a given local industry. What varies among industries and over time is the relative mix of local demand fulfillment, importation, and exportation. The processes of import substitution and export growth are clearly linked, however, because any circumstances that increase the ability of firms to serve a local area will also assist sales to customers outside the area's boundaries. Moreover, the initial existence of importation implies that the function in question is amenable to interregional trade.

For these reasons the problem of stimulating service activity is often considered simply in terms of export development, even though import substitution is heavily involved and tends to be more important for areas with an underdeveloped service base. Import substitution yields the same multiplier effects for a region's overall economy as export growth. In addition, the increased ability of an area to serve its own needs creates a higher multiplier on all subsequent export growth in both service-producing and goods-producing sectors. This has led the urban theorist Jane Jacobs to consider import substitution, not export growth, as the key element of the city-building process.

Interregional trade is relatively more important for producer-oriented services than for consumer-oriented services. The level of interregional trade in an industry is determined by tradeoffs between economies of scale and agglomeration on the one hand and the required number of direct customer contacts on the other. Part of the reason for recent increases in the overall volume of service trade is that progressively greater specialization is increasing the relative importance of economies of scale and agglomeration.

The magnitude of interregional trade in services was very poorly appreciated until recently. Important work in this area has been conducted by Beyers and colleagues.[1] Their survey research found that service industries including government accounted for close to half of all export jobs in the Central Puget Sound region, which is the home of Boeing and usually thought of as a manufacturing center.

Whereas manufacturing exportation from moderate-sized economies typically involves establishments that have always been mostly export-oriented, service establishments appear to be oriented at first toward local sales unless they are explicitly designated as regional offices. Building upon a base of local patronage, service firms acquire nonlocal customers over time if they are organized, motivated, and positioned to do so. This means that export growth in a service industry tends to be linked to growth in local demand. For this reason, stimulating service exportation would seem to be a difficult proposition in areas that are not growing. If demand limitations are to be overcome, the community must bring its full economic development resources to bear upon services as well as manufacturing.

Source: Thomas R. Hammer, *Evaluation of Development Potentials for Metropolitan Flint*, Evanston, Ill.: NCI Research, 1986.
[1] W. B. Beyers, M. J. Alvine, and E. G. Johnsen, *The Service Economy: Export of Services in the Central Puget Sound Region*, Central Puget Sound Economic Development District, Seattle, 1985.

Those non-specializations that are strong performers are of the most interest because they may represent emerging industries. The significance of these growth sectors should be evaluated. For example: What accounts for the local strength of these industries? What are their sources of competitive advantage? What relationship do they bear to the local area's traditional industry strengths?

Industries that are not current specializations, which are growing in absolute but not comparative terms, are growing due to larger economic or industry trends rather than local competitive advantage. In the absence of either a strong local presence or improving competitiveness, the local prospects for these industries are likely to be limited, notwithstanding current employment growth. These industries represent a lower priority target for development attention unless there is reason to think that local competitive performance can be turned around.

Similarly, industries with a limited local presence that are losing employment but gaining competitive share are an unlikely focus for development attention. In most cases there would be little rationale for efforts to bolster local strength in a declining industry that is not an important component of the local export base.

Finally, industries that are not local specializations and that have been declining in both comparative and relative terms would appear to offer little leverage for stimulating economic growth.

This type of analysis can be expanded to consider other industry characteristics for which published data are available. For instance, the Cook County analysis cited below had an industry size criterion: only industries with more than 1,500 local employees were considered. In lieu of a size threshold for inclusion, industries that are expanding could be screened to ensure that the number of added jobs meets a minimum level. This would prevent attaching undue significance to growth that is actually a result of the "small base effect"—situations where a large percentage increase in employment reflects an extremely small starting base. Another criterion that is sometimes used to screen industries is earnings per worker, an indicator of the quality of employment opportunities. Employment projections prepared by agencies such as DOL's Bureau of Labor Statistics can also be consulted to assess overall industry growth prospects.

EXAMPLE: COOK COUNTY
TARGET INDUSTRY STUDY

The example that follows is adapted from an industry targeting analysis performed for Cook County. The analysis focused on two segments of the local industry base: the manufacturing sector and the so-called "producer" services (Table 5.1). Producer services are sectors that tend to serve business and government markets rather than the final consumer.

Table 5.1
Industry Growth Analysis
Cook County, 1983-87[1]

A. Manufacturing

		1987 Employment	1983-87 Employment Change Cook Cty	U.S.	1983-87 Competitive Shift
	Manufacturing	490,863	-6.1	4.2	-10.3
20	Food & Kindred Products	43,623	-8.3	0.6	-8.9
[203	**Preserved Fruits & Vegetables**	**4,216**	**20.7**	**6.4**	**14.3]**
23	**Apparel & Fabricated Textile (232)**	**9,836**	**0.4**	**-4.7**	**5.1**
24	Lumber & Wood Products	4,037	-15.4	17.9	-33.3
25	**Furniture & Fixtures (all)**	**11,089**	**5.8**	**16.8**	**-11.0**
26	Paper & Allied Products	18,859	-0.5	5.6	-6.1
[264	**Misc. Converted Paper Prod.**	**8,529**	**5.4**	**10.4**	**-5.1]**
27	**Printing & Publishing (all)**	**61,673**	**4.0**	**16.6**	**-12.6**
28	**Chemicals & Allied Products (284, 286)**	**19,955**	**6.2**	**-5.6**	**11.8**
29	Petroleum & Coal Products	1,990	-1.2	-14.7	13.5
30	Plastic & Rubber Products	16,843	-1.7	18.3	-20.0
31	Leather & Leather Products	1,525	-10.0	-29.3	19.3
32	**Stone, Clay & Glass Products**	**9,697**	**1.0**	**6.4**	**-5.4**
33	Primary Metal Industries	18,514	-21.2	-9.1	-12.1
[336	**Nonferrous Foundries**	**3,400**	**5.2**	**13.8**	**-8.6]**
34	Fabricated Metal Products	63,526	-4.2	6.1	-10.3
[344	**Fabricated Structural Metal Prod.**	**7,357**	**4.7**	**3.0**	**1.7]**
[345	**Screw Machine Products**	**7,495**	**6.3**	**8.0**	**-1.7]**
[347	**Metal Services, n.e.c.**	**6,871**	**5.1**	**24.5**	**-19.4]**
35	Nonelectrical Machinery	47,905	-6.8	-1.7	-5.1
[359	**Misc. Nonelectrical Machinery**	**8,972**	**27.5**	**24.4**	**3.1]**
36	Electrical Machinery	63,042	-9.6	6.2	-15.8
[361	**Electric Distributing Equipment**	**5,770**	**2.8**	**-6.6**	**9.5]**
[364	**Electric Lighting Equipment**	**10,111**	**2.6**	**7.7**	**-5.1]**
37	Transportation Equipment	15,369	-13.8	17.0	-30.8
38	Instruments & Related	17,186	-11.9	-0.4	-11.5
39	Misc. Manufacturing	14,615	-13.1	6.2	-19.3
--	Admin., Aux., & Misc.	(est.) 50,000	-34.2	n.a.	n.a.

Note: Industries in bold face experienced employment growth in Cook County over the period.
Source: County Business Patterns, 1983, 1987. Adapted from J.F. McDonald, *Targeting Industries for Economic Development Marketing*, Evanston, Ill.: NCI Research, 1990.

In identifying producer services, the analysts generally followed the "Service Industry Classification Framework" that appears above in Unit 4. Excluded from consideration were service sectors devoted almost exclusively to serving the local population. Also excluded were services related to recreation, tourism, and cultural activities (which were outside the purview of the agency sponsoring the study) and nonprofit services such as health care, education, and social services. However, there is no inherent reason why recreation-tourism services or nonprofit services should not be

B. Producer Services[2]

		1987 Employment	1983-87 Employment Change		1983-87 Competitive Shift
			Cook Cty	U.S.	
	Producer Services	739,032	9.5	24.5	-15.0
42	Trucking & Warehousing (all)	34,861	5.3	25.5	-20.2
45	Air Transportation (all)	31,752	35.5	28.8	6.7
47	Transportation Services (all)	13,642	28.6	36.4	-7.8
48	Communication	26,656	-17.7	-9.8	-7.9
50	Wholesale-Durables (all)	110,226	13.1	15.2	-2.1
51	Wholesale-Nondurables (all)	62,080	4.1	12.2	-8.1
AA	Wholesale	16,440	10.3	8.2	2.1
60	Banking	55,040	-4.7	5.6	-10.3
61	Credit Agencies (all)	27,043	32.5	39.0	-6.5
62	Security, Commodity Brkrs. & Svcs. (all)	27,163	21.1	48.5	-27.4
63	Insurance Carriers (632 Medical)	57,201	2.2	8.6	-6.4
67	Holding & Investment Offices (all)	7,401	5.0	45.8	-40.8
AA	FIRE	2,730	28.0	?	?
73	Business Services (all exc. 7374)	153,124	6.4	47.8	-41.4
[731	Advertising	13,595	16.0	33.4	-17.4]
[737	Computer & Data Processing	13,228	-58.2	51.0	-109.2]
[7372	Computer Programming	3,757	68.4	91.7	-23.3]
[7392	Management & Public Relations	24,844	33.2	53.3	-20.1]
81	Legal Services (all)	30,766	27.6	35.5	-7.9
86	Membership Organizations (all exc. 863)	44,497	10.6	36.5	-25.9
89	Misc. Professional Svcs. (893, 899)	38,410	27.1	43.6	-16.5
AA	Services	12,746	16.6	22.5	-5.9

[1] Covers industries of 1,500 or more employees in Cook County in 1983 and 1987. Notations in parentheses indicate growth components within a particular sector. Bracketed items are three- or four-digit industries that run counter to their parent industry.

[2] Excludes SIC sectors that primarily serve the local population, nonprofit services, and recreation and tourism-related services, specifically: Local and Interurban Passenger Transit (41), Electric, Gas, and Sanitary Services (49), Retail Trade, Insurance Agents (64), Real Estate (65, 66), Hotels and Lodgings (70), Personal Services (72), Auto Repair (75), Misc. Repair Services (76), Motion Pictures (78), Amusement and Recreation (79), Health Services (80), Educational Services (82), Social Services (83), Museums, Art Galleries and Zoos (84).

analyzed as part of an overall economic assessment, since these industries—like producer services—may be important parts of the economic base in some areas.

The analysis began by deriving location quotients to identify Cook County's industry specializations (see Table 4.4 and the accompanying analysis in the previous unit). Next, measures of growth performance were derived (see Table 5.1). First, the 1983-87 change in industry employment was calculated for industries at the two- and three-digit levels (and also at the four-digit level in the case of business services.) The difference between the growth rate of an industry in Cook County and the national growth rate for that industry was also derived as a measure of change due to local factors (i.e., the local competitive shift).

Industry Growth Analysis. Table 5.1 reports the results of the analysis of industry employment growth for Cook County's manufacturing sector (Part A) and producer services sector (Part B). Because the 1983-87 period was one of economic recovery, the cyclical tendency would be for industries to show growth rather than decline. Indeed, the nation as a whole exhibited growth in manufacturing as well as producer services. However, Cook County experienced an overall 6.1 percent decline in manufacturing and lagging growth in producer services, so that the local competitive shift in both of these key sectors was negative.

Closer examination shows that only a few Cook County manufacturing industries experienced broad-based growth, notably furniture and fixtures (SIC 25) and printing and publishing (SIC 27). Several others, including apparel (SIC 23) and chemicals (SIC 28), increased employment only in selected subsectors. The metals and machinery industries (SICs 33-36), which employ a large number of people in Cook County and are historically important components of the economic base, did not perform well in the 1983-87 period. These industries lost employment overall, although selected subsectors ran counter to the general trend (see those listed within brackets).

Central areas have been losing manufacturing employment since at least the 1970s, so it is not too surprising to see manufacturing declines in Cook County in the period under examination. A key question is whether manufacturing losses were being offset by gains in sectors such as producer services that have been expanding in central areas in recent years. In fact, Cook County's 9.5 percent increase in producer services employment over the 1983-87 period generated about 64,000 additional jobs, more than offsetting the loss of some 31,600 manufacturing jobs during the same period. As shown in Part B of Table 5.1, almost all two-digit sectors within producer services gained employment in Cook County, the exceptions being Communication (SIC 48) and Banking (SIC 60). However, the right-most column of the table forewarns of trouble ahead. Despite Cook County's broad-based employment gains in producer services, almost all of these sectors were losing competitive share.

Analyzing Competitiveness. Table 5.2 arrays industries according to the screening criteria outlined above, so that the data may be compared from the standpoint of shifts in local competitiveness. Most of the manufacturing subsectors that gained employment in Cook County are local industry specializations; however, only two of these specializations gained share and could be considered strong performers—Electric Distributing Equipment (SIC 361) and Miscellaneous Nonelectrical Machinery (SIC 359). Four other local specializations in the metals and equipment sectors exhibited lagging growth, while one closely-related segment showed promise as an emerging industry (Fabricated Structural Metals, SIC 359). Meanwhile, the performance of the respective parent industries was poor in all cases.

A reasonable strategy for manufacturing development would be to focus on the strong and lagging performers within the metals and equipment industries to identify ways to retain and build on these pockets of strength within major local sectors that are otherwise in decline. This could be complemented by a closer look at the local chemicals industry (SIC 28), an emerging industry that may have potential as a major employer. Furniture is another segment that may represent an emerging specialization. Compared to other urban counties of the Northeast and North Central regions, Cook County has a noticeably higher concentration of employment in this growth sector (see comparisons to Super County, Table 4.4). Lagging performance may not be a concern if local firms have developed a niche within an industry that is not usually concentrated in major urban areas.

Cook County's printing and publishing industry (SIC 27) is best considered in relation to the producer services sector, since commercial printing accounts for the largest share of employment in the county's printing industry. Indeed, the pattern of lagging growth in this industry tallies with the lagging growth of industries that generate heavy demand for printing services such as advertising, management and public relations, and securities/commodities. The larger question, then, is why Cook County was losing share in these advanced corporate services, all of which represent important local specializations.

Cook County's sharp drop in employment in business services (SIC 73) also bears further examination, because this is a large and varied sector that has exhibited strength in central areas. This drop can be traced to a

Table 5.2
Assessment of Industry Development Status, Cook County[1]

A. Local Industry Specializations[2]

SIC	Industry	1987 L.Q.	1987 Employment	1983-87 Employment Change (%)	1983-87 Competitive Shift
	Strong Performers				
	Manufacturing				
[361	Electric Distrib. Equip.	2.49	5,770	2.8	9.5]
[359	Misc. Nonelec. Machinery	1.16	8,972	27.5	3.1]
	Services				
45	Air Transportation	2.40	31,752	35.5	6.7
AA	Wholesale	2.27	16,440	17.2	2.1
	Lagging Performers				
	Manufacturing				
[345	Screw Machine Products	3.15	7,495	6.3	-1.7]
[364	Electric Lighting Equip.	2.31	10,111	2.6	-5.1]
[264	Misc. Converted Paper	1.43	8,529	5.4	-5.1]
[336	Nonferrous Foundries	1.62	3,400	5.1	-8.6]
27	Printing & Publishing	1.70	61,573	4.0	-12.6
[347	Metal Services n.e.c.	2.33	6,871	5.1	-19.4]
	Services				
50	Wholesale-Durables	1.41	110,226	13.1	-2.1
AA	Services	1.88	12,746	16.6	-5.9
63	Insurance Carriers	1.77	57,201	2.2	-6.4
61	Nonbank Credit Agencies	1.26	27,043	32.5	-6.5
47	Transportation Services	1.79	13,642	28.6	-7.8
81	Legal Services	1.56	30,766	27.6	-7.9
51	Wholesale-Nondurables	1.13	62,080	4.1	-8.1
89	Misc. Prof. Services	1.10	38,410	27.1	-16.5
62	Security, Commod. Svcs.	2.6	27,163	21.1	-27.4
67	Investment Offices	1.28	7,401	5.0	-40.8
73	Business Services	1.27	153,124	6.4	-41.4
[731	Advertising	2.59	13,595	16.0	-17.4]
[7392	Management & P.R. svcs.	1.46	24,844	33.2	-20.1]
	Constrained Performers				
	(none)				
	Poor Performers				
	Manufacturing				
26	Paper & Allied Products	1.25	18,859	-0.5	-6.1
34	Fabricated Metals	1.82	63,526	-4.2	-10.3
38	Instruments	1.18	17,186	-11.9	-11.5
33	Primary Metals	1.12	18,514	-21.2	-12.1
36	Electrical Machinery	1.32	63,042	-9.6	-15.8
39	Misc. Manufacturing	1.56	14,615	-13.1	-19.3
	Services				
60	Banking	1.49	55,040	-4.7	-10.3
AA	Manufacturing	1.56	(est.) 50,000	-4.0	n.a.

B. Other Local Industries

SIC	Industry	1987 L.Q.	1987 Employment	1983-87 Employment Change (%)	1983-87 Competitive Shift
	Strong Performers				
	Manufacturing				
[203	Preserved Fruits & Veg.	0.82	4,216	20.7	14.3]
28	Chemicals	1.02	19,995	6.2	11.8
23	Apparel	0.38	9,836	.4	5.1
[344	Fabricated Struc. Metal	0.73	7,357	4.7	1.7]
	Lagging Performers				
	Manufacturing				
32	Stone, Clay, Glass	0.74	9,697	1.0	-5.4
25	Furniture	0.91	11,089	5.8	-11.0
	Services				
42	Trucking & Warehousing	1.01	34,861	5.3	-20.2
86	Membership Orgs.	1.05	44,497	10.6	-25.9
	Constrained Performers				
	Manufacturing				
29	Petroleum & Coal	0.68	1,990	-1.2	13.5
31	Leather	0.48	1,525	-10.0	19.3
	Poor Performers				
	Manufacturing				
35	Nonelectrical Machinery	1.04	47,905	-6.8	-5.1
20	Food & Kindred Prod.	1.07	43,623	-8.3	-8.9
30	Rubber & Misc. Plastics	0.89	16,843	-1.6	-19.9
37	Transportation Equip.	0.35	15,369	-13.8	-30.8
24	Lumber & Wood	0.24	4,037	-15.4	-33.3
	Services				
48	Communication	0.92	26,656	-17.7	-7.9
[737	Computer & Data Proc.	0.83	13,228	-0.6	-51.6]
[7372	Computer programming	0.54	3,757	68.4	-23.3]

Notes

[1] Industries are listed within categories in order of competitive shift, from strongest gainer to weakest decliner.

[2] Location quotient for industry in Cook County versus the U.S. is 1.1 or more.

[3] Bracketed items are industry segments that run counter to their parent industry or that are of special interest (i.e., professional components within business services).

---

rapid loss of jobs in data processing, an example of decentralization occurring in so-called "back office" operations. Advances in information technology have made it possible to decouple the routinized information-processing segments of certain services from those that require the face-to-face contacts or specialized services and skills most likely to be found in central urban locations. As happened in manufacturing, labor- or space-intensive routine service activities may split off, gravitating toward locations where the costs of space, energy, and labor are lower than in major urban centers.

Within producer services, Cook County's greatest current strength is in the "distributive" services, the grouping that includes transportation, communication, and wholesale trade. Transportation-related activities and wholesaling are local specializations with sizable employment. Among these industries are two of the area's strongest performers (Air Transportation and A&A activities in wholesaling), as well as several others that are lagging only moderately (Wholesale-Durables, Transportation Services, and Wholesale-Nondurables).

This cluster of industries reflects historic locational strengths of the Chicago area, notably its central location relative to the rest of the United States and its function as a distribution point for the major products of the Midwest, especially agricultural commodities and durable goods. The strengths of Cook County's central location have persisted into the present with the development of a strong concentration in air transportation, a key element of infrastructure in today's service- and consumer-oriented economy. Development strategy for the Cook County area should investigate ways to retain and consolidate its strengths in distributive services. For example, signs of weakness in Trucking and Warehousing (SIC 42) could have a bearing on the local growth prospects of this cluster.

Limitations of Targeting Analysis

The type of targeting analysis described above will help focus attention on a small set of significant local industries. However, this process is not without its drawbacks. First, the sole performance criterion used to identify these target industries is employment growth. Other criteria, such as sales or investment, could be just as relevant in evaluating industry performance. Thus, focusing only on employment may result in some industries being overlooked. Unfortunately, industrially detailed data are not available for other variables.

Second, the analysis of industry performance is backward looking. For instance, the most current industrially detailed data available at this writing are CBP data for 1989. Because it is based on historical patterns, this type of targeting analysis may miss significant recent trends. For example, in the Cook County case, more recent data would have been helpful in evaluating segments within the finance-insurance-real estate sector, which has been in turmoil in the past few years.

Third, in many rural areas, the data may be quite limited for this type of screening. Many small and mid-sized economies are highly concentrated in a limited number of industries or dominated by a few major employers.

Data disclosure problems may preclude target industry analysis unless the scope is expanded to encompass a larger region. In such cases, the analyst can turn to alternate methods of evaluating the local business base, such as those reviewed below.

EXAMINING THE BUSINESS BASE

The foregoing analysis is especially important for what it might reveal about the development of local industry clusters. Industries do not grow and develop at random, although historical accident does play a part. Nor do they grow in isolation; they develop as part of a nexus of related and supporting firms and industries, in a location that offers necessary inputs and access to customers and suppliers.[1] The right mix of attributes offers a competitive advantage to the industry's operations in that location. Competitive advantage is highly industry-specific and the sources of an area's competitive advantage are best understood in terms of particular industry clusters, rather than as isolated characteristics of the local area.

In an extensive cross-national study of the evolution of industry clusters at the national scale, economist Michael Porter (1990) develops insights that seem to apply equally well at the regional or local scale. In exploring why some areas are better than others at fostering leading firms in a particular industry, he identifies four aspects of the environment for industry growth that influence competitive advantage (see Figure 5.2). These "determinants of competitive advantage" comprise the operating environment and operating characteristics of an industry in a particular area.

In addition to production inputs ("factor conditions"), this model of industry competitiveness includes the role of industry clusters ("related and supporting industries"), the influence of market demand ("demand conditions"), and the goals and orientation of firms themselves ("firm strategy, structure, and rivalry"). Chance plays a role in the evolution of industries by disrupting the established order and creating openings for new competitors, products, and markets to emerge. Government also influences the system. In the case of local government, influence is typically directed to "factor conditions," alternatively known as factors of production. The next two units focus on ways to assess the local availability of such factors, including labor and nonlabor resources. Here we consider ways to evaluate the other three key determinants of industry competitive advantage.

---

[1] See, for example, Norse (1968), Ó hUallacháin and Satterthwaite (1988), Porter (1990), Satterthwaite (1992).

Figure 5.2
Determinants of Competitive Advantage

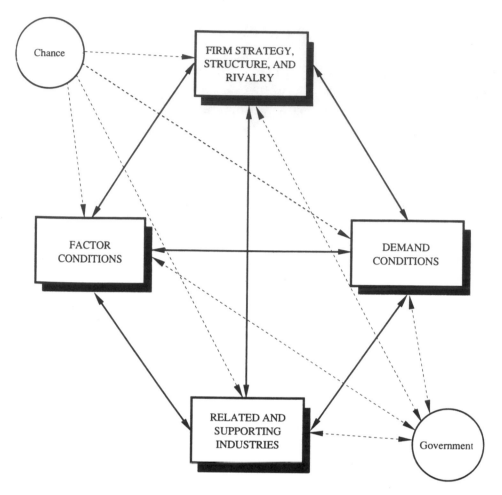

Reprinted with permission of the Free Press, a Division of Macmillan, Inc. from *The Competitive Advantage of Nations* by Michael E. Porter. Copyright 1990 by Michael E. Porter.

This stage of the analysis involves investigating the characteristics of the local business base as they relate to the nature of local industry clusters and the dynamism and market strength of local firms. Examples of things to examine include customer and supplier linkages, the nature of firms' markets, and the level of local entrepreneurship and innovation. Published data on these characteristics are scarce, although industry input-output tables and data on establishments are sometimes helpful (see below).

Specialized publications and reference sources are also worth consulting for industry-specific information. For example, the SIC Code

Manual can be consulted to gain a better understanding of the types of activities included in particular industries. The *U.S. Industrial Outlook*, published annually by the U.S. Department of Commerce, assesses the current situation and short- and long-term prospects of several hundred manufacturing and non-manufacturing industries and provides a list of additional references. It is a good source of information on the dynamics and outlook for particular industries, though its coverage of service industries is not as strong as its coverage of manufacturing. Industry trade groups and market research organizations (e.g., *Predicasts Forecasts*) are other sources that can be used to refine understanding of local industry clusters. There may be local public or university libraries with subscriptions to such market research services.

At this point, it will also be worthwhile to talk to people knowledgeable about particular industries in the local area. A business survey or interviews with local firms may be the only source for some types of information. A business survey can be used to gather a great deal of information on relationships among local businesses, suppliers and markets, and perceptions and problems with the local business environment.

Assessing Local Industry Clusters

Economic development involves building from the existing local industry base. One way to strengthen the industry base is to encourage the development of backward (supplier) and forward (customer) linkages. Examining interindustry linkages can reveal potential niches for locally supplied goods and services. It can also highlight vulnerabilities—such as the potential secondary impact on suppliers of a decline in an important local industry—which may help focus retention efforts.

Input-Output Analysis. One method for identifying these linkages is input-output analysis, which at its most basic level is an accounting framework. Input-output analysis examines the portion of its input an industry receives from other industries and the portion of its output that it sells to other industries. It can be used to assess what types of goods and services are needed to produce products in a given SIC sector. The analyst then can examine whether industries in a local economy supply basic inputs into the production process or whether these inputs are being imported into a local economy. This sort of analysis can help identify import substitution opportunities with the potential to stem leakages of local dollars for outside business purchases.

Table 5.3

**Major Inputs in Electrical Machinery Industries:
Direct Requirements per Dollar of Output**

	SIC					
	361,2	363	364	465,6	367	369
Primary iron and steel manufacturing (SIC 33)	.065	.085	.062	—	—	.026
Primary nonferrous metal manufacturing (SIC 33)	.067	.045	.066	.026	.049	.116
Screw machine products & stamping (SIC 345,6)	.015	.023	.029	—	.017	.014
Other fabricated metals (SIC 34)	.010	.026	.021	.012	.025	.025
Service industry machines (SIC 358)	—	.018	—	—	—	—
Electrical including equipment (SIC 361,2)	.077	.053	.018	—	—	.010
Household appliances (SIC 363)	—	.013	—	—	—	—
Electric lighting & wiring equipment (SIC 364)	—	.010	.020	—	—	—
Radio, TV and communications equipment (SIC 365,6)	—	—	—	.057	—	—
Electrical components (SIC 376)	.019	—	.014	.164	.144	.033
Miscellaneous electrical (SIC 369)	—	—	.019	—	—	.042
Scientific instruments (SIC 38)	—	.026	—	—	—	—
Transportation & warehousing (SIC 40-42, 44-47)	.015	.013	.017	.010	.016	.022
Utilities (SIC 49)	.012	.013	.012	—	.014	.012
Wholesale & retail trade (SIC 50-59)	.053	.053	.060	.045	.052	.046
Finance & insurance (SIC 60-64)	.010	—	.011	—	.010	.011
Business services (SIC 73, 89)	.020	.041	.026	.034	.030	.021
Value added	.510	.401	.462	.461	.468	.479

Source: 1977 U.S. Input-Output Table

Although a region-specific input-output table is unavailable for most communities and clearly impractical to construct, some states may have developed input-output tables. A useful alternative can be to utilize the U.S. Department of Commerce's national input-output table, published periodically in the Survey of Current Business. Table 5.3 above provides an example of such a table, showing input-output relationships among electrical machinery industries.

Surveying Customer-Supplier Relationships. Surveying or interviewing firms in a local economy is another way to identify linkages among area firms. For instance, firms could be asked to identify the five most important goods and services needed in their operations and to identify where they currently purchase these goods and services. Likewise, firms could be asked to identify the markets in which they sell their goods and services.

This type of effort can help identify local industry clusters. In one local area, investigation of recent industry growth patterns identified input linkages between food processing subsectors and several other growing industries. Growth in grain mill products (SIC 204) was found to be related to the growth of bakery products manufacturers (SIC 205). In addition, paperboard containers and boxes (SIC 265) was growing, as was food products machinery (SIC 3556). Thus, growth was occurring in a complex of activities related to the particular type of food processing in the area.

Markets of Local Firms

Firms that are aggressive in seeking out new customers and in responding to demand are the most likely to expand their markets. From a development perspective, a local environment that encourages market leadership will stand the best chance of long-term economic growth.

Other than information available from proprietary research services, data on the markets of local firms is apt to be sparse. This is a topic that is often covered in a business survey. As part of asking firms about their customer-supplier relationships, questions can be framed to elicit information useful in assessing firms' market position and market development activities. Firms can be asked to identify their major customers and suppliers by industry, by location and distance away, and by annual volume of purchases or sales. Things to consider include whether a firm is highly dependent on one or two firms or has a diverse customer base, the extent to which it sells within the local area or outside, and the extent of regional, national, and international markets.

Other items of interest include whether a firm is pursuing, or would consider, special marketing opportunities, such as export sales, government procurement, or joint ventures (e.g., joint bidding, licensing agreements, shared use of specialized equipment). Firms should also be asked about product development and whether they have introduced any new products recently or have any new products under development. Modernization needs also merit attention. Firms can be asked about technological change in their industry and how it is affecting them. It may be helpful to identify firms' primary sources of information about marketing, technology, and product innovations.

This kind of information will help assess the market status of local firms and suggest ways to focus business development programs.

Considering Value-Added. A special issue in many resource-based economies, where many of the raw materials are sent to other areas for further processing, involves the potential to shift to higher-value activity. Thus, it may be possible to identify opportunities for additional processing that involve a more productive use of local resources.

Evaluating Entrepreneurship

One of the most important characteristics of any local economy is its ability to generate new business. Research has shown that the death rate of existing firms is nearly constant in most areas of the country, but the birth rate of firms varies considerably (Birch, 1979). Successful economies are likely to have high birth rates of new firms and a high degree of entrepreneurship. Porter (1990) cites the importance of new business formations in supporting vigorous domestic rivalry, which was found to be strongly associated with the creation of competitive advantage in an industry.

Unfortunately, business birth rates by area are not readily available from published data sources. Some information on start-ups may be available from the state office that handles new firm incorporations. Unfortunately, these data are an extremely unreliable guide to new business starts. Many incorporations simply represent the legal incorporation of already existing establishments, usually as a means for the owners to gain personal protection against the firm's legal liability. Dun and Bradstreet's *DMI Indicators* also provides data on new businesses by area as a byproduct of their credit rating analysis of firms. However, their coverage of new firms, while reasonably comprehensive for manufacturers, is quite spotty for businesses in other sectors. Another possible data source is the state employment commission, which regularly tracks unemployment and employment data.

Using Establishment Data. In lieu of better sources, establishment data reported in *County Business Patterns* can be used to assess industry structure, employment concentration, and growth patterns as they may bear on the local environment for entrepreneurship. For example, an economy dominated by a single large firm—such as Caterpillar in Peoria, Illinois—or by a few large firms will perform differently from an economy with no dominant employer and a large number of small firms. The former economies are obviously highly dependent on the economic fortunes of the dominant firm. Similarly, business outreach efforts and development strategies can be expected to differ depending on whether employment in an industry is highly concentrated in a few firms or dispersed among many smaller firms.

The available data on establishments includes the number of establishments by size category, reported by county. Breakdowns are available by detailed size category as indicated in Table 5.4 below, which compares data for two counties in 1986:

Table 5.4
Number of Establishments
by Size Category

Establishment Size Category	County A	County B
1-4	2399	4138
5-9	1092	1741
10-19	694	1073
20-49	495	641
50-99	158	182
100-249	79	101
250-499	23	19
500-999	8	3
1000 or more	7	13

Source: 1986 County Business Patterns

To aid analysis, establishment size categories are often aggregated into groups such as small establishments (1-19 employees), medium-sized establishments (20-99 employees), large establishments (100-499 employees), and very large establishments (500 or more employees). Then the percentage of an area's businesses in each size category can be calculated and compared with that of other areas; changes over time in the area's distribution of establishments by size can also be examined. As shown in Table 5.5, this step indicates that the two counties have a roughly similar share of establishments in the "small" category.

Table 5.5
Percent of Total Establishments
by Size Category

Size Category	County A	County B
Small (1-19)	84.5	87.8
Medium (20-99)	13.2	10.5
Large (100-499)	2.1	1.5
Very Large (500+)	0.3	0.2

Source: 1986 County Business Patterns

Table 5.6
Percentage of Total Employment
by Establishment Size Category

Size Category	County A	County B
Small (1-19)	26.9	24.7
Medium (20-99)	32.8	23.2
Large (100-499)	25.5	16.0
Very Large (500+)	14.8	35.8

Source: 1986 County Business Patterns

Obviously, it would reveal more about a local economy if we knew the percentage of employment by establishment size group. These data are not reported, but by making a few assumptions we can come up with a reasonable estimate. If we assume that each establishment in a size group employs the median number of employees in that size category (i.e., all establishments in the five-nine employee size group employ seven people), then we can estimate the number of employees by size group simply by multiplying the median number of employees for that size group by the number of establishments in that group. Obviously, this cannot be done with the final size group (500 or more employees) because we do not know the midpoint. But, we can estimate the number of employees in this group simply by adding the estimated number of employees in all the other size groups and subtracting the result from the total number of employees in the area (also provided in *County Business Patterns*.)

Using this procedure we can see that the economies of the two counties differ substantially (Table 5.6 above). Employment in County B is much more concentrated than in County A; approximately 36 percent of County B's total employment is in very large establishments compared with about 15 percent for County A.

Establishment data can also help in evaluating the characteristics of individual industries. For example, Table 5.7 displays the distribution of establishments by size category in air transportation and transportation services industries in Cook County. A comparison of SICs 45 and 47 illustrates how industry structure can differ: SIC 45, which includes airlines, is much more concentrated than SIC 47, which includes travel agencies.

Assessing Changes in the Size Distribution of Establishment. As shown in Table 5.7, it is possible to calculate the change in the number of establishments in an area or industry between any two points of time.

Table 5.7

Table 5.7
Air Transportation and Transportation Services:
Number of Establishments by Employment Size

SIC		Total 1987	1 - 19		20 - 99		100 - 499		500 +	
			1987	Change 1983-87	1987	Change 1983-87	1987	Change 1983-87	1987	Change 1983-87
45	Air Transportation	144	90	-3	30	+4	19	+11	5	-5
451	Certified air transportation	121	76	+3	25	+3	15	+11	5	-5
458	Air transportation services	23	14	-3	5	-1	4	0	0	0
47	Transportation Services	1,269	1,157	+208	93	+13	18	+6	1	0
471	Freight forwarding	150	120	+20	23	+1	7	+2	0	0
472	Arrangement of Transportation	1,048	981	+186	60	+17	6	+2	1	+1
4722	Passenger	877	827	+129	44	+13	5	+2	1	+1
4723	Freight	170	154	+57	16	+4	0	-1	0	0
474	Rental of RR cars	15	12	+2	1	-1	2	+1	0	0
478	Misc. transportation services	37	26	+1	8	-3	3	+1	0	0

Source: County Business Patterns

Sometimes analysts look at change in the number of small firms (1-20 employees or 1-50 employees) as an indicator of entrepreneurship. However, it is possible that some of the change represents not "net" new firms in the area but existing firms that were previously medium-sized but lost employment so that they now fall into the category of small-sized firms. However, if the number of establishments is increasing across all size categories, it can be interpreted as a positive sign of strength for the local economy or the particular industry under examination.

The general difficulty with interpreting changes in establishment size distribution is that this simple calculation represents a "net" change and tells us nothing about the actual number of new businesses started. For this purpose "gross" changes are necessary. Suppose the number of establishments in a county increased by 100 over a five year period. This could have occurred through the birth of 200 new establishments and the closing of 100 or through the birth of 500 new establishments and the closing of 400. The latter situation suggests a much more entrepreneurial and dynamic economy. Researchers such as Birch (1987) and Hicks (1991) are among those developing techniques for analyzing underlying components of establishment change.

Firm Ownership Characteristics and Establishment Function. The ownership characteristics of local firms and the economic functions of individual establishments may also influence their entrepreneurial orientation.

Establishments may be independent single location firms, the headquarters site of a multi-location firm, or a branch plant of a multi-location firm. There is some evidence that areas whose economies are characterized primarily by headquarters establishments and independent firms may be more in control of their own destinies and less susceptible to sudden disruptions (such as plant closures and relocations) than areas dominated by branch plant establishments.

Unfortunately, data on the ownership characteristics and function of establishments are not available from any public data source. The best private data source is the Dun and Bradstreet *DMI File*. Other alternative sources of information include industry directories and Chamber of Commerce data. These sources of information can also be used to fill gaps when data from federal sources are withheld.

Conducting a Business Survey

As the preceding discussion indicates, there are many types of information that can be obtained only from surveys or interviews with local firms. Although a comprehensive business survey entails a fair amount of effort, it is worth undertaking periodically since there is no substitute source for the kind of in-depth information that can be obtained about local firms. A less ambitious undertaking might involve surveying only selected industries or even convening a "focus group" of industry representatives to outline issues for industry development in the local area.

There are many excellent treatments of survey research methods that can be consulted when planning such a survey. In addition, examples of survey instruments for economic development purposes are available from a number of sources (see the references at the end of this unit).

One aspect of business surveys that is often overlooked is their function in establishing contact between local employers and the local economic development community. The survey can do more than generate information, it can be a basis for developing a closer relationship between local firms and the staff of business development programs or public officials. It is sometimes suggested that business surveys be carried out with the participation of business groups such as local chambers of commerce, both to reduce labor costs and because local business people may be more inclined to deal with other local business people than with public officials. Whether or not this is the case probably varies depending on local circumstances. One consideration is that such a survey may generate timely information (e.g., notice that a firm plans to relocate or that it is unable to secure financing) that should be passed on to local development officials. Procedures should be in place to ensure that the survey sponsor realizes the maximum benefits of this type of outreach effort.

ANALYZING ECONOMIC GEOGRAPHY

Economic geography refers to the location and economic function of a city within the constellation of other communities in a larger region. Analysis of economic geography may be especially important for local economies that are dominated by larger regional forces, whose scope of effective action may consist largely of site-specific development opportunities.

Areas in close proximity exchange significant flows of goods, services, people, and income. Geographic patterns of development and trade within and around the study area can be examined to identify the function of the local economy within the regional economy and ways local functions might be strengthened. Things to consider include:

- Population characteristics and trends and implications for population-support functions (e.g., housing, retail trade)

- Location of employment centers and policy implications of commuting patterns

- Special regional functions (e.g., airports, universities, recreation facilities) and ways they might be leveraged

Adjacent communities often compete with the study area for consumer and producer markets in the region. At the same time, adjacent communities are potential consumers of goods and services produced locally. The types of analysis outlined below can help clarify these relationships for purposes of development planning.

Who Lives in the Local Area?

Population analysis explores overall trends, components of population change, and demographic characteristics of the local population. This will reveal the nature of local markets and the potential need or demand for particular types of goods and services. The analysis focuses on the following issues:

- Overall population increases or decreases and whether they are due to natural causes (births and deaths) or migration into or out of the area

- The age distribution of the population

- Whether certain segments of the population (by age, race, sex) are increasing or decreasing

- Characteristics of migrants

Broad population trends should already be familiar from the earlier analysis of income statistics as part of the assessment of economic performance and condition (see Chapter 3). For a more detailed analysis of population characteristics and trends, the best source of data is the decennial Census of Population. Local area population statistics with breakdowns by age, sex, and race are scheduled for release in 1991-92; data on social and economic characteristics including migration and commuting should be available in 1993 (see Appendix B, *Census '90* for reports and projected release dates).

For intercensal years or toward the end of a decade, analysis will have to be carried out using estimates from other sources such as the Census Bureau's Current Population Reports (Series P-26) or state sources. In working with census data, keep in mind that the data cover those who live in a local economy and not necessarily those working there. Care must be exercised in reconciling population data with employment information based on place-of-work.

Overall Trends and Components of Change. To gauge long-term trends, the analyst should assemble total population figures from the last two decennial censuses (e.g., 1970 and 1980) along with the most current estimates available until 1990 census data are released. The percentage change over each period can be calculated and compared to similar data for the nation, state, and comparison areas. This will answer basic questions with potential policy implications. For example, has the local population been growing rapidly or slowly compared to other areas? Has the direction or magnitude of population change shifted from one period to the next? Beware of assigning too much importance to small differences, which might reflect imperfections in how the numbers were generated.

Aggregate population change can be broken down into two basic components: natural increase/decrease and net migration. *Net natural increase (or decrease)* is the difference between the number of births and deaths that occur in an area. *Net migration* is the difference between the number of people who move into an area (in-migrants) and the number who move out (out-migrants).

To illustrate, consider the following comparison of population changes in two rural counties over the 1980-88 period (Table 5.8). Both experienced a roughly similar percentage change in population: County A's population rose by nearly 1,300 persons (16.7 percent) while County B's population increased by roughly 1,600 persons (15.9 percent). However, the components of change were very different for the two areas.

In County A, the increase in total population is due entirely to net migration—more people moved into the county than moved out. At the same time, the number of deaths exceeded births, dampening overall population growth. In County B, on the other hand, the population increase was due in almost equal parts to net migration (more people moved in than moved out) and net natural increase (an excess of births over deaths). The two counties, then, proceeded along separate paths to reach the same general outcome.

Analyzing Demographic Change. While this information is useful, it raises as many questions as it answers. For example, what is the age distribution in the two counties? Does County A's natural decrease reflect a population comprised primarily of older residents? What are the characteristics of the in- and out-migrants? Are the people moving into County A retirees and those in County B younger families? If so, County A may need to consider the adequacy of health and nursing care facilities or

---

Table 5.8
Change In Population
1980-88

	Population		Absolute Change 1980-88	Percent Change 1980-88	Net Migration 1980-88	Natural Increase 1980-88
	1980	1988				
County A	7,711	9,000	1,289	16.7%	1,300	-11
County B	10,009	11,600	1,591	15.9%	800	791

Source: U.S. Census Bureau (1980) and state estimate (1988).

specialized transportation, while County B may have to worry about whether the schools in the area can absorb more students and the adequacy of services needed by families. An area with in-migrants may be gaining new workers (good if jobs are available) or perhaps retirees (who bring new income into the area, but may increase the demand for services for the older population).

Clearly, the age distribution of the local population influences local markets for goods and services and also affects the size and composition of the potential labor force (see Chapter 6). In the case of the two counties analyzed above, a quick comparison (not shown) focused on the "tails" of the age distribution—those over 65 and those under 18. The comparisons confirmed the hypotheses. In 1980, 21 percent of the residents of County A were over the age of 65 compared to only 12.5 percent in County B and only 9.8 percent in the state. Conversely, the percentage of persons under 18 in County A was only 27 percent, compared to 32 percent in County B and 30 percent in the state.

The sum of these two categories—percent of people over 65 and under 18—is sometimes used as a measure of dependency, since these people are not normally in the labor force. For example, in County A almost 48 percent of the population fell into these two categories compared to only 38.5 percent in the state. Areas such as County A may have a greater demand for government services than other areas, but a more limited working age population to support public services through taxes.

It is often useful to examine changes in the age distribution over time. For example, which is the fastest-growing age category? Is the number of persons of "prime" working age (21-65) declining? The implications of such changes for the local economy and for policy should be explored. To assist in analyzing age characteristics of the population, detailed age breakdowns are often displayed as an "age pyramid" (see example, Figure 5.3).

Analyzing Migrants. The contribution of migration to the changing age distribution of the local population is often of interest. For example, if the economy is performing poorly, the prime working age population may be declining as people move in search of better economic opportunities. Areas experiencing such declines may find it difficult to respond to the need for additional labor without having to "import" workers from other areas. Another consideration is whether the area is gaining, or losing, retirees— especially the more affluent segments with stable sources of unearned income.

Figure 5.3
Age Structure of the Population,
Home County vs. U.S.
1970 and 1980

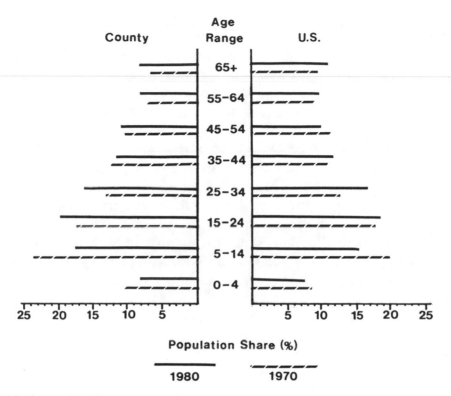

Source: U.S. Bureau of the Census

Unfortunately, other than census data, information for examining the characteristics of migrants is quite limited. Until the 1990 census data become available, the best source of information is the 1980 census data (which covers the characteristics of people who moved between 1975 and 1980). The Internal Revenue Service's Statistics of Income Division can provide counts of the number of in- and out-migrants to and from all U.S. counties and states for every two-year period using its master file of all income tax returns. However, this source does not provide any information on the characteristics of those who moved other than where they moved to and from.

Population dynamics can provide significant insight and help identify local needs or market opportunities that should be considered in strategic planning.

Where Do People Work?

Analysis of area industrial structure typically relies on data reported by place of work (e.g., CBP and BEA data). However, the economic integration achieved by commuting can have major policy implications.[2] For example, one city that is a small part of a larger urban area found that only 12 percent of all jobs in the city were held by city residents, while only 23 percent of the city's residents were employed there. Such findings do not mean that attracting new businesses is unimportant, but they suggest that business development programs should probably focus more on tax base and population support objectives than job-related objectives.

In another case, location quotient analysis suggested that a county was fully satisfying its internal requirements for retail trade and was probably a major exporter of food retailing. However, the area's industrial structure was found to be unusual in that half the county's resident jobholders work outside the county. In such a case, data on total at-place employment substantially understates local demand for consumer services. Analysis of other data confirmed that far from being an exporter of retailing, the area was fulfilling only between half and two-thirds of its retail trade requirements.

In the case of Flint, analysis of area income data revealed income leakages due to commuting (see Chapter 3). A strong net in-commuting pattern, perhaps as a result of a large local manufacturing plant as in the case of Flint, can bias a local economy. Manufacturing employment may be high, but service expenditures and employment may be lower than expected because many workers leave the area after work and spend their earned income elsewhere. To stem such leakages, the area may want to consider improving residential or shopping opportunities. Alternatively, it may decide to focus on its function as an area employment center.

Data Availability. The decennial census is the major source of data on commuting flows, reported in its "Place of Work" and "Journey to Work" series. The projected release date for commuting data from the 1990 census is 1992 or early 1993. Printed reports will present data on net commuting flows from one county to another within metropolitan areas and flows into and out of metropolitan areas. For comprehensive and detailed cross-tabulations of data at the local level (e.g., age, race, sex, and earnings associated with various commuting flows), it may be necessary to purchase the Census Public Use Tapes and run the cross-tabs locally.

---

[2] Examples of the role of commuting are drawn from Thomas R. Hammer, *Technical Support for Strategic Planning in Small Michigan Communities*, Evanston, Ill.: NCI Research, July 1990.

Where Do People Shop?

As with commuting, area geography and land use can profoundly affect trade patterns within a region. Flint, for instance, suffers a market disadvantage with respect to consumer purchases. While it is too far away from Detroit for an easy work commute, it is sufficiently close that it loses much of its "central-placc" function in relation to the surrounding hinterland. If Flint were a bit more remotely located, residents of adjacent counties would have fewer choices: they would have to make retail and service purchases within the local area. However, the relative proximity and good access to a much larger urban center means that income is siphoned off.

This type of income leakage is especially likely to occur with more significant purchases of goods and services for which individuals will travel some distance, such as big ticket retail items, highly specialized services, and upscale consumption. These purchases have a bit of a multiplier cffcct, so losses are both direct and indirect.

Some baseline data on regional competition and markets can help place the study area economy in perspective. Two useful data sources arc *Sales and Marketing Management Magazine*, which provides data on Effective Buying Income (EBI) or total after-tax personal income, and Rand McNally's *Commercial Atlas and Marketing Guide*, which provides data on total retail sales by county. These data can be used to determine whether income from a particular county is leaking out for purchases of retail goods in adjacent counties. The first step involves calculating the home county share of the total EBI for the home county plus all surrounding counties where local residents might conceivably shop. The next step is to calculate the home county share of total retail sales in the same area. If the home county accounts for half of the area's total EBI, it should likewise account for half of the area's total retail sales assuming there is no nct leakage. If the home county's share of retail sales exceeds its share of area EBI, it is capturing income from other areas (retail trade represents an export good). Conversely, if the home county's share of retail sales falls below its share of area EBI, it is leaking income to adjacent areas.

Trade Capture Analysis. Another potentially useful technique is a "trade capture" analysis. Trade capture analysis compares an area's retail sales per capita by retail industry to state retail sales per capita in the same industry, after adjusting for differences in per capita income between the area and the state. A score of less than one suggests that a local economy is losing customers to other areas, while a score greater than one indicates it is attracting customers from outside the area.

Special Functions

Another aspect of economic geography is the presence of specialized facilities serving the region. It may be useful to compile an inventory of regional facilities, such as airports, convention centers, stadiums, major tourist attractions, theaters and cultural facilities, and universities and colleges. Local planning departments, chambers of commerce, and economic development groups are likely sources of information.

Other types of information to include in this review include information on land-use zoning patterns and development planned in the near future, to identify major concentrations of manufacturing firms, commercial development or specialized aggregations (e.g., high-tech clusters). Potential sources include area realtors as well as local planning departments.

SUMMARY: DRAFTING A MISSION STATEMENT

The results of the industry targeting assessment will identify local industries that merit special attention because of their concentration or recent growth patterns. Indications of changing competitive advantage can be explored further by supplementing the quantitative analysis with information from other sources. Things to consider include the nature of industry linkages, the presence and strength of industry clusters, the nature of firms' markets, and the entrepreneurial orientation of industries and firms. Some of this information is available only from interviews or surveys of local businesses.

Some local economies function largely within the sphere of influence of a larger metropolitan or regional economy. Unless the area functions as an employment center for the region, it may be more appropriate to focus analysis on population support functions that the area may perform as a residential or retail center.

At this stage of the analysis, the issues that represent primary areas of need or opportunity for the local economy should be fairly evident. This is an appropriate time to present the findings of the economic audit to the strategic planning committee for review. At this point, the committee or community representatives should attempt to reach a consensus on the main focus for the rest of the planning effort. Ideally, this consensus can be articulated as a "mission statement" that informs the next stage of the analysis—a review of resources and response options.

Additional Reading

Location and Growth of Services

Beyers, William B. "Producer Services and Metropolitan Growth and Development," in *Sources of Metropolitan Growth*, Edwin S. Mills and John F. McDonald, eds. New Brunswick, N.J.: Center for Urban Policy Research Press, 1992.

Moss, Mitchell L. and Andrew Dunau. "Will the Cities Lose Their Back Offices?" *Real Estate Review*, Spring 1987, New York: Warren, Gorham & Lamont, Inc.

Ó hUallacháin, Breandán. "The Location and Growth of Business Services in U.S. Metropolitan Areas," in *Assessing the Development Status of Metropolitan Areas* by John F. McDonald, Breandán Ó hUallacháin and Thomas M. Beam. Evanston, Ill.: NCI Research, 1989.

Agglomeration and Industry Clusters

Nourse, Hugh O. *Regional Economics*. New York: McGraw-Hill, 1968.

Ó hUallacháin, Breandán and Mark Satterthwaite. *Sectoral Growth Patterns at the Metropolitan Level*. Evanston, Ill.: NCI Research, 1988.

Porter, Michael E. *The Competitive Advantage of Nations*. New York: Macmillan-The Free Press, 1990.

Satterthwaite, Mark A. "High Growth Industries and Uneven Metropolitan Growth," in *Sources of Metropolitan Growth*, Edwin S. Mills and John F. McDonald, eds. New Brunswick, N.J.: Center for Urban Policy Research Press, 1992.

Input-Output Analysis

For basic overviews of input-output analysis, see:

Jackson, Randall. "Input-Output Analysis For The Uninitiated." DeKalb, Ill.: Center for Governmental Studies, 1984.

Miernyk, William H. *The Elements of Input-Output Analysis*. New York: Random House, 1965.

Assessing Entrepreneurship

For discussion and examples of approaches for analyzing the local base of business establishments see:

Birch, David L. *The Job Generation Process*. Washington, D.C.: Economic Development Administration, 1979.

_____. "The Rise and Fall of Everybody." *INC*. September, 1987, pp. 18-19.

Hicks, Donald A. "Tracking Economic Turnover and Adjustment." *Economic Development Commentary* 15 (Summer, 1991): 28-29. Published by National Council for Urban Economic Development.

Survey Research Methods

For an excellent in-depth treatment of survey research, see

Bailey, Kenneth D. *Methods of Social Research*. New York: Macmillan/Free Press, 1978.

For examples of business surveys, see

Gregerman, Alan. *Competitive Advantage: Framing a Strategy to Support High Growth Firms*. Washington, D.C.: National Council for Urban Economic Development, July 1984.

Michigan Modernization Service. Research Analysis Group, "Local Area Modernization Plan - LAMP Project Questionnaire." Ann Arbor: Industrial Technology Institute, June 1989.

Trade Capture Analysis

Hustedde, Ron, et al. *Community Economic Analysis*. Ames, Iowa: North Central Regional Center for Rural Development, 1984.

CHAPTER

6

PROFILING LOCAL HUMAN RESOURCES

Earlier units have focused upon economic activity or the "demand" side of an area economy. This unit and the next focus on the "supply" side of the economic development equation. First we consider the role of human resources and how they can be evaluated. In the next unit, attention turns to the nonlabor resources that support the local economy.

Labor force trends and characteristics are as important to examine as the structure of the local economy. An area's human resources—the skills, education, knowledge and aptitudes of its population—represent one of the most important resources available to existing and potential investors. As Robert Reich has observed,

> ". . . The industries of the future will not depend on physical 'hardware,' which can be duplicated anywhere, but on the human 'software,' which can retain a competitive advantage . . . [T]he skills, knowledge, and capacity for teamwork within a nation's labor force will determine the collective standard of living."[1]

In assessing local human resources, three broad topics need to be investigated: 1) trends in the labor force and its components, 2) labor force characteristics such as occupational mix and quality, and 3) labor cost. Key questions to answer include:

- What is happening to the size of an area's labor force?

- How many people are working and how many are looking for work? How have these changed over time?

- What is happening to labor force participation rates and how have they changed?

---

[1] Robert C. Reich, *The Next American Frontier*, New York: Basic Books, 1983, p.236.

- What is the current and past mix of occupations in a local economy? How has this changed over time and in comparison to other areas?

- How do local labor quality and costs compare to those elsewhere?

LABOR AVAILABILITY

The analysis of the local population base described at the end of the preceding unit provides a starting point for a closer examination of local human resources. As with the population analysis, the basic data source is the decennial Census of Population. When current decennial census data are not available, the analyst may have to rely on supplementary sources to update the census figures.[2] In addition, private vendors such as CACI, Polk, and others sell more detailed estimates of population (but not the labor force per se), with breakouts by age, race, sex, and income level for census tracts and zip code areas. Since these estimates are based on proprietary methods, their accuracy is hard to determine.

Size of the Labor Force and
Numbers Employed and Unemployed

The first step in determining labor resources is to identify the size of the "potential" labor force, defined as the local population in the 16-65 age range. Changes in the size and composition of the labor force can be calculated using data for the past two census years or appropriate mid-point estimates to compare trends (e.g., 1970-1985/90; 1970-80, and 1980-85/90). Data may also be available to compare trends in recent years (see example below, Table 6.1)

Knowledge about changes in the size of the working-age population may clarify aspects of an area's economic performance. For instance, some areas have experienced stubbornly high unemployment rates even though the number of jobs available has grown at a rapid rate. Analysis may reveal that the area's working-age population is expanding more quickly than jobs are being created.

---

[2] These include the Census Bureau's annual *Local Population Estimates*, for basic population data, and the BLS *Employment and Earnings* series, with monthly labor force and occupational data for the 30 largest MSAs and selected central cities.

As the foregoing suggests, an area's unemployment rate provides a broad indication of tightness or slackness in the local labor market but reveals little about underlying labor market dynamics. The significance of area unemployment rates can be explored by examining the numbers of employed and unemployed residents in light of the size of the potential labor force.

For example, Table 6.1 shows January labor force, employment, and unemployment totals and January to January changes for residents of the Chicago PMSA in 1988, 1989, 1990, and 1991. In the 1988-89 period, growth in the labor force was being exceeded by growth in employment resulting in a decline in the number unemployed and a reduction in the unemployment rate. But in the 1989-90 period, strong growth in employment was exceeded by even stronger growth in the labor force, producing an increase in the number of unemployed and a rise in the unemployment rate. This illustrates that rising unemployment does not always reflect declines in the number of jobs. In the 1990-91 period we see the effects of recession. The size of the labor force has declined, but not so much as the number of jobs (e.g., the number employed). As a result, the number unemployed continued to climb and so did unemployment rates.

Table 6.1
Labor Force Analysis, Chicago PMSA*
1988, 1989, 1990

	Labor Force	Number Employed	Number Unemployed	Unemployment Rate (%)
January 1988	3,151,404	2,947,702	203,702	6.5
January 1989	3,181,152	3,001,043	180,109	5.7
(Change 1988-89)	(0.9%)	(1.8%)	(-11.6%)	
January 1990	3,305,539	3,102,298	203,241	6.1
(Change 1989-90)	(3.9%)	(3.4%)	(12.8%)	
January 1991	3,275,748	3,056,740	219,008	6.7
(Change 1990-91)	(-0.9%)	(-1.5%)	(7.8%)	

* The Chicago primary metropolitan statistical area (PMSA) consists of Cook, DuPage, and McHenry counties

Source: Illinois Department of Employment Security

Labor Force Participation

In the preceding example, we observed rising unemployment accompanied by shrinkage in the size of the local labor force. Changes in the size of the local labor force are not only a function of changes in the working-age population due to natural increases and decreases or migration; the local labor force may also be affected by changes in labor force participation.

Not all of those in the potential labor force are working or seeking work. The overall labor force participation rate is the percentage of the population aged 16-65 that is working or actively seeking work (i.e., registered as unemployed).[3] Labor force participation rates often vary by demographic group or over time.

Some care must be taken when calculating labor force participation rates, especially in areas with a large institutional population (residents in health care facilities, prisons, colleges, etc.). Because most of these residents are unlikely to be actively seeking work, the potential labor force may be overstated. If their numbers can be ascertained, they can be subtracted from the total population aged 16-65 years (the denominator of the ratio) before calculating participation rates.

A number of factors may influence local labor force participation and cause variations over time. First, a dynamic, growing local economy may draw many people into the labor force who would otherwise not be actively seeking employment. Similarly, in a depressed, declining economy, labor force participation rates can be expected to fall as discouraged workers cease looking for work and no longer show up on the unemployment rolls. Labor force participation rates also may change as social changes occur—for instance, as more women enter the labor force. The relationship between migration and labor force participation rates is another factor to explore. Young adults of prime working age (21-65) are most likely both to move and to be in the labor force.[4]

---

[3] Some analysts use the ratio of total employment to total population as a proxy for labor force partipation rates. However, this would seem to be an inferior measure because it omits the number of unemployed seeking work and fails to take into account the age structure of the population.

[4] See, for example, Donald R. Haurin and R. Jean Haurin, "The Migration of Youth and the Business Cycle: 1978-1984," *Economic Development Quarterly*, May 1987, pp 162-175.

Assessing Discouraged Workers. Unemployment rates do not capture those who have given up looking for work and dropped out of the labor force. Although there is no direct way to measure the presence of these discouraged workers, analysis of labor force participation rates in light of overall economic trends or participation rates elsewhere can be revealing.

Labor force participation rates by age, sex, and race in the city of Chicago for each year from 1980 to 1988 are shown in Table 6.2. Overall employment in the city of Chicago was growing throughout most of this period, increasing 7.5 percent between 1983 and 1989 (not shown). Labor force participation ordinarily increases when an economy is growing. The table shows that this has generally been the case for the white population in Chicago. Except for teenagers, labor force participation of whites was up about two percent in 1988 over its level in the mid-1980s. The labor force participation rate for nonwhites shows the opposite trend, with a two percent decline between 1987 and 1988. The pattern suggests an increasing number of discouraged workers. Among the possible explanations for the observed decline are mismatches between workers' skills or educational levels and those needed in the contemporary workplace.

Table 6.2
Labor Force Participation Rates
City of Chicago, by Percent of Participation

	16-65	16-19	20-65	Male 16-65	Female 16-65
White Population					
1980	64.5	61.6	64.8	79.1	50.9
1981	64.4	58.1	65.0	78.6	51.5
1982	61.9	54.3	62.5	76.8	48.9
1983	60.2	NA	NA	74.5	47.5
1984	60.1	NA	NA	72.6	49.3
1985	61.9	57.8	62.3	75.2	50.2
1986	62.4	54.4	62.9	75.9	50.5
1987	63.0	47.6	64.2	76.1	51.8
1988	64.1	50.0	65.2	77.2	52.8
Non-white Population					
1980	55.7	27.7	59.8	64.6	48.2
1981	56.3	33.3	60.0	65.8	48.9
1982	59.9	36.1	62.9	69.0	52.6
1983	60.1	NA	NA	69.8	52.7
1984	57.3	NA	NA	66.4	49.7
1985	60.0	35.5	61.7	69.1	50.6
1986	58.3	37.9	60.8	67.5	51.0
1987	58.4	34.4	60.9	67.7	50.8
1988	56.5	31.0	59.8	66.6	48.8

Source: U.S. Bureau of the Census, Current Population Survey

Comparisons of local labor force participation rates to those elsewhere may also indicate the presence of discouraged workers or signal labor force segments that are underutilized. Table 6.3 compares labor force participation rates by age and sex in the Flint MSA to those in the state and nation using 1980 census data. The 1980 participation rates for males were somewhat higher than the corresponding U.S. rates for the three age groups covering years 16 through 54. Flint also exceeded Michigan except in the case of teenagers. Beyond age 54, however, labor force participation was much lower in Flint than in either the state or the nation. The relatively high labor force participation rates of "prime" working age males in Flint reflect conditions prior to the initiation of GM's downsizing, ongoing through the 1980s.

In contrast to male labor force participation rates, rates of labor force partipation among women in Flint were lower than the corresponding Michigan and U.S. rates in all age categories. The lowness of the values suggests that the area's female productive resources were substantially underutilized.

Table 6.3
Labor Force Participation Rates by Age and Sex in 1980,
Flint, Michigan, and U.S.

	Age Group				
	16-19	20-24	25-54	55-64	65+
Male:					
Flint	51.8	87.1	93.1	61.6	11.8
Michigan	53.7	82.7	92.5	69.9	14.9
United States	51.2	81.8	92.4	71.3	19.3
Flint-U.S.					
Difference	0.6	5.3	0.7	-9.7	-7.5
Female:					
Flint	42.8	64.5	58.1	32.9	5.0
Michigan	49.0	67.6	59.7	37.4	6.2
United States	45.6	67.6	63.1	41.6	8.2
Flint-U.S.					
Difference	-2.8	-3.1	-5.0	-8.7	-3.2

Source: U.S. Census of Population, 1980. Table adapted from *Evaluation of Development Potentials for Metropolitan Flint, Michigan* by Thomas R. Hammer, Evanston, Ill.: NCI Research, 1986, p. 136.

Employment Patterns by Demographic Group. Variations in the labor force participation of demographic groups may reflect local employment structure. An assessment of the distribution of employment by demographic group may clarify the labor force implications of employment shifts.

For example, Table 6.4 shows the number of workers in manufacturing and nonmanufacturing industries in the Flint MSA in 1980, with breakdowns by race and sex. Some 40 percent of resident workers in 1980 were employed in manufacturing, primarily at GM. However, manufacturing employed a much larger share of nonwhite workers (53 percent) than white workers (38 percent). The relative concentration of nonwhite workers in manufacturing means the area's nonwhite population is most affected by cyclical shifts and long-term decline in local manufacturing industries.

The data also reveal a polarization of male and female labor in manufacturing versus service activity that is characteristic of economies with a metal-industry specialization. Only about 20 percent of the area's female workers were engaged in manufacturing in 1980, compared to 53 percent of all male workers. As a result, the manufacturing sector was 21 percent female and 79 percent male. The sex distribution for all nonmanufacturing employment was 54 percent female and only 46 percent male.

The analyst observed that differences in the distribution of employment by demographic group would cause the various groups to fare differently in light of economic trends. The ongoing shift to services could be expected to draw additional female workers into the workforce, while

---

Table 6.4
Demographic Profile of Flint Resident Workers, 1980

	Manufac- turing	Nonmanu- facturing	Total	Percent Mfg.
Workers by Race:				
Nonwhite	12,485	11,134	23,619	53%
White & other	55,934	92,250	148,184	38%
Total	68,419	103,384	171,803	40%
Workers by Sex:				
Female	14,434	55,907	70,341	21%
Male	53,985	47,477	101,462	53%
Total	68,419	103,384	171,803	40%

Source: 1980 Census of Population. Table adapted from Thomas R. Hammer, Ibid., p. 134.

declines in manufacturing would impact negatively on males generally and nonwhites generally (and would presumably have the largest impact on nonwhite males, although statistics did not permit evaluating this segment directly).

Analysis of employment patterns by demographic group can be helpful in targeting employment and training programs of various types. Other implications of this type of analysis may be less obvious. For example, in the Flint case, the analyst observed that the dominant role of women in service production means that the more footloose service functions will tend to locate in places where women want to be. This observation led to insights on downtown stagnation:

> If a downtown area is perceived by women as dangerous, such services will tend to locate elsewhere; and if no alternative locations are strong from a competitive and operations standpoint, there may be net losses of service activity from the region as a whole. Flint may have suffered from leakages of this type.[5]

As these examples indicate, the analysis of the size and demographic composition of the labor force will be most useful if it is informed by consideration of the area's industrial structure and economic geography.

LABOR FORCE QUALITY

How can you assess the quality of the labor force in your area? The concept of labor force "quality" or "skill" is extraordinarily difficult to capture and measure. In addition, skill requirements obviously differ from job to job. This section presents some of the techniques that can be used to assess the knowledge and skill levels of the local labor force. While it is difficult to measure the skills and training of the workforce directly, insights can be gained by analyzing the area's occupational mix and from such measures as educational attainment and standardized test scores.

Analyzing Occupational Mix

One way to assess the skills available in the local workforce is to examine the occupational composition of employment. This will permit comparisons in terms of the percentage of the area's labor force in higher-skilled professional, managerial, and technical occupations and the percentage in lower-skilled occupations (such as manual laborers and operatives).

---

[5] Ibid., p. 137.

Sources of Data. *County Business Patterns* provides some limited data on occupational employment, reporting the number of employees in each broad (one-digit) sector who work in central administrative offices and auxiliary establishments. This employment primarily represents white collar administrative occupations rather than production occupations.

More comprehensive data on employment by occupation for local areas are available on a place-of-residence basis from the decennial Census of Population. Local area occupational data from the 1990 census are expected to be released in 1992-93. As noted elsewhere, the prevalence of work-related commuting in an area may have implications for the use of this data.

A more serious disadvantage with the census data is that they become dated toward the end of a census interval. Updated estimates of occupational employment are sometimes derived by applying the old census percentages (e.g., 1980 percentages of employment by occupation) to more recent data on employment by industry. For example, if 200 of 1,000 local manufacturing employees in 1980 were in the professional, managerial, and technical occupational category, that same percentage (20 percent) can be applied to the number of manufacturing employees in the area in the most recent year for which data are available (say 1989) in order to derive updated estimates of the number of professional, manager, and technical workers. (The assumption that the occupational employment percentages will be the same is clearly wrong; they will have changed as a result of changes in production processes, changes in the employment base, etc.).

State departments of employment sometimes publish updated estimates of occupational employment during intercensal periods. However, area coverage varies from state to state. Some states present breakdowns by county, others by multi-county subregions, and still others by Service Delivery Area (SDA) designated under the federal Job Training Partnership Act (JTPA).

Another alternative is for a local area to derive its own updated estimates, using an occupation-industry matrix developed for the state (if available) or for the nation as a whole. Table 6.5 shows the 1986 industry-occupational matrix depicting the distribution of occupational employment by industry for the nation as a whole. Using this matrix, local occupational employment can be estimated as follows:

- Obtain employment figures by industry for the study area. The *BEA Employment and Income* data are most appropriate since they include government employees and the self-employed.

- 117 -

Table 6.5
Industry-Occupational Matrix for the U.S., 1986

Occupation	Agriculture (Wage & Salary Only)	Mining	Const.	Manf.	Trans. Comm. & Util.	Wholesale & Retail Trade	Finance Ins, Real Estate	Service	Gov't	Self-Empl. & Unpaid Family Wkrs.
All Occupations (thousands)	100.00%	100.00%	100.00%	100.00%	100.00%	100.00%	100.00%	100.00%	100.00%	100.00%
Managerial & Management-Related	2.39%	9.45%	9.57%	8.19%	8.04%	9.12%	19.29%	7.39%	11.59%	13.52%
Engineers, Architects & Surveyors	0.71%	**	0.94%	3.64%	1.62%	—	—	1.23%	2.29%	0.81%
Natural, Computer and math scientist	0.57%	4.56%	—	0.80%	—	—	1.11%	0.73%	1.82%	—
Teachers, librarians and counselors	—	**	**	—	—	—	—	14.75%	1.14%	1.26%
Health diagnosing and treating occupations	1.38%	**	**	—	—	—	—	6.33%	1.98%	2.99%
Other professional specialists	0.68%	**	**	1.35%	2.50%	0.63%	1.16%	5.09%	8.29%	7.51%
Technician occupations	0.88%	3.87%	0.79%	3.17%	3.03%	0.64%	1.85%	6.43%	4.80%	0.88%
Marketing & Sales	1.15%	1.14%	1.41%	3.00%	4.89%	34.87%	13.34%	2.43%	0.68%	18.42%
Admin. Support incl. clerical	4.78%	12.37%	**	11.90%	24.63%	13.38%	52.66%	19.57%	30.68%	4.23%
Service occupations	1.11%	0.87%	0.73%	1.79%	3.38%	24.24%	5.22%	25.94%	19.04%	10.53%
Agriculture, forestry fishing & related	79.34%	**	—	0.51%	—	—	1.42%	0.96%	1.39%	16.63%
Blue-collar worker supervisors	0.60%	5.10%	4.46%	4.21%	3.59%	0.67%	—	—	1.38%	1.26%

Table 6.5 (cont'd)

Occupation	Agriculture (Wage & Salary Only)	Mining	Const.	Manf.	Trans. Comm. & Util.	Wholesale & Retail Trade	Finance Ins., Real Estate	Service	Gov't	Self-Empl. & Unpaid Family Wkrs
Construction trades & extractive workers	—	22.00%	40.57%	1.45%	1.53%	—	0.55%	0.56%	3.71%	9.15%
Mechanics, installers & repairers	1.01%	7.19%	5.97%	4.12%	12.77%	4.58%	2.41%	2.58%	3.57%	4.72%
Precision production & plant systems	—	2.04%	2.54%	9.51%	3.83%	1.53%	—	0.78%	1.81%	2.26%
Machine setter & set-up operator	1.12%	2.80%	0.53%	23.17%	—	—	—	1.04%	—	0.90%
Assemblers and other handwork	—	**	0.84%	12.23%	—	—	—	—	—	0.84%
Transp. and material moving machine & vehicle operators	2.24%	15.78%	6.85%	3.93%	23.25%	4.93%	—	1.83%	2.95%	3.45%
Helpers, laborers and material movers	2.74%	6.25%	15.45%	7.57%	6.52%	3.45%	—	1.56%	2.98%	0.82%
Misc. Occupations	—	6.58%	9.36%	—	—	—	—	—	—	—

— less than 1%
** The share of employment for these occupations cannot be determined from the source data. The aggregate missing data is accounted for under miscellaneous occupations.

Source: U.S. Bureau of Labor Statistics

- Generate a local industry-occupational matrix by multiplying the industry employment figures from BEA by the percentages shown in the matrix.

- Sum the occupational rows in the matrix to arrive at an estimate of total employment in each occupational category in the local area.

Once data have been assembled, the analyst can examine the current occupational mix and changes that have been occurring.

Analyzing Occupational Distribution. The occupational mix can be expressed in terms of that portion of employment falling into each occupational category. In the example below (Table 6.6) employment by occupation has been aggregated into six broad categories. The first and second categories represent "white collar" occupations and the last two would generally be considered "blue collar" occupations. The table compares the occupational mix of the Lansing MSA to that of Michigan in 1980 and 1985.

The data indicate that the mix of occupations in the Lansing MSA differs from that of the state. For instance, managerial, technical, and other professional occupations were a more important source of employment in Lansing than in Michigan in both 1980 and 1985. Lansing's higher concentration of employment in this category probably reflects its role as a government and education center, since it is the state capital and the home of Michigan State University.

Table 6.6
Distribution of Employment by Occupational Category
1980 and 1985

Occupational Category	1985		1980	
	Lansing	Michigan	Lansing	Michigan
Managerial, Technical, Other Prof.	29.7%	25.0%	30.0%	25.2%
Sales & Administrative Support	27.6	26.3	25.6	26.3
Services	15.8	16.2	15.4	16.0
Farm & Farm-related	3.4	2.9	2.8	2.4
Precision Production, Craft, Repair	11.7	12.0	9.8	11.7
Operatives & Laborers	11.8	17.6	16.4	18.4
Totals	100.0%	100.0%	100.0%	100.0%

Source: Michigan Employment Security Division

Similarly, the proportion of employment in blue-collar occupations (the "precision production, craft, and repair" and "operatives and laborers" categories) is higher in the state than in Lansing. Moreover, the state employment base is more concentrated in semiskilled and unskilled blue collar occupations, with 17.6 percent of 1985 employment statewide in the "operatives and laborers" category compared to only 11.8 percent in Lansing.

Shifts in the occupational mix of employment are also of interest. Referring again to Table 6.6, we see that the state's distribution of employment by occupation changed little from 1980 to 1985. However, the data for Lansing show a reduction in the share of employment in the "operatives and laborers" category and gains in the "precision production" and "sales and administrative" categories, suggesting that the Lansing area was restructuring ahead of the rest of the state.

Occupational Trends. Patterns of occupational growth and decline can be as revealing about strengths and weaknesses in the local economy as patterns of growth or decline in industrial sectors. Moreover, information on growing and declining occupations is needed to focus workforce training and retraining efforts.

Table 6.7 shows the percentage change in occupational employment for the Lansing MSA and the state between 1980 and 1985. The percentage changes reveal the extent of decline in Lansing in "operative and laborer" occupations—one in five of these jobs were lost in Lansing while statewide this category grew slightly from 1980 to 1985. The trend data also highlight the rapid growth in the skilled blue collar occupations in the Lansing MSA. Other findings that were not evident from the examination of shifts in occupational mix include Lansing's above average growth in white-collar occupations.

Table 6.7
Percentage Change in Occupational Employment
1980-1985

Occupational Category	Lansing	Michigan
Managerial, Technical, Other Prof.	9.4%	5.1%
Sales & Administrative Support	18.9	6.3
Services	13.3	7.2
Farm & Farm-related	31.0	27.3
Precision Production, Craft, Repair	32.6	8.2
Operatives & Laborers	-20.7	6.0

Source: Michigan Employment Security Division

Measuring Education Levels

Analysis of local occupational mix will reveal much about the general aptitudes of the local workforce. This can be supplemented by other types of information, reviewed below.

Educational Attainment Measures. Information on education levels of the local population is available from the decennial Census of Population, which tracks "years of education" of persons over age 25. Aside from infrequent coverage and the omission of younger workers, the data do not differentiate between those who are in the labor force and those who are not. Further, in those areas that are home to educational institutions with sizable graduate programs, the data should be approached with some care, because an indeterminate number of highly educated residents may be transient.

With these caveats in mind, the analyst can use the data to identify the percentage of the population in the following types of categories:

- The percentage of persons over 25 with less than 12 years of schooling (those without a high school diploma)

- The percentage of persons over 25 with 13 or more years of schooling (high school graduates)

- The percentage of persons over 25 with 16 or more years of schooling (college graduates)

In the past, a high school diploma was considered adequate training for many jobs. But given the significant transformations occurring in the nature of work in many occupations and industries, this is no longer the case. Individuals with less than a high school education are at a significant disadvantage in today's society.[6] In the U.S. as a whole, the share of the over-25 population with a high school diploma increased from about half (52.3 percent) in 1970 to two-thirds (66.5 percent) in 1980. The share of the population with a college degree increased from 10.7 percent in 1970 to 16.2 percent in 1980 and the 1990 census figures can be expected to show a continued rise.

A comparison of differences in unemployment rates and educational attainment among one state's MSAs suggests the nature of linkages between

---

[6] See, for example, Frank Levy (1968).

an educated workforce and local economic conditions (see Table 6.8 below). An inverse relationship is clearly evident: unemployment rates tend to be lower as the share of college-educated residents increases.

Areas having highly educated populations may have an advantage in attracting various types of "high-tech" manufacturing, research and development, and advanced service firms. In addition, they may be attracted to areas having the sorts of amenities they desire.

Standardized Test Scores. Scores on standardized tests are sometimes used to assess the quality of local educational preparation and the educational attainment of labor force entrants. However, it is known that test scores reflect the socioeconomic backgrounds of students in the school system as well as the quality of the system's educational programs and instruction. Unfortunately, there is no easy way to sort these out. As a result, it is important to keep in mind that test scores measure student knowledge and that school system quality plays only a part in how much knowledge students display.

Standardized test scores may be available in some states for local areas within the state. In addition, the National Assessment Governing Board, a federal agency, conducts an annual survey known as the "Nation's Report Card." The tests cover a cross-section of eighth graders within each participating state and track student performance in a number of areas,

---

Table 6.8
Educational Attainment and Unemployment Rates,
Michigan MSAs

MSAs Ranked by Unemployment Rate (Low to High)	Unemployment Rate, 1987	Percent of Population with College Degree, 1980
Ann Arbor	4.2%	36.1
Kalamazoo	5.3	23.0
Grand Rapids	6.3	15.9
Lansing	6.7	21.7
Battle Creek	7.9	11.9
Jackson	7.9	12.2
Detroit	8.0	14.0
Saginaw-Bay-Midland	8.8	12.6
Benton Harbor	8.9	13.3
Muskegon	10.0	10.6
Flint	12.2	10.9
Michigan	8.2	14.3
United States	6.2	16.2

Source: Census of Population and Michigan Employment Security Commission.

including math.[7] All but 13 states participate in the national survey, but state-by-state comparisons were made available only in 1991 (although the survey has been conducted for 20 years).

Scores on college entrance exams such as the Scholastic Aptitude Test (SAT) and those of the American College Testing (ACT) program also are available for state-by-state comparisons. These measures were relied upon before the federal state-by-state data became available. However, their relevance is unclear since they measure only the college-bound population, whose participation in the local workforce is likely to be intermittent or delayed even if they pursue studies in the local area.

Dropout Rates. Local school dropout rates generally are available from the public school system. The rates usually are reported as annual dropout rates for each grade (e.g., 11 percent of ninth graders dropped out in a given year). The figures must be compounded to arrive at a total dropout rate for a class of students as they progress from one grade to the next over a period of years.

Only a few local areas have systems for tracking an entering class over the long term, including monitoring those who continue in school past their scheduled graduation date. Since New York City began such monitoring in 1986, it has identified a trend among students who do not graduate on time to continue in school for additional years.[8] Eventually, however, many of these students do drop out. Nationally the dropout rate is about 30 percent.[9]

Worker Productivity and Motivation

It would be useful to have information on worker productivity, labor-management relations, and the local work ethic as indicated by such things as turnover and absenteeism or working hours and work rules. However, such information is spotty and generally unavailable for comparative analysis of local conditions.

---

[7] Karen DeWitt, "Math Survey in Public Schools Shows No State Is 'Cutting It,'" New York Times, June 7, 1991.

[8] Joseph Berger, "Dropout Rate in New York Shows Decline," New York Times, June 13, 1991, B1.

[9] Census Bureau, *School Enrollment: Social and Economic Characteristics of Students - October, 1990*, Current Population Reports P20, Population Characteristics No. 460, (Washington, D.C.: Government Printing Office.)

The five-year Census of Manufactures reports value added by sector in manufacturing for MSAs, counties, and selected places. The Bureau of Labor Statistics (BLS) publishes some national productivity figures by industry, which appear in new releases and various special reports, and occasionally some data is released for large metropolitan areas. But generally, local productivity measures are simply unavailable.

Similarly, objective comparative indicators of the quality of labor-management relations are limited. The only widely available measure of unionization is the percent of a state's nonagricultural employment with union membership, reported by the Department of Labor for states. The DOL also tracks work stoppages within states, indicating their frequency and the number of workers involved. Another possible indicator is the number of contested worker compensation claims per 1,000 wage and salary employees. Some data may also be available, usually on a state-by-state basis, from private sources such as the Industrial Relations Data and Information Service (West Orange, New Jersey) or the Bureau of National Affairs (Washington, D.C.).

Because information on worker productivity and reliability is rarely available from published sources, this information may need to be gathered directly from local employers. As part of a local business survey or focus group, employers can be asked about their workforce needs and how easy it is to find workers of various types; turnover and absenteeism; and aspects of the local labor climate that may affect productivity, such as restrictive work rules. The box below illustrates the types of questions that might be covered in discussions with local employers to identify their labor requirements and special problems or opportunities related to local human resources development.

Local Education and Training Institutions. The reputation of area technical schools among employers is an indirect measure of labor force quality, since it reflects the degree of employer satisfaction with at least that part of the workforce they have hired from those institutions. This applies in particular to area community colleges and technical-vocational schools, which draw primarily from the local population and which are a major source of entry and post-entry level job applicants for a wide range of industries and occupations.

Local areas can play a major role in upgrading human resources through their support for local education and training institutions. As part of the evaluation of local competitiveness, the committee should evaluate opportunities for post-secondary education and vocational training. These might range from apprenticeship programs, to short-term technical training, to offerings at community colleges, four-year colleges, and universities.

- 125 -

In assessing local educational institutions, some comparisons should be approached with care. For example, placement rates are as likely to measure the relative ability of job markets in different areas to absorb additional employees as the quality of institutional training received by students. Aside from objective measures such as courses offered, number of graduates, and comparative rankings in particular fields, interviews with faculty and administrators of local educational institutions may reveal relative strengths and weaknesses and suggest ways such institutions could be improved to strengthen local competitive advantage.

LABOR FORCE COSTS

Local wage rates have long been considered a primary factor in local ability to attract investment. This is less the case today, as the availability of specialized labor with appropriate skills is apt to receive equal consideration with wage rates per se in employers' labor cost calculations. This section reviews data sources and considerations in assessing local labor costs.

Local economic analysts are often interested in knowing how local wage rates for particular occupations in important local industries compare to those elsewhere. However, wage data by occupation are rarely available for comparisons among local areas. State employment departments can be contacted to check on the availability of comparable wage data for localities within the state. It may also be possible to obtain information on the pay scales of major local employers. The BLS also publishes special bulletins and news releases that report occupational wage data for some metropolitan areas. Another option is to conduct an area wage survey or include questions related to wages by occupation and the wage distribution within local industries as part of a business survey. Such surveys, if conducted periodically, can provide very useful information on changes in labor cost. However, it may be difficult to identify other areas that collect similar data, limiting comparisons.

The primary sources of comparative data for labor cost analysis are payroll by industry, reported in *County Business Patterns*, and earnings by industry, reported by BEA. These figures can be divided by industry employment figures to derive pay-per-worker or earnings-per-worker for use in making comparisons. One drawback with these measures is the possibility of variations due to differences in the number of hours worked; for example, some industries are characterized by substantial part-time employment or substantial amounts of overtime. If possible, employment figures should be adjusted to full-time equivalents.

There are some differences between the two data sources to keep in mind when making comparisons. The CBP figures exclude government and the self-employed, as well as employee benefits compensation. The BEA earnings figures are in some respects more comprehensive—since they cover government and the self-employed and include "other labor income" or benefits—but they are available only for one-digit industries. More detailed industry breakdowns permit more meaningful comparisons.

Analyzing Pay-Per-Worker

The example that follows is drawn from an analysis of pay competitiveness comparing Chicago to 10 other large central cities.[10] The data source was a special tabulation of *County Business Patterns* data for 1987.

The analysis began by comparing average annual pay per worker overall and by major sector (Table 6.9). At $24,604, Chicago's average pay is relatively high, exceeded only by average pay levels in New York and San Francisco. However, there is some variation in relative pay levels by industry. Chicago's average manufacturing pay of $26,134 was less than the average manufacturing pay in five of the nine comparison cities. Chicago ranks third or fourth out of 10 in average pay in the other major sectors of the economy. Average pay in Boston is quite similar to the pay figures for Chicago: the table shows that the two cities differ by less than $1,000 in each broad industry category.

Table 6.9
Average Annual Pay in Chicago and Selected Other Cities: 1987

	Total	Manuf.	TCU	Wholesale Trade	Retail Trade	FIRE	Services
Chicago	24,604	26,134	32,614	28,589	12,972	33,303	22,183
Baltimore	20,953	24,568	29,679	25,383	10,738	25,926	18,560
Boston(Suffolk Cty)	24,152	27,070	32,169	28,931	12,115	33,654	21,194
Denver	23,163	25,019	31,292	25,850	12,934	30,679	19,619
Kansas City, MO	20,537	27,989	27,652	24,049	11,529	24,269	17,787
New Orleans	19,643	24,762	26,219	22,539	10,496	23,743	17,385
New York(Manhattan)	32,156	30,567	35,066	35,251	17,197	44,604	26,492
Philadelphia	21,960	25,277	28,846	26,854	11,861	28,789	20,502
San Francisco	26,591	28,719	31,888	30,230	14,172	34,413	24,021
St. Louis	23,770	30,010	31,923	26,750	14,033	24,792	18,400
Average of Other Nine Cities	23,658	27,131	30,526	27,315	12,786	30,097	20,440

Source: County Business Patterns, Special Tabulation

---

[10] John F. McDonald, "Employment Growth, Payrolls, and Wage Competitiveness," *Chicago Economic Update*, Report prepared for the Economic Development Commission of Chicago, Evanston, Ill.: NCI Research, 1990.

Adjusting for Differences
in the Cost of Living

The data in Table 6.9 are informative, but cost of living differences are ignored. A better way to compare pay levels in an industry across regions is to make the comparison relative to the overall average pay in the region. Such comparisons are shown in Table 6.10 for two-digit SIC industries.

Table 6.10
Pay in Chicago Compared to Other Cities: 1987

| SIC | | Chicago | | Comp. City Average* | | Ratio of |
		Payroll per Worker	Relative PPW	Payroll Per Worker	Relative PPW	Chicago to CCA Relative PPW
----	Total	24,604	1.000	23,658	1.000	1.000
15--	Contract Construction	31,151	1.266	27,816	1.176	1.077
19--	Manufacturing	26,134	1.062	27,131	1.147	0.926
2000	Food and Kindred Products	25,079	1.019	22,393	0.947	1.077
2200	Textile Mill Products	17,902	0.728	18,932	0.800	0.909
2300	Apparel and Other Textile Products	17,944	0.729	15,168	0.641	1.138
2400	Lumber and Wood Products	16,335	0.664	22,978	0.971	0.684
2500	Furniture and Fixtures	20,064	0.815	20,046	0.847	0.962
2600	Paper and Allied Products	23,624	0.960	23,741	1.003	0.957
2700	Printing and Publishing	26,521	1.078	27,299	1.154	0.934
2800	Chemicals and Allied Products	27,293	1.109	30,086	1.272	0.872
2900	Petroleum and Coal Products	29,012	1.179	32,928	1.392	0.847
3000	Rubber and Misc. Plastics Products	20,415	0.830	20,132	0.851	0.975
3100	Leather and Leather Products	16,436	0.668	16,762	0.709	0.943
3200	Stone, Clay, and Glass Products	24,995	1.016	23,929	1.011	1.004
3300	Primary Metal Industries	25,867	1.051	22,082	0.933	1.126
3400	Fabricated Metal Products	24,699	1.004	26,624	1.125	0.892
3500	Machinery, Except Electrical	21,847	0.888	25,876	1.094	0.812
3600	Electric and Electronic Equipment	21,724	0.883	26,603	1.124	0.785
3700	Transportation Equipment	30,920	1.257	27,449	1.160	1.083
3800	Instruments and Related Products	21,481	0.873	24,163	1.021	0.855
3900	Miscellaneous Manufacturing Industries	21,542	0.876	19,442	0.822	1.065
40--	Transportation and Other Public Utilities	32,614	1.326	30,526	1.290	1.027
4100	Local and Interurban Passenger Transit	15,380	0.625	11,639	0.492	1.271
4200	Trucking and Warehousing	24,411	0.992	21,853	0.924	1.074
4400	Water Transportation	30,690	1.247	30,013	1.269	0.983
4500	Transportation by Air	34,424	1.399	29,016	1.226	1.141
4700	Transportation Services	23,668	0.962	21,491	0.908	1.059
4800	Communication	38,394	1.560	34,123	1.442	1.082
4900	Electric, Gas, and Sanitary Services	0.000	0.000	34,873	1.474	NA
50--	Wholesale Trade	28,589	1.162	27,315	1.155	1.006
5000	Wholesale Trade-Durable Goods	29,345	1.193	27,649	1.169	1.021
5100	Wholesale Trade-Nondurable Goods	27,380	1.113	25,181	1.064	1.046

(Excerpted)

* The comparison cities are Baltimore, Boston (Suffolk County), Denver (Denver County), Kansas City, Missouri, New York (Manhattan), New Orleans, Philadelphia, San Francisco, and St. Louis.

Source: County Business Patterns

The table shows average pay in each industry in Chicago and the average for the other nine cities. The table also displays the pay in each industry relative to a city's overall average. For example, average overall pay in Chicago was $24,604 and average pay in manufacturing was $26,134. Thus, the relative pay in manufacturing was $26,134/24,604 = 1.062. The corresponding figure for the comparison cities' average is $27,131/23,658 = 1.147. The right-most column of the table shows the relative pay in the industry in Chicago divided by the industry's relative pay in the nine comparison cities. In the case of manufacturing, this index figure is 1.062/1.147 = .926. This figure implies that average pay in Chicago in manufacturing is 92.6 percent of the average for the other nine cities.

The index figures resulting from this type of calculation can be used to determine which industries in an area pay well (or poorly) compared to elsewhere.

SUMMARY

An area's labor force represents the human capital an area offers to existing and potential business investors. This chapter has presented techniques for assessing the availability, quality, and cost of labor resources in a local economy. A variety of comparative analyses can be conducted using regularly published data available from federal sources. For some types of data, the analyst will have to seek out state, local, or private sources. State and local employment divisions as well as business organizations such as chambers of commerce are potential sources of specialized information on the local labor market. In addition, an area business survey can provide useful information on labor force quality and characteristics.

The information gathered on local human resources will aid the strategic planning committee in identifying issues for local economic development and appropriate policy or programmatic responses.

Additional Reading

Occupational Analysis

Thompson, Wilbur R. "Policy-Based Analysis For Local Economic Development" *Economic Development Quarterly* 1 (1987): 203-213.

Thompson Wilbur R. and Phillip R. Thompson, "National Industries and Local Occupational Strengths: The Cross Hairs of Targeting," *Urban Studies* 24 (1985): 547-560.

Upgrading the Workforce

Levy, Frank. *Dollars and Dreams*. New York: W. W. Norton & Company, 1988.

Wozniak, G. "Human Capital, Information, and Early Adoption of New Technology," *Journal of Human Resources* 22 (1987): 101-12.

EVALUATING NONLABOR RESOURCES

An area's human resources are clearly an important attribute of the local area. What other local characteristics are important to economic growth? The question of what factors support economic activity and account for differences in growth among areas has absorbed numerous researchers, theoreticians, and policymakers. Since the seminal work of Lösch and others in the post-WWII period, an extensive body of literature has accumulated on the determinants of industrial location.

Below we review some of the current thinking about why economies grow or stagnate and the role of different "location factors." Then we consider ways to assess the locational advantages and disadvantages of a particular area for economic activity of different types.

LOCATION THEORY AND
COMPETITIVE ADVANTAGE

Classical location theory, which was developed to explain the location of trade and heavy manufacturing, has been less successful in explaining the location of today's high-growth industries. The central truism of location theory—that in making location decisions, firms balance cost and demand considerations to maximize profits—is not in question. The problem, some argue, has to do with changes in the relevant cost factors. Costs have proved more elusive to quantify as information—embodied in technology and human expertise—has become an increasingly important production input.[1]

In the past, natural advantages linked to geography—such as natural resources deposits, or favorable growing conditions, or locations along waterways or transportation routes—were often decisive in giving rise to cities and towns. Transportation costs were an important influence on

---

[1] See Mark A. Satterthwaite, "Location Patterns of High-Growth Firms," *Economic Development Commentary*, Spring 1988, pp. 7-11.

location. Firms whose products lost considerable weight in processing—as in metal refining or agricultural processing—would locate near sources of supply to minimize transportation costs. Operations that added weight in processing—like bottling—would locate closer to final markets. Manual labor was a significant production input and productivity growth was usually achieved by taking advantage of production economies of scale.

New Patterns of Agglomeration. Many of today's growing service and high-tech industries have turned these traditional relationships on their head. High-tech products often have a high ratio of value to weight, reducing the significance of transportation costs. Resource inputs (e.g., silica for silicon chips, petroleum for plastics) are ubiquitous or readily acquired even at a distance, as a result of rapid improvements in global communication and transportation systems. Labor, too, can be readily obtained, since there is abundant surplus labor in developing countries around the globe that can be trained for semi-skilled and skilled production tasks. With few ties to input locations, production facilities are relatively footloose and move easily to the lowest-cost area.

For communities in advanced economies like the United States, attempts to compete on the basis of low input costs simply drive down wages and reduce the standard of living. Sustained economic growth depends less on reducing basic input costs (traditionally defined) than on adding value through innovation. In this context, industry-specific "localization economies" become a major source of productivity growth. These are the savings that accrue to a firm from locating in an established industry cluster.

For innovating firms, the most important "costs" are things like the availability of key personnel with specialized skills, access to specialized products and services, and access to specialized information or technology. These needs can be met most cheaply and efficiently if a firm locates near others in the same or related industries.

The phenomenon of industry clustering has been very apparent in the U.S. semiconductor industry in recent years. In the mid-1980s, it spawned a "rush to technology," as areas aspired to emulate the growth of Silicon Valley or Boston's Route 128. But experience with research parks, venture capital funds, and similar tools have demonstrated that the conditions for industry growth are not so easily replicated.[2]

---

[2] Karen Grassmuck "Wariness Dampens 1980's Craze for Building University-Sponsored Technology Parks," *Chronicle of Higher Education*, June 27, 1990.

Product Cycle Theory. Many of the policy responses that have emerged in the past decade reflect recognition of the "product cycle" as an additional influence on firm location and growth. As applied to economic development, product cycle theory differentiates firms' locational requirements according to the stage of product development.

In the earliest stage of product development, firms are highly dependent on knowledge resources, such as cutting-edge technology and individuals with highly specialized expertise (scientists, physicists, and theoretical engineers). As the product moves beyond the prototype stage into mass production, resources for capital investment and the availability of a reliable, trainable workforce assume importance. Research and quality control personnel are still important, but less so than in the product development stage. Ultimately, as the product technology diffuses and the market matures, price-based competition takes over and location decisions are most apt to reflect sensitivity to input costs.[3]

Sources of Industry Competitive Advantage. One of the most successful attempts to integrate the various strands of theory explaining industry location and economic growth is recent work by Michael E. Porter, referenced earlier in Chapter 5.[4] In exploring why industries grow or decline in particular areas, he underscores the distinction between "absolute" advantage and "comparative" advantage. A region enjoys an absolute advantage in trade when it is the lowest-cost producer of a product. However, a region's comparative advantage is determined by the most productive use of its assets in relative terms. Thus a region that is a low-cost producer of an item may still import that item if its assets can be deployed more productively in another industry.

Traditionally, "factor-based" comparative advantages that result from different endowments of land, labor, capital, and natural resources have been emphasized in explaining patterns of trade as well as industry location. But Porter faults this narrow view of the sources of competitiveness:

> A new theory must move beyond the comparative advantage to the competitive advantage of a nation. . . . [It] must reflect a rich conception of competition that includes segmented markets, differentiated products, technology differences, and economies of scale. Quality, features, and new product innovation are central in advanced industries and segments. Moreover, cost advantage grows as much out of efficient-to-manufacture product designs and leading product technology as it does out of factor costs or even economies of scale.[5]

---

[3] See for example Robert M. Ady (1983) and R. D. Norton and J. Rees (1979).

[4] Michael E. Porter, 1990.

[5] Ibid, p. 20.

This emphasis on the multiple sources of innovation and upgrading is also evident in much of the recent literature exploring entrepreneurship and innovation.[6]

Though Porter's discussion refers to nations, it is also pertinent for regions or local areas. In Chapter 5 we considered three important aspects of the operating environment and operating characteristics of an industry in a particular area: the strength of local industry clusters, the nature of firms' markets, and the local climate for entrepreneurship. Now we turn to the fourth point of the so-called "diamond" of competitive advantage: local factor conditions and ways they can be assessed.

ASSESSING FACTOR CONDITIONS

Factors of production are the basic inputs needed by an industry. Most of the characteristics that have been identified in the literature as important location factors can be grouped into the following five broad categories:

- Physical resources — The natural resources and geography of an area, including climate and location in relation to customer and supplier markets

- Human resources — The availability, skills, cost, and productivity of workers, including top level personnel

- Knowledge resources — The availability of scientific, technical, and market information to support industry development

- Capital resources — The availability and cost of investment capital in various forms

- Infrastructure — The type, quality, and cost of infrastructure as it pertains to both residents and businesses

To these groupings another might be added that pertains to the distinct culture of the local area:

- Civic culture — Community attitudes and perceptions that influence and reflect the political environment, local business climate, and quality of life.

---

[6] See, for example, Peter E. Drucker (1985).

In assessing the location factors that support or inhibit economic activity in the local area, the following distinctions can be kept in mind. The factors that are important to industries in an area may include "basic" factors as well as "advanced" factors, developed as a result of substantial investment. Basic factors are those that an area inherits, such as natural resources, or those that represent only limited investment (e.g., basic literacy, low-skilled labor). Basic factors tend to be broadly comparable across many areas or readily sourced from elsewhere, so that competitive advantage stemming from basic factors is vulnerable in today's economy. More important than endowments of basic factors is the ability to create factor advantages. The Japanese have demonstrated a remarkable ability to overcome disadvantages in basic factors (e.g., limited natural resources, limited population base, distance from markets) by creating advanced factors through investment in human resources and technology.

In addition to identifying basic and advanced factors, the analyst should note whether factors are "generalized" or "specialized." Specialized factors or factor-creating mechanisms are industry-specific and help strengthen the position of a particular industry in the local area. They are often, but not always, the same as advanced factors. For example, a university degree program in engineering would represent a mechanism for creating advanced factors of a generalized nature; a sequence for automotive engineers would represent a specialized factor-creating mechanism.

In the preceding chapter we considered some of the ways to assess human resources, a critical location factor in today's economy. Below we review some of the things to consider in assessing other locational characteristics of a particular area.

Assessing Physical Resources

As noted above, the most basic types of advantage often relate to the physical attributes of an area. The evaluation should consider the current advantages and disadvantages represented by the following types of physical attributes.

Natural Resources Deposits. Advantage in this area shifts as new supplies are discovered and others are depleted. This type of advantage is highly sensitive to global markets and changes in technology and products that alter demand. Sometimes, a declining resource-based industry can be rekindled through advances in technology or changes in industry economics.

For example, as oil becomes more scarce, prices may rise sufficiently to make it feasible to use advanced recovery technology in depleted "oil patch" regions of states like Texas and Oklahoma. As a result of air quality concerns, the coal-producing regions of the eastern U.S. have experienced severe decline in competition with regions producing cleaner-burning low-sulfer coal. It is possible that new technology might help the region overcome this relative disadvantage. In both these cases, advantage would have to be regained through investment to upgrade basic factors. The risk of relying on natural resource-based advantages is illustrated by the mining "ghost towns" of the western U.S., whose futures ran out along with the ore.

Geographic Location. Historically, geographic location has been a major source of competitive advantage particularly as it pertains to location along transportation routes and access to customer and supplier markets. However, this attribute is quite sensitive to changes in transportation technology. For example, at one time many of the areas in Michigan offered access to port facilities on the Great Lakes, a competitive advantage. However a change in technology to containerized shipping has rendered this feature less of an advantage. Competitiveness may require a significant investment to upgrade facilities. Whether this would be justified in light of declines in traffic on the Great Lakes points to the need to consider the regional influences on competitive advantage.

Access to markets is another aspect of geographic location that may affect competitive advantage. For instance, the Foreign Trade Agreement with Canada may offer a special opportunity for border communities. In many rural communities, the distance from markets must be reckoned with as strategies for economic development are developed. One way to evaluate access to markets is to estimate the distance one can reasonably travel in a day by car or truck, generally an area between 250 to 500 miles depending on natural barriers, and examine the potential markets within that area. However, it is not simply the size of the surrounding market area but access to it through an efficient transportation network that determines an area's market potential. Once again, the need to upgrade basic factors comes into play.

Natural Features. A waterway, mountain, or forest may provide an area with a special advantage for tourism and recreation development, but investment in facilities and marketing is necessary to gain competitive advantage. A mild climate may also be a source of competitive advantage—it can help keep energy costs down and attract population. However, the city of Minneapolis, notorious for its cold weather, illustrates how climate disadvantages can be offset. A recent ad campaign asserts "We like it here!" with copy that reads "In Minneapolis we have something more. An Attitude.

It's friendly, it's proud and it's personable." Minneapolis sells its people and their attitudes in an effort to neutralize a negative over which it has little control. Nevertheless, a mild climate, attractive scenery, or opportunities for outdoor recreation are natural features whose amenity value may contribute indirectly to competitive advantage by attracting residents and workers.

If tourism emerges as a focus of the strategic planning effort, it will be useful to inventory all natural resources and events that attract visitors and all public and private facilities that currently support visitation. The relative strengths and weaknesses of these resources, events, and facilities should be evaluated. Planners should estimate the total tourist spending in the community if possible. Profiles of typical trips, visitor parties, and spending patterns should be developed. Tourism development can then be addressed in terms of:

1. Stimulating additional expenditures by existing categories of visitors

2. Attracting more or longer trips by the same types of visitors

3. Creating new types of tourism in the area

Proposed projects then can be compared in terms of their ability to achieve one or more of these outcomes.

Availability of Developable Sites. As part of the assessment of physical attributes, the community should identify the extent and characteristics of developable land or vacant sites. In addition, it may be necessary to catalog environmental problems such as contaminated sites or constraints imposed by air and water pollution. A land-use analysis may be an essential starting point for smaller communities.

The availability of development sites can be considered with respect to such broad categories of activity as manufacturing development and downtown development. Often the investigation will touch upon infrastructure issues.

For example, if the concern is manufacturing development, it will be important to analyze industrial sites in the community and nearby areas to assess whether site availability is currently a limiting factor for industrial growth. Not to be overlooked is the potential to serve smaller operators who may have limited space requirements or seek flexible tenancy arrangements.

The market for industrial space resembles other markets in that sellers need an inventory of items to offer. The existence of one or two persistent vacancies does not mean that there would be no customers if the community had 10 or 20 available sites. The asking prices for industrial land and building space may constitute a strength or weakness of the community relative to other areas. Of the possible measures to increase the availability of industrial sites, providing infrastructure to vacant land is a common approach. More aggressive programs—underwriting the construction of speculative building space, developing industrial incubators, or recycling older industrial buildings—may make sense in some circumstances, though risks should be carefully identified.

Downtown retail and commercial areas are sometimes a logical focus for community strategic planning. The key competitive factors for downtowns—convenience and coordination of functions—are external to individual businesses and so must be addressed by common action. Nearly all downtowns have been affected by competition from malls and strip development elsewhere. The effects of competition tend to be greatest for retail trade, somewhat less for consumer services, and least for general office functions (although this distinction may not apply for small downtowns that were never office centers). The challenge is to capture some of the advantages of unified facilities such as shopping malls without losing the benefits of diversity. Even when this challenge is difficult, downtown development initiatives can have substantial long-term benefits because they stabilize and enhance values that already exist.

Most communities have paid some attention to the problems and prospects of their downtowns, but it is usually beneficial to analyze downtown issues in an organized fashion. The most basic step is to prepare a map of existing land and building uses, noting all vacant parcels and unused building space. Other steps can include surveys of parking availability, structure condition, storefront attractiveness, and public open space. Questionnaire or interview surveys can be useful to solicit the opinions of downtown business operators about current needs and prospects. Business customers can also be interviewed.

This should provide a general understanding of the functions, limits, and potentials of the downtown area, which may suggest development options. It may be that infrastructure or open space improvements would create new development opportunities. Or there may be limitations involving site assembly problems that the public can address. There may be a strong need to find new uses for currently vacant space. The analysis may suggest types of establishments that would strengthen downtown functions or fill an apparent market demand.

Downtown projects involving a combination of public and private actions usually require some time to plan and negotiate. The major output of the assessment may be to indicate the need for a longer-term planning process, for example, a project-specific feasibility analysis. Or there might be a need for institutional changes, such as establishment of a downtown development authority to pursue a long-term improvement program. Options that emerge from the analysis become grist for the strategy development process outlined in the next chapter.

Infrastructure

The various aspects of community infrastructure should also be evaluated in terms of such measures as capacity and cost. This should include assessments of the adequacy of the community's basic systems—transportation systems of all types, systems that ensure local environmental quality such as water and wastewater systems and solid waste disposal systems, energy utilities, and communications systems.

Water and sewer systems that are approaching capacity represent a constraint for economic development. Increasingly, solid waste disposal presents a problem. In some areas, particular utilities have not fully upgraded to the "state-of-the-art." For instance, some areas may not have access to digit switching telephone networks or touch-tone dialing.

A transportation network—including access to interstate highways, railroads, airports, and ports—is an important aspect of an area's infrastructure. The capacity to move people, goods, and services from one area to another is a critical factor in determining an area's access to markets and to other needed resources. Recent changes in transportation regulation have adversely affected both smaller metropolitan areas and rural areas throughout the United States, placing them at a disadvantage compared to larger metropolitan areas.

Since the advent of the interstate highway system in the 1950s, most products have been shipped via this highway network. Location on major interstate highway routes may play an important role in an area's economic fortunes. Local areas can assess their relative transportation advantages and disadvantages by deriving comparative data from maps (for the distance to nearest east-west and north-south interstate highway interchanges, distance to nearest airport and rail service, etc.) and timetables (for destinations and frequency of service).

Community infrastructure, in a broad sense, also refers to the availability of infrastructure to support the local population: the quality and cost of housing, the quality of education, the quality of local public services, and the presence of amenities such as cultural or recreational facilities.

Capital Resources

Maintaining and upgrading competitive advantage requires sustained investment to transform basic factor advantages into more advanced and productive factors. The availability of investment capital is in large part a function of national capital markets and larger economic forces affecting credit, currency values, and the money supply. Nevertheless, there is sufficient sub-national variation to suggest that a local community evaluate the relative availability and cost of capital of various types.

Debt capital probably will be available at prevailing regional rates, but the committee should assess whether local lending practices differ in any respect and whether firms themselves have indicated any difficulty in obtaining commercial or industrial financing. One issue that may need to be explored is mismatches between the types of financing required by firms in growth sectors of the economy (e.g., service or information-intensive industries) and the types of financing that are available (see "Investing in Information Capital").

The committee should also note the regional and local availability of early-stage financing (seed or venture capital). Compendiums such as *Pratt's Guide to Venture Capital Resources*, published annually, and the magazine *Venture Economics* can be examined for information on local or regional availability of seed capital. Special public financing programs should also be noted.

The level of taxation represents an influence on firm finances over which local governments have some control. Investigations of the impacts of taxation on firm location generally indicate that the level of taxes is not apt to be a deciding influence on a firm's choice of a particular region. However, once a firm has selected a suitable region for investment, tax considerations may affect decisions to invest in one community versus another one nearby. Moreover, firms are apt to consider taxes in light of other factors such as the adequacy of public services in making investment decisions.

INVESTING IN INFORMATION CAPITAL

In today's economy, the principal generator of productivity increases, which create value, is information capital. Unlike the industrial era when physical capital stoked the engines of growth, information capital is the key factor of production in a knowledge-based economy. The problem with acknowledging information's role in today's industries is that we have limited means of assessing its contribution to productivity and value added. It has been called the invisible asset. Today's accountants ignore it or list it under the 19th century heading of 'good will.'

Because of the mystery surrounding information capital, it is difficult to finance innovative industries in which information capital is the principal production factor. Similarly, we underinvest in measures that would increase information capital though human resource development, or provide infrastructure support to lower the cost and increase the flow of information.

Economists have been trying to develop formulas or ratios to assess the value of information. One method is Tobin's q. Devised by James Tobin of Yale, Tobin's q is the ratio between a company's market value (stock price times shares outstanding) and the replacement value of physical assets. It is, however, a very rough measure of whether or not an industry's information capital is expanding or contracting. Most innovative growth industries have ratios ranging between 2:1 and 8:1, while industrial-era industries hover around a 1:1 ratio.

A cursory look at Tobin's q for growth firms is enough to convince the casual observer that most of the wealth in this country is the result of the innovation, productivity, efficiency, and value created by information capital. In the industrial era, value was created by developing products from natural resources. Today value is created from ideas—from information.

Consider that one of the world's wealthiest families has derived their riches from discount sales. The Wal-Mart system provides its suppliers with up-to-the-minute information on sales trends. This reduces supplier costs by permitting more efficient production schedules and lower inventory costs. Wal-Mart's efficient distribution logistics cut overhead costs dramatically. The Wall Street Journal has reported that in the average department store, 40 to 50 percent of the selling price of a product goes to cover the store's inventory, distribution handling, and administration costs. In a warehouse store that cost is reduced to eight percent, which can reduce the selling price of a product by 25 percent and still have profits 15 to 20 percent above department stores. This is value created from information capital.

Economic development practitioners must look for ways to reduce the barriers to investment in information capital if they are to encourage growth in their community. Working with local financial institutions to develop better information on needs in this area is one place to start. Traditional approaches to subsidizing land, taxes, labor, and standard types of infrastructure may have little impact on investment decisions of growth industries.

Source: James E. Peterson, President, NCI Research

Knowledge Resources

Knowledge resources can be thought of as the pool of scientific, technical, and market information available to support industry development. Because much knowledge resides in individuals, the presence of so-called "stimulus" labor—a concentration of individuals with specialized skills—represent an area of overlap with human resources. However, knowledge resources also reside in institutions and information networks whose local presence should be noted and explored.

Local colleges and universities are valuable not only because they upgrade human resources generally, but because they often support the development of specialized industry-specific information. In assessing local educational institutions, the analyst should note course offerings or research specializations that may contribute to the local knowledge base for particular industries. If a community hopes to acquire or retain a position as an industry's "home base"—or the area where the industry's competitive advantage is created or sustained—then there must be support for the development of specialized expertise.

Knowledge resources are also developed via government and private research labs, university-affiliated research parks, trade and professional associations, and specialized trade literature and databases. Industry clustering in an area is both cause and consequence of the presence of industry-specific knowledge.

Over the past ten years, many communities have adopted policies to support particular industries through development of the local technology base for that industry. As part of the assessment, the committee can consider the availability of and need for services in such areas as industry R&D, product and process development, or modernization.

Knowledge of markets is also important to industry competitiveness as a way to upgrade products and services. Communities should note the presence or absence of specialized sources of market information (e.g., literature or activities of trade and professional associations, databases on contracting or exporting opportunities). An often-overlooked, but potentially significant, mechanism for building knowledge resources is a local trade or professional association.

Civic Culture

An intangible but important aspect of a local area is its civic culture, including such things as the quality of local leadership, public-private cooperation, and positive or negative perceptions of the local business climate and quality of life.

Recognizing this issue, business surveys often ask businesses to comment on the local "business climate." Employers can be asked to rate the overall business climate of the area as excellent, good, fair, or unsatisfactory. They can also include more specific questions regarding whether firms encounter any problems with public services or whether any county or local laws, regulations, or procedures make it difficult to operate profitably.

SUMMARY

The location factors that support economic growth and their relative importance vary by community. In this chapter we have identified some of the most important factors to consider. Different measures for assessing local or state comparative standing have been developed for many of these location factors and are often published as "rating schemes" by groups like Rand-McNally, the *Places Rated Almanac*, and others (see "Additional Reading").

The process of compiling information on an area's labor and non-labor resources sets the stage for the next phase of the strategic planning process: strategy development.

Additional Reading

Location Theory

Lösch, A. *The Economies of Location*. New Haven: Yale University Press, 1954.

Schmenner, Roger W. *Making Business Location Decisions*. Englewood Cliffs, N.J.: Prentice Hall, 1982.

Sources of Agglomeration

Mills, Edwin S. "Sectoral Clustering and Economic Development." In *Sources of Metropolitan Growth*. Edwin S. Mills and John F. McDonald, eds. Rutgers: Center for Urban Policy Research, 1992.

Ó hUallacháin, Breandán and Mark Satterthwaite. *Sectoral Growth Patterns at the Metropolitan Level: An Evaluation of Economic Development Incentives*. Report to the U.S. Economic Development Administration. Evanston, Ill.: NCI Research, 1988.

Product Cycle Theory

Ady, Robert M. "High-Technology Plants: Different Criteria for the Best Location." *Economic Development Commentary*, Winter 1983, p. 9. Published by National Council for Urban Economic Development, Washington, D.C.

Norton, R.D. and J. Rees, "The Product Cycle and the Spatial Decentralization of American Manufacturing."*Regional Studies* 13 (August 1979): 141-51.

Competitive Advantage

Porter, Michael E. *The Competitive Advantage of Nations*. New York: Macmillan-The Free Press, 1990.

Reigeluth, George A. and Harold Wolman. *The Determinants and Implications of Communities' Changing Competitive Advantages: A Review of Literature.* Washington, D.C.: The Urban Institute, 1979.

Entrepreneurship and Innovation

Drucker, Peter E. *Innovation and Entrepreneurship.* New York: Harper and Row, 1985.

Infrastructure

National Council on Public Works Improvement, *Fragile Foundations: A Report On America's Public Works.* Washington, D.C.: U.S. Government Printing Office, February 1988.

Comparative Measures of Location Factors

For a comprehensive review of sources, see

Neithercut, Mark E. et al. *Local Economic Development Research: A Guide to Data Sources.* Detroit: Wayne State University, Center for Urban Studies, 1989.

Capital Resources

Mt. Auburn Associates. "How to Analyze the Local Financial Market" in *Design and Management of State and Local Revolving Loan Funds: A Handbook.* Washington, D.C.: Economic Development Administration, 1987.

LINKING ANALYSIS AND PLANNING: STRATEGY DEVELOPMENT[1]

The types of data collection and analysis described in this handbook should not take place in a vacuum; they should be part of a purposeful and participatory process that involves community decisionmakers in discussions about a local area's economic prospects and future. The overall goal is to develop information on the local economy that can be used to set priorities for efforts to promote economic growth. Therefore, the analysis should be part of a consensus-building process that leads to the commitment of resources and assignment of responsibility for implementation.

STRATEGIC PLANNING: PARTICIPANTS AND SEQUENCING OF ACTIVITIES

Strategic planning is sometimes initiated by business leaders who are concerned about local economic directions and hope to mobilize a community response. In other cases, governmental leaders may be the ones to begin the process, sometimes in response to funding agency mandates. Regardless of who acts first, success will depend on the involvement and support of community leaders from both the public and private spheres.

The process can get underway with the organization of a steering committee of key decisionmakers and opinion leaders representing the various political, economic, and community interests that must be "brought on board" for the plan to be implemented. Involvement must be broad enough to build credibility and marshal support for the plan, yet not so broad that the process becomes unwieldy and incapable of yielding consensus. The value of the process depends in large part on its ability to forge agreement on a plan of action.

---

[1] Portions of this chapter are adapted from Norton L. Berman, *Local Strategic Planning: A Handbook for Community Leaders*, Lansing: Local Development Services Bureau, Michigan Department of Commerce, 1990.

For the best chance of success, analysis and planning should be integrated, so that the direction of the analysis is shaped by local insight, even as debate is informed by objective fact. Many excellent planning studies fail to influence policy because their insights are not shared with the broader public; the results are not disseminated or presented in a way that engages public debate. Conversely, planning efforts often founder upon a lack of solid information; if parties disagree about basic facts, they are unlikely to be able to resolve differences about what is needed, much less commit to act.

The six-phase process depicted earlier in Figure 1.1 represents a typical sequence of activities in strategic planning. Analysis is central to the first step: the community economic audit. This encompasses the techniques described in Chapters 3, 4, and 5—the assessment of economic performance and condition, the analysis of local industrial structure, and the evaluation of local growth prospects.

Results of these analyses should be presented to the steering committee for their review and deliberation. With information on economic trends and industry structure and growth prospects, the committee can take the next step of identifying key issues for economic development. Hammering out a "mission statement" is a way to begin to build a common vision and sense of purpose. The results of the economic audit and the mission statement can be released to the press to lend substance to the planning process and stimulate public debate.

Once priority issues have been identified, the analysis continues with a focused examination of the resources or "location factors" that support local economic activity, including both labor and nonlabor resources. The audit of local resources should suggest problems or opportunities as they relate to the local business environment and industry base.

In the next phase of the process, planning and analysis become fully integrated. The local steering committee should convene to formulate development strategy that translates problems or opportunities into a specific plan of action.

FORMULATING STRATEGY

At this stage, the information that has been developed should be evaluated from two perspectives. One constitutes an "external" evaluation: How are events and trends in the larger society and economy likely to impact the local community and local economy? Are there steps that can be taken at the local level to mitigate threats or take advantage of opportunities arising from external developments? This in turn focuses attention back to the "internal" characteristics and resources of the community: Do they represent assets or liabilities? Are there ways to leverage positive attributes or to correct weaknesses in order to encourage economic growth, particularly in light of larger trends?

One author offers the following explanation of the logic behind this evaluative process:

> People and organizations involved in economic development are in the business of coping with economic change. Your community's strategic condition (competitive position) is a function of two sets of factors: *outside forces* that are generally beyond local control, and *locational characteristics of the community* that local action may or may not be able to influence. These factors combine to drive the community's economy and shape its economic development prospects.[2]

At this point it may be useful to restructure the steering committee into issue-oriented task forces, based on the critical issues identified in the mission statement. This will help ensure that the process is clearly focused on finding solutions. To build commitment to the results, committee participants should be allowed to choose the task force they want to serve on. One member with expertise and interest in a specific critical issue should serve as chair.

The steering committee should also seek to expand participation to other persons or institutions not previously involved in the process, particularly those with professional competence in the issues of major concern (e.g., industrial adjustment, commercial revitalization, residential development, infrastructure development and finance). They might include industry experts or trade group representatives, city and county economic development staff, real estate developers, mortgage bankers, or job training specialists, among others.

Enlarging the group of participants will have several advantages: it will increase the knowledge base of the group, it will involve new participants who may add to the resources available to implement the plan, and it will add to the credibility of the strategic planning process.

The focus of the external and internal evaluations is to identify both "actionable issues"—circumstances that can be addressed by local-level

---

[2] Alan Gregerman. *Competitive Advantage: Framing A Strategy to Support High Growth Firms*, Washington, D.C.: National Council for Urban Economic Development, 1984, p.30.

- 151 -

actions—and potential community responses. The process of defining issues and identifying response options provides a basis for articulating goals and objectives and developing strategies to achieve them.

The business base characteristics and location factors discussed in previous units provide a framework for evaluating external trends, pinpointing the community's strategic assets and liabilities, and identifying options for capitalizing on development opportunities or overcoming constraints. They can be arrayed as an assessment matrix to guide the committee's discussion (see Figure 8.1). Also included on the matrix is a set of factors termed "civic culture;" these also merit evaluation, since such factors as the quality of local leadership and community attitudes—positive or negative—can be important influences on the ability to implement development strategies.

As discussed in more detail below, the evaluation proceeds as follows:

1. Identify external trends that are affecting or likely to affect the local economy. What opportunities or threats do they present? Note whether the impact is likely to be positive, negative, or neutral for the community and whether there is the potential for a local response.

2. For each of the characteristics that have been the focus of data collection and analysis, consider whether and in what respect it represents an asset or a liability in terms of prospects for economic growth. Note whether an asset represents a major or minor strength and whether particular liabilities can or cannot be corrected.

In the course of these discussions, any suggestions regarding options for the local community to enhance and capitalize upon strengths or ameliorate weaknesses should be noted for further consideration in establishing priorities for action.

Figure 8.1
Formulating Development Goals:
Exploring Critical Issues and Response Options

	External Trends	Local Assets & Liabilities	Response Options
BUSINESS BASE CHARACTERISTICS			
Industry Clusters • Competitiveness of key industries • Presence of related & supporting industries			
Demand Conditions • Extent of current markets • Market development activity (new products, customers)			

Entrepreneurial Orientation
• Dominant firm culture
• Start-up or spin-off activity
• Enterprise development networks
   (lawyers, accountants, venture
   forums, incubators, etc.)			

LOCATION FACTORS			
Physical Resources • Natural resources • Geographic location and access to customers and suppliers • Natural features • Availability of developable sites			
Community Infrastructure • Transportation networks & facilities • Environmental systems and quality (water and wastewater, solid waste) • Communications networks • Energy costs • Public services • Housing costs and quality • Amenities			
Knowledge Resources • Presence of R&D facilities or programs • Specialized trade associations • Specialized databases for market or technology development			
Capital Resources • Availability of reasonably-priced debt • Availability of equity or seed capital • Public sector financing programs • Local tax levels			
Human Resources • Labor availability & skill mix • Education levels • Local work ethic • Worker productivity/value-added • Labor costs • Mechanisms for upgrading (education and training institutions, etc.)			
CIVIC CULTURE			
• Community leadership & vision • Public-private cooperation • Perceptions of business climate • Perceptions of quality of life			

Evaluating External Factors

The effort to identify threats and opportunities arising from changes in the external environment is a distinguishing feature of strategic planning. This external evaluation should encompass not only the regional and national spheres, but the international one as well. Many external influences will be beyond local control. Nevertheless, their likely effects on the local economy are an important consideration in strategic planning. Examples of factors that might be considered are outlined below.

Economic Changes. Although the data analysis provides basic information about the local economy, the committee should also consider economic forces operating at the regional, national, and international levels. For instance, issues involving capital investment (such as housing, infrastructure, or industrial parks) will be affected by the availability and cost of capital. The globalization of the economy has affected the location and nature of job-creating investments and the skills required of the labor force. Similarly, the increasing dominance of services in advanced economies has profound implications at the local level.

Regulatory and Legislative Changes. A locality may have little or no control over changes in state or federal laws and regulations. Yet those changes may have a major impact on the local economy or particular sectors. For example, banking deregulation in the 1980s substantially changed the way housing is financed, affecting housing programs throughout the nation. Environmental protection policies have affected the operations and economics of all forms of manufacturing and may limit opportunities to recycle older industrial sites for new investment, a key concern for urban communities.

Social and Political Changes. These include such things as political shifts (e.g., state and Federal budget limitations and reduced willingness to share revenues with local communities, heightened environmental concerns and their interjection into policy debates); changing values; and social/cultural developments (e.g., increases in drug-related crime, growth in homelessness, increasing pressures on the social safety net, the emergence of an urban "underclass").

Demographic Changes. As discussed in Chapter 5 (see section on *Analyzing Economic Geography*), demographic shifts influence the market for goods and services. Demography also shapes the local work force. The committee should consider the implications of demographic shifts such as declining household size, the influx of women in the workforce and the rise of two-earner families, middle-class flight from older urban centers, and variations in birth and migration rates. Currently, for example, the aging of the U.S. population is creating increased demands for medical care and is also contributing to growth in leisure travel by retirement-aged persons.

Technological Changes. These are among the most often discussed changes that affect local economies. Employment in some industries may be directly affected by automation, which reduces the need for unskilled and semi-skilled labor. At the same time, employers may have difficulty finding adequately trained skilled and semi-skilled workers. Technology, particularly advances in communications and information technology, are affecting every conceivable issue. Consider, for example, the impact of such technological innovations as computers, fiber optics, fax machines, cellular telephones, VCRs, and microwaves on how business is conducted and on recreational and cultural goods and services.

In analyzing the external environment it is useful to distinguish issues at the regional/state scale from those at the national/global scale. Many regional and state issues revolve around dominant industries. At the national/global scale, some issues like tight credit will affect most communities in a similar way. Other influences may be highly selective, such as technological changes in specific industries.

A common approach to external analysis is to brainstorm about the forces that are having an important influence on the local economy. Participants should take advantage of written material and studies that may be available from specialized sources such as regional or state planning agencies and departments of commerce, university centers, and business and industry experts. Alternatively, representatives from these organizations and institutions can be invited to make presentations to the steering committee or specific task forces. There are also consultants who specialize in evaluating the significance of regional, national, and global change for community development efforts.

The thrust of the external assessment is to identify those circumstances and trends that are important for the subject community and to try to clarify their implications for local action. This process should help identify those issues that the community may be able to address, provided a suitable response can be identified. The process of identifying potential responses continues with the analysis of internal factors.

Evaluating Internal Factors

Earlier units have discussed ways to assess key factors that influence local economic prospects, including business base characteristics and labor and nonlabor resources or "location factors." We have also mentioned that "civic culture"—including local leadership, community institutions, and community attitudes and perceptions—should also be considered in developing a strategic plan. All of these factors should be systematically considered to identify local strengths and weaknesses and implications for development strategy.

The data and analysis that have been produced should be made available to the steering committee or task forces to guide their discussions. The internal evaluation plays a pivotal role in strategic planning because most of the proposals for specific actions are likely to originate at this stage. Examples of how to approach this type of assessment are given below for business base characteristics and human resources.

Example: Evaluating the Business Base. As discussed in Chapter 5, the competitiveness of a particular industry in a local area depends in part on the availability, cost, and quality of necessary factors of production. However, these factors are not the only important consideration; other influences on industry competitiveness include demand conditions, the presence of related and supporting industries, and industry structure and rivalry. Though these are less susceptible to local influence, they are characteristics of local industry that can be considered in evaluating development options.

Assessing Important Industry Clusters. One result of the analysis of industry structure should be a fairly good idea of the industries or clusters of industries that underpin the local economy. The earlier analysis of competitiveness will have indicated whether a particular industry has been gaining or losing competitive position in the local economy. Reasons for these shifts should be considered in light of external trends and in terms of the actions that might be taken locally to strengthen the industry's position in the area.

In general, policies will be more effective if they seek to reinforce an existing or emerging cluster than if they seek to create a new industry in the absence of any prior base. Also, efforts to identify and build on a core of industry strength will offer more synergy and growth potential than offering assistance to firms on an ad hoc basis. It is not easy to discern an emerging industry concentration. Once it is recognized, however, a community can take steps to signal its presence and begin to invest in specialized factors that will support its growth.

Demand Conditions. Sophisticated home demand for an industry's output can push that industry to innovate so that it gains or maintains industry leadership. There are a number of ways that local policies can stimulate home demand. Government procurement policies can provide markets for local firms and can push innovation if technical requirements are sufficiently advanced. Local regulations, such as stringent health or environmental standards, can also push an industry to upgrade.

San Francisco, for example, recently enacted the nation's first ergonomic standards for video display terminals in the workplace. Although motivated by concern for worker health and safety, the regulations would also push the domestic computer industry, centered in nearby Silicon Valley, to upgrade in a direction that could ultimately make it more competitive (since such standards are bound to become more widespread). This kind of local activism is on the cutting edge, however. Computer manufacturers have sued to block the San Francisco regulations and in January 1992 they won a court ruling that under state law, California localities are not empowered to legislate worker health and safety. The ruling is being appealed by the city and the Service Employees' International Union.

Seattle provides another example of potential local influence on home demand. Having experienced rapid growth over the past decade in part because of its natural amenities, Seattle leads the nation in recycling as a result of city mandates. Seattle's environmental awareness is creating the conditions for recycling industry leadership. Industries that become complacent and unresponsive to emerging demand segments, like the U.S. auto industry, may see competitiveness erode.

Entrepreneurial Orientation of Firms. This aspect of the local environment for industry relates to what can be called the "culture" of dominant firms and industries and their propensity toward entrepreneurship and innovation. The local community may have very little influence over this aspect of industry competitiveness, although it may be strongly affected by it.

One example is the effect of General Motors on the climate for entrepreneurship in Flint, Michigan. An analysis of reasons for Flint's lack of economic diversity noted that for a major corporate employer, GM had generated few spin-offs in Flint. There were a number of plausible contributing factors, aside from the possibility that in a mature industry opportunities for new business formation are more limited. Flint, which was where GM started, had lost its position as GM's "home base" to Detroit. Upper-level personnel were rotated in and out, which may have precluded the commitment to Flint that would have caused them to start companies there rather than elsewhere. It also seemed that a "big institution" mind set had taken over, dampening entrepreneurial initiative generally.

This situation can be compared with that of Fairchild Industries, an aerospace and defense contractor in Chantilly, Virginia, which is estimated to have spawned more than 30 companies. Obviously communities need to be aware of how their dominant firm or industry culture may be supporting or retarding new business formation.

Evanston, Illinois, a northern suburb of Chicago, is an example of a community that has crafted a development strategy aimed at providing a supportive environment for entrepreneurs, particularly those with ideas for products or services that involve emerging technology. Through a partnership involving business, government, and the research and educational community centered at nearby Northwestern University, Evanston has created a number of organizations and resources to aid entrepreneurs. Spearheaded by Evanston Inventure, a nonprofit economic development corporation formed in 1984, the effort has included the following components: a nonprofit seed capital fund for new business development; a small business incubator offering affordable space and shared services for start-up and emerging companies; a small business development center providing counseling, financial packaging, and referral services for the broad spectrum of small businesses in the area; a technology commercialization center geared to the specific needs of technology-based companies; and a university-linked center for applied research and development. To date, this activity is credited with the establishment in Evanston of some 40 emerging technology firms.[3]

Example: Evaluating Human Resources. Human resources are a location factor that will be relevant in all communities. The analyses of population and labor force characteristics will provide basic information useful in evaluating overall labor availability, as well as the mix of skills as evidenced by the occupational composition of the workforce.

If an area's human resources are characterized by a large complement of relatively unskilled workers, the main issue may be ensuring the "trainability" of the local labor force. Industry competitiveness today calls for adaptable workers who can be retrained as products and processes are upgraded. This assumes competence in basic reading and math, as well as good reasoning ability. Once U.S. literacy rates were the envy of the world, but that is not the case now. Other nations, like Korea, have surpassed us.

If workers are not being adequately prepared through the local educational system, the burden of preparation will fall on industry. For

---

[3] For a discussion of ways to create a more entrepreneurial environment in a local area see Gregerman (1991).

example, a survey of 10,000 employees at one auto plant found that 22 percent said they needed help in "understanding simple words, signs and labels" and 31 percent needed help in "understanding basic written directions, charts, procedures and instructions." At another auto plant, classes in statistical process control to improve quality were a failure because half of the trainees lacked sufficient math or reading skills to understand the material. It was necessary to first institute a reading program.[4] Obviously the quality of K-12 education is a generalized factor that affects competitive advantage through its influence on basic workforce skills.

Other aspects of the local labor force that affect competitive advantage include worker productivity and labor costs. As the labor content of many products diminishes with technological advances in production processes, the relative productivity and reliability of an area's workforce may be more important to employers than wage rates per se.

The availability of mechanisms for upgrading local human resources deserve special attention in community discussions since this is an area over which the community may exert some influence. Of special interest are educational or training programs that support the development of specialized human resources or "stimulus labor" that may represent an advanced factor for supporting economic growth.

The presence of four-year colleges or universities in an area can contribute to labor force quality in several ways. First, to the extent that students remain in the area after completing their education, such institutions result in a more highly educated labor force. Secondly, institutions offering four-year college programs or graduate programs bring into the community not only the highly educated employees of those institutions but often their highly educated spouses, who may be available for employment. Also, such institutions may offer amenities, such as cultural and athletic events, or research spin-offs that make it easier to attract other highly educated people to the area.

Identifying Response Options

In identifying response options, it is important to consider ways to support factor *creation*. The traditional approach to economic development is to seek to reduce factor *costs* by writing down land or buildings, subsidizing

---

[4] *Business Week*, September 29, 1986.

capital, or subsidizing training costs. But seeking to reduce costs to industry through subsidization may only undercut innovation and delay the process of needed adjustment to more advanced competitive advantages. Better results may be obtained by concentrating resources to aid firms indirectly, by investing in education to upgrade human resources or investing in infrastructure. Alternately, investments in combination with industry (e.g., tax incentive programs, business-government-university cooperative research programs) can help impose market discipline so that investments translate into true competitive advantage.

There are a number of professional organizations that provide information on the use of specific development techniques and incentives. They include the National Council for Urban Economic Development, in Washington, D.C., and—for a stronger focus on industrial development—the American Economic Development Council in Rosemont, Illinois. The Urban Land Institute, in Washington, D.C., is a source of information on real estate development in general. Also in Washington, D.C., are a number of organizations that specialize in selected aspects of economic development: The Corporation for Enterprise Development, which focuses on small business development; the International Downtown Association; the National Congress for Community Economic Development (for grass-roots community development techniques); and the National Trust for Historic Preservation, a good source of information on commercial revitalization as well as historic rehabilitation. Also, the publications of the American Planning Association and the International City Management Association often address various aspects of economic development. All of these sources can be consulted for ideas about specific initiatives that might be appropriate in a given situation.

In considering response options, further analysis may be required to evaluate relative costs and benefits. It also may be helpful to obtain or prepare forecasts of population and employment, to provide a context for assessing the potential impacts of different proposals.[5] Other types of analyses that may be required include assessments of local fiscal capacity, infrastructure studies, or feasibility studies for particular types of projects.

For example, the analysis of the Flint, Michigan economy, used as an example in several earlier units, led to the general conclusion that Flint should place as much emphasis on expanding service production—and producer services in particular—as it does on efforts to expand and diversify the area's industrial base. The study recommended several follow-on

---

[5] For use of microcomputers in projecting population or employment see Brail (1987) or Ottensmann (1986).

- 160 -

investigations to explore ideas raised by the initial assessment. These included a feasibility study to assess options for building on local strengths in health services; a detailed labor market study to document attributes of the local workforce that might help combat negative employer perceptions; a land use plan to spur development of a self-reinforcing growth center for light industrial and producer services firms in an area identified as optimal for such development; a feasibility study for a "technology center" to build on and reinforce area capabilities in applied engineering; and an organizational plan for an entity to provide area-wide coordination of economic development services. These follow-on studies helped to narrow the range of potential actions to those that represented local consensus about the best way to proceed.

THE ACTION PLAN:
MOVING TO IMPLEMENTATION

The external and internal assessments described above should generate a list of options for responding to critical economic development issues. This becomes the basis for developing an action plan that spells out goals, objectives, and strategies that are realistic and can be achieved.

It is useful to define these three terms, which often cause confusion. *Goals* are specific statements of what the community would like to be or to attain; they derive from the community's vision of its future and provide a frame of reference in making decisions on objectives and strategies. *Objectives* quantify the goals and, where possible, include deadlines or timeframes. *Strategies* are the action plans that spell out how the goals and objectives are to be achieved.

Identifying Goals, Objectives, and Strategies

Goals. Goals must be based on more than wishful thinking and should incorporate a strong sense of reality. A task force working on job creation and economic development must take into consideration the economic resource base, the community's competitive advantages and disadvantages, the external environment that limits or expands the community's opportunities, and the locational requirements of industrial and service sector firms in arriving at realistic goals.

The statement of goals must be clear and concise and provide direction. Therefore, a goal to "diversify the local economy" would not be very helpful. However, a goal of "assisting firms to expand nonlocal markets" or "increasing office employment opportunities" would be explicit and guide the effort to identify relevant objectives to meet these goals. For example, the goals articulated as a result of Flint's strategic planning effort are summarized in the box below.

Objectives. Goals are aspirations; objectives are targets. Therefore, goals must be capable of being translated into specific objectives or performance targets. If this cannot be done, it will be difficult to measure progress in achieving the goals and it will be almost impossible to determine what strategies or actions are most likely to produce the desired results.

Objectives should identify 1) the key result to be achieved, 2) numerical or other measurable indicators of progress, and 3) a target date for completion. As stated above, there will be more than one objective for each goal. Some may be short-term, others longer-term but within the approximately three-year time frame appropriate for strategic planning.

Objectives should be realistic and attainable. The human, financial, and institutional resources necessary to achieve them must be on hand, accessible, or at the very least, identifiable. Some may be found within the community. Others may be available from county, state, or federal government agencies, the private sector, or more likely a combination of these sources. Finally, objectives must be capable of being explained to the community as a whole, which will be asked to pay the price to achieve them.

Referring to the goal of "assisting firms to expand nonlocal markets" mentioned above, one objective might be to "expand government contracting by local firms over the next two years." Another might be to "identify new national and international markets for local products within a year."

Strategies. Once goals and objectives have been agreed upon, each task force must begin to develop strategies that spell out how the goals and objectives are to be achieved. A strategy usually consists of a project or activities to be undertaken to accomplish the objective. One key characteristic of a strategy is that it can be assigned to someone or some institution to carry out. It is at this point that the "nuts and bolts" practicalities take on major importance.

STRATEGIC DEVELOPMENT GOALS
FLINT-GENESEE COUNTY, MICHIGAN

BASIC STRENGTH: "Making things," in particular, expertise in the production of durable goods

BASIC WEAKNESS: Dependence on a mature industry (automotive)

OVERALL STRATEGIC GOAL: Economic diversification

SUBGOALS:

1. *Manufacturing* — a) regain and maintain a competitive lead as a center for goods manufacturing, with a new emphasis on production process innovation; b) increase the value-added component of local manufacturing output by increasing local ability to apply new knowledge and new technology to goods production.
   - Build on GM presence to increase local base of engineering, design, and marketing professionals
   - Increase applied research capabilities
   - Seek new ways to integrate human capabilities and productivity-enhancing computer and information technologies
   - Build on non-GM manufacturing base by developing local ability to compete in the area of specialized batch production

2. *New Growth Industries* — Develop a supportive environment for firms in growth sectors (e.g., technology-based industries, selected services such as health, education, engineering)
   - Develop Genesee County as a center for technology commercialization, with specialized abilities to develop and bring to market applications of basic research conducted elsewhere.
   - Increase availability of equity and near-equity capital for innovative firms through measures to expand local access to early-stage seed capital, venture financing, and working capital.

3. *Entrepreneurial Development* — Strengthen the local support systems that can help firms identify and respond to entrepreneurial opportunities.

4. *Business Retention and Expansion* — Reduce dependence on GM and vulnerability to auto industry cyclicality by assisting firms to expand nonlocal markets and improve product offerings.

5. *Economic Development Capacity* — Mount a coordinated, well-funded county-wide business development effort that draws on both the public and private sectors.

6. *Human Resources* — Build the quality of the Genesee County labor force by supporting programs to increase basic educational competencies and develop occupational skills matched to emerging requirements.

Source: Based on recommendations made in area economic and feasibility studies.

Returning to our previous example, one strategy might be "the establishment of a 'procurement assistance' program, including a database with information on state and federal contract opportunities and bidding procedures and requirements, developed and maintained by the local community development office." This strategy may include other components, such as a newsletter or advisories to potential users. There may be additional, equally appropriate strategies aimed at the objective of expanding the markets of local firms.

One good way to develop strategies is to convene task force members (or sub-groups within the task force who are familiar with the external and internal evaluations) for free-wheeling brainstorming sessions. New ideas and new ways of dealing with old ideas are likely to surface. The involvement of task force members representing diverse disciplines and interests will increase the likelihood of innovative ideas.

It is likely that more strategies will be suggested than the community could possible implement. Therefore, the following information should be developed for each proposed strategy:

- Cost
- Personnel requirements
- Agencies or organizations that will be responsible for implementation
- Time frame
- Expected impact
- Legal implications

By using these criteria to compare strategies, members will have a basis for ordering preferences and some strategies will be eliminated, thus assisting the task force in developing its issue-specific action plan in a realistic and credible manner.

Each task force should report its results to the overall strategic planning committee at a meeting called for the purpose of reviewing the proposed objectives and strategies and selecting those that are to be included in the action plan. There are many criteria that might be used to make the selection. The set of criteria presented in the box below are adapted from those used in the San Francisco strategic planning process.

The meeting at which the goals, objectives, and strategies are presented, discussed, and agreed upon is one of the most exciting events of the entire process. Each task force naturally tends to present its report as an advocate for its particular critical issue, and the competition and consensus-building dynamics are a real test of the cohesiveness and commitment of all involved.

STRATEGY SELECTION CRITERIA

Impact
What effect will this strategy have on the goal of the task force?
+ Major
0 Medium
- Minor

Feasibility
How likely is it that the strategy can be successfully implemented?
+ Very likely
0 Neither likely nor unlikely
- Very unlikely

Private Sector Ability
What is the private sector's ability to bring expertise or influence to bear on the strategy?
+ Great ability
0 Some ability
- Very little ability

Public Sector Acceptability
Will this strategy be supported by local government?
+ Definitely
0 Not sure
- No

Compatibility With Other Strategies
Will this strategy also contribute to the achievement of strategies or goals of other task forces?
+ Yes
0 No effect
- Negative effect on others

Timing
Does this strategy respond to an urgent need or time-sensitive opportunity?
+ Timing of immediate concern
0 Timing a factor but not immediate
- Timing not a concern

Developing the Action Plan

Once consensus is reached as to goals, objectives, and strategies it is possible to specify a plan of action. The action plan is the document that will guide implementation. Therefore it should cover agreements that are reached, identify resources, and assign responsibilities. This in turn will minimize misunderstandings about who is supposed to do what, when, and with what resources.

Generally, an action plan includes the following elements:

- Chronology of the strategic planning process
- Mission statement
- Statement of goals, objectives, and strategies
- Organizational responsibilities for each strategy
- Funding requirements, including identification of sources and accessibility of financial resources
- Evaluation and monitoring process

Identifying Resources. In writing the action plan, the committee will be dealing with the real limits of available resources, perhaps for the first time. Although the task forces will have discussed the costs of different strategies, an accurate assessment of overall costs is not possible until the plan is viewed in its entirety. There must be a link between strategy and budget. Although some strategies may address policy changes and removal of administrative barriers and not involve cash outlays, successful strategic planning will require allocation of scarce financial resources to implement the project-oriented strategies.

Potential public sector resources include budgetary allocations from local governments (city and county), grants and loans from state government agencies, and funds from federal sources such as the Economic Development Administration (EDA), the Environmental Protection Agency (EPA), the Small Business Administration (SBA), and the Department of Housing and Urban Development (HUD). Of equal importance will be the financial and human resources commitments of the business community, including financial institutions.

Sorting all this out will not be easy, particularly since care must be taken in committing resources over which the committee has no control. Timing is often difficult because some resources may not become available until it is clear that they are essential for the success of the program. This is especially true where private resources are need to "match" public funds. Thus the action plan must be assembled by the committee with the recognition that circumstances may change and that revisions may be required in the course of implementation. A carefully-crafted plan should be flexible enough to withstand change with minimum disruption to the community's program as a whole.

Gaining Support. The action plan should be shared with the general public prior to its formal adoption by the committee. If it is to represent the community's "shared vision," it must be subject to public review. There are two ways to ensure widespread awareness of the action plan: 1) publication in the local newspaper and 2) presentation at a public meeting co-sponsored by public and private sector leaders. It is important to encourage public comments and to convey that these are being solicited before the plan is finally adopted by the strategic planning committee and the community's legislative body.

Many of the financial and human resources required to implement the various strategies will be controlled, directly or indirectly, by local government. It is therefore important that elected officials formally adopt the action plan and commit their offices to implementing it.

Assigning Responsibility for Implementation. If the strategic planning process has been done well, there will be a broad consensus about what the critical issues are, how the external environment is affecting the community, and what the community's key strengths and weaknesses are. Also, if the process has been successful, a new coalition of business, government, and community leaders will be committed to specific strategies and the action plan. Finally, the process will have produced "champions," the leaders who will assume the responsibility of making sure that the strategies are implemented and the objectives met.

The key to implementation is organization and the preparation of an organization chart is an early requirement. The various community organizations that have helped to develop the action plan will now be involved in getting the job done, and the specific strategies proposed in the plan must be clearly assigned.

This requires a specific commitment from each organization, whether it be the city public works department, a community-based nonprofit housing corporation, the chamber of commerce, the city's economic development organization, the downtown development authority, or others. Each participant should:

- Know its responsibility for action
- Know the desired results
- Accept responsibility for those actions and results
- Know the timeframe within which the actions are to be taken and completed
- Be committed to achieving the desired results

A useful technique is to request that each responsible organization prepare a work plan with a one-year time frame. For each strategic action, the work plan should identify the responsible agency and project manager and include a breakdown of specific tasks involved in implementing the strategy. The requirements for completing each task should be noted, including the schedule, staffing requirements, other resource requirements, estimated budget, and sources of funds.

The importance of creating an effective organizational structure within the community to implement the action plan cannot be overemphasized. In smaller communities, the players will be more easily identified because of the scale and the high visibility of the strategic planning process. Also, peer pressure will be more of a factor than in larger communities. Turf conflicts, organizational jealousies, and duplication of effort must be avoided. The process of consensus-building and negotiation that led to the action plan is intended to help circumvent such problems. Otherwise, they must be resolved as organizational responsibilities are assigned. The chair of the strategic planning committee and the chief elected official are well placed to resolve them.

MONITORING AND UPDATING THE PLAN

The process of strategic analysis and strategic planning does not end with the adoption of an action plan, though that is obviously a major milestone. Implementation may not be swift or easy and plans must be monitored and adjusted to reflect changing circumstances. Economic development is not a one-time thing. Similarly, the process of analyzing economic change and framing a community response is best viewed as an ongoing one.

The first requirement for monitoring is that an individual or organization be assigned that responsibility. One of the benefits of the strategic planning process is the involvement of the community's leadership with the strategic planning committee and the visibility that the process gives to those who have served. Therefore, the planning committee or a smaller group of members may be the logical ones to keep track of results and maintain momentum. Both public officials and private interests should be represented, with the latter in the majority. This will reflect the continuing importance of the public-private partnership as the key to consensus building and implementation.

The monitoring process should track the following activities:

- Progress on each strategy compared with the scheduled progress according to the action plan and individual work plans

- Time and financial resources spent compared with resources allocated

- Changes in individuals and organizations that may affect their abilities to complete assignments

- Changes in the external environment that might sabotage the plan

Because each action plan will consist of a number of strategies, this monitoring function can be burdensome. However, it is necessary because it ensures that actions are taken and that the effort is kept on target by providing a way to adjust to changes in available or needed resources or in the environment itself. If the environment should change abruptly (e.g, by the closing of a major plant, an unexpected loss of infrastructure, the arrival of a major new employer) the monitoring group can reconvene the planning committee to consider adjusting strategies.

Within one year after implementation has begun, the monitoring group should reconvene the strategic planning committee for a formal progress review. This will provide an opportunity to update the strategies and to make certain that the assumptions underlying the strategic plan still hold. This review is also a way to maintain interest within the community's leadership group.

If the critical issues selected are truly the important ones, and if the mission statement reflects fundamental priorities, the strategic plan should—with periodic updating—last three to five years. Of course, given the rapidly changing environment in which all communities now operate, keeping track of external factors will be an important ongoing function of the monitoring group. When a major revision of the action plan is needed, the process begins all over again with the community economic audit.

The methods that have been described in this handbook can help a community develop its own capacity to engage in ongoing monitoring and evaluation of the local economy. The more sensitive and responsive community institutions are to changing economic conditions, the better the community's chances of identifying and implementing appropriate policy and programs to stimulate local economic growth.

Additional Reading

Entrepreneurship Development

Drucker, Peter E. *Innovation and Entrepreneurship: Practice and Principles*. New York: Harper & Row, 1985.

Gregerman, Alan S. "Rekindling the Future." *Economic Development Commentary* 14 (Winter 1991): 7-14. Washington, D.C.: National Council for Urban Economic Development.

Feasibility Analysis, General

Barrett, G. Vincent and John P. Blair. *How to Conduct and Analyze Real Estate Market and Feasibility Studies*. Chicago: American Planning Association, 1981.

Matzer, John, ed. *Capital Projects: New Strategies for Planning, Management, and Finance*. Washington, D.C.: International City Management Association, 1989.

Patton, Carl V. and David S. Sawicki. *Basic Methods of Policy Analysis and Planning*. Chicago: American Planning Association, 1985.

Planning Advisory Service. *Analyzing the Economic Feasibility of a Development Project*. PAS 380. Chicago: American Planning Association, 1984.

Forecasting Techniques

Brail, Richard K. *Microcomputers in Urban Planning and Management*. New Brunswick, N.J.: Center for Urban Policy Research, 1987.

Ottensman, John R. *Basic Microcomputer Programs for Urban Analysis and Planning*. New York: Chapman and Hall, 1986.

Boyle, M. Ross. *Developing Strategies for Economic Stability and Growth*. Information Service Report No. 37. Washington, D.C.: National Council for Urban Economic Development, 1987.

See also the listing at the end of Chapter 1.

BIBLIOGRAPHY

Ady, Robert M. "High-Technology Plants: Different Criteria for the Best Location." *Economic Development Commentary* (Winter 1983): 8-10. Washington, D.C.: National Council for Urban Economic Development.

Balfe, Kevin P. *A Comprehensive Methodology for Labor Market Analysis*. Evanston, Ill.: NCI Research, 1989.

Bailey, Kenneth D. *Methods of Social Research*. New York: Macmillan-The Free Press, 1978.

Barrett, G. Vincent and John P. Blair. *How to Conduct and Analyze Real Estate Market and Feasibility Studies*. Chicago: American Planning Association, 1981.

Bendavid-Val, Avrom. *Regional and Local Analysis for Practitioners*. New York: Praeger Publishers, 1983.

Berman, Norton. *Local Strategic Planning: A Handbook for Community Leaders*. Lansing, Mich.: Michigan Department of Commerce, 1990.

Beyers, William B. "Producer Services and Metropolitan Growth and Development." In *Sources of Metropolitan Growth*, Edwin S. Mills and John F. McDonald, eds. New Brunswick, N.J.: Center for Urban Policy Research, 1992.

Beyers, William B.; Michael J. Alvine; and Erik G. Johnsen. *The Service Economy: Export of Services in the Central Puget Sound Region*. Seattle, Wash.: Central Puget Sound Economic Development District, 1985.

Birch, David L. *The Job Generation Process*. Washington, D.C.: Economic Development Administration, 1979.

_____. "The Rise and Fall of Everybody." *INC.* (September 1987):18-19.

Blakely, Edward J. *Planning Local Economic Development*. Newbury Park, Calif.: Sage Publications, 1989.

Bosscher, Robert A. and Kenneth P. Voytek. *Local Strategic Planning: A Primer for Local Area Analysis*. Lansing, Mich.: Michigan Department of Commerce, 1990.

Boyle, M. Ross. *Developing Strategies for Economic Stability and Growth*. Washington, D.C.: National Council for Urban Economic Development, 1987.

Brail, Richard K. *Microcomputers in Urban Planning and Management*. New Brunswick, N.J.: Center for Urban Policy Research, 1987.

Chambers, John C. "How to Choose the Right Forecasting Technique." *Harvard Business Review*, May-June 1971, pp. 45-74.

Doeringer, Peter B. et al. *Invisible Factors in Local Economic Development*, New York: Oxford University Press, 1987.

Drucker, Peter E. *Innovation and Entrepreneurship: Practice and Principles*. New York: Harper and Row, 1985.

Erickcek, George. "Growth Potential of Services in West Michigan." *Business Outlook*, Vol. 6, No. 4 (1990): 1-5.

Galambos, Eva C. and Arthur F. Schreiber. *Economic Analysis for Local Government*. Washington, D.C.: National League of Cities, 1978.

Gardocki, B.C. and J. Baj. *Methodology for Estimating Nondisclosure in County Business Patterns*. Dekalb, Ill.: Center for Governmental Studies, Northern Illinois University, 1985.

Gillis, William R. "Can Service Producing Industries Provide a Catalyst for Regional Economic Growth." *Economic Development Quarterly*, Vol. 1, No. 3 (1987): 249-256.

Goldstein, Harvey. "A Practitioner's Guide to State and Substate Industry Employment Projections." *Economic Development Quarterly*, Vol. 4, No. 3 (1990): 260-275.

_____. *Projecting Industry and Occupation Employment for State and Substate Areas*. Washington, D.C.: National Occupational Information Coordinating Committee, 1988.

_____. and Edward M. Bergman. *Methods and Models for Projecting State and Area Industry Employment*. Washington, D.C.: National Occupational Information Coordinating Committee, 1983.

Grassmuck, Karen. "Wariness Dampens 1980's Craze for Building University-Sponsored Technology Parks." *Chronicle of Higher Education* (June 27, 1990).

Greenberg, Michael R. et al. *Local Population and Employment Projection Techniques*. New Brunswick, N.J.: The Center for Urban Policy Research, 1978.

Gregerman, Alan S. *Competitive Advantage: Framing a Strategy to Support High Growth Firms*. Washington, D.C.: National Council for Urban Economic Development, 1984.

Gregerman, Alan S. "Rekindling the Future." *Economic Development Commentary* 14 (Winter 1991): 7-14. Washington, D.C.: National Council for Urban Economic Development.

Hammer, Thomas R. *Data Needs for Regional Analysis and Economic Development*. Evanston, Ill.: NCI Research, 1986.

_____. *Evaluation of Development Potentials for Metropolitan Flint, Michigan*. Report to the Mott Foundation. Evanston, Ill.: NCI Research, 1986.

_____. *Technical Support for Strategic Planning in Small Michigan Communities*. Evanston, Ill: NCI Research, 1990.

Haurin, Donald R. and R. Jean Haurin. "The Migration of Youth and the Business Cycle: 1978-1984." *Economic Development Quarterly*, Vol. 1, No. 2 (1987): 162-175.

Heilbrun, James. *Urban Economics and Public Policy*. New York: St. Martin's Press, 1987.

Helman, Daryl A. "Shift-Share Models as Predictive Tools." *Growth and Change*, 1976, pp. 3-8.

Hewings, Geoffrey J.D. *Regional Input-Output Analysis*. Newbury, Calif.: Sage Publications, 1985.

Hicks, Donald A. "Tracking Economic Turnover and Adjustment." *Economic Development Commentary* 15 (Summer 1991): 28-29.

Hirschorn, Larry. "Scenario Writing: A Development Approach." *APA Journal*, Vol. 46, No. 2(1980)172-183.

Hustedde, Ron et al. *Community Economic Analysis*. Ames, Iowa: North Central Regional Center for Rural Development, 1984.

Isard, Walter. *An Introduction to Regional Science*. Englewood Cliffs, N.J.: Prentice Hall, Inc., 1975.

Jackson, Randall. "Input-Output Analysis for the Uninitiated." DeKalb, Ill.: Center for Governmental Studies, 1984.

Johnston, J. *Econometric Methods*. New York: McGraw-Hill, 1963.

Kasarda, John D. and Michael D. Irwin. "National Business Cycles and Community Competition for Jobs." September 1988, unpublished manuscript, University of North Carolina-Chapel Hill.

Kmenta, J. *Elements of Econometrics*. New York: Macmillan, 1971.

Kolzow, David. *Strategic Planning for Economic Development*. Chicago: American Economic Development Council, 1988.

Krueckberg, Donald A. and Arthur Silvers. *Urban Planning Analysis: Methods and Models*. New York: John Wiley and Sons, 1974.

Levy, Frank. *Dollars and Dreams*. New York: W.W. Norton & Company, 1988.

Lipman, Barbara J. and Ted R. Miller. *Feasibility Study to Update, Define, Enhance, or Replace EDA's Industrial Location System*. Washington, D.C.: The Urban Institute, 1987.

Lösch, A. *The Economics of Location*. New Haven: Yale University Press, 1954.

Matzer, John, ed. *Capital Projects: New Strategies for Planning, Management, and Finance*. Washington, D.C.: International City Management Association, 1989.

McDonald, John F. "Employment Growth, Payrolls, and Wage Competitiveness." *Chicago Economic Update*. Report to the Economic Development Commission of Chicago. Evanston, Ill.: NCI Research, 1990.

_____. *Targeting Industries for Economic Development Marketing*. Evanston, Ill.: NCI Research, 1990.

McDonald, John F.; Breandán Ó hUallacháin; and Thomas M. Beam. *Assessing the Development Status of Metropolitan Areas*. Report to the U.S. Economic Development Administration. Evanston, Ill.: NCI Research, 1989.

McKee, William L. and Richard C. Froeschle. *Where the Jobs Are*. Kalamazoo, Mich.: W.E. Upjohn Institute for Employment Research, 1985.

Michigan Modernization Service, Research Analysis Group. *Local Area Modernization Plan, Montcalm and Ionia Counties*. Ann Arbor, Mich.: Industrial Technology Institute, June 1989.

Miernyk, William H. The Elements of Input-Output Analysis., New York: Random House, 1965.

Milkman, Raymond H. et al. *Evaluating Economic Development Programs*. Washington, D.C.: Lazar Management Group, 1978.

Mills, Edwin S. "Sectoral Clustering and Economic Development." In *Sources of Metropolitan Growth*. Edwin S. Mills and John F. McDonald, eds. New Brunswick, N.J.: Center for Urban Policy Research Press, 1992.

Monti, Lorna. "The Uses and Misuses of Metropolitan Area Employment and Unemployment Numbers." *Economic and Business Issues of the 1980's*. J.E. Pluta, ed. University of Texas at Austin: Bureau of Business Research, 1980, pp. 96-104.

Moriarity, Barry M. *Industrial Location and Community Development*. Chapel Hill, N.C.: University of North Carolina Press, 1980.

Morrissett, Irving. "The Economic Structure of American Cities." *Papers and Proceedings of the Regional Science Association* 4 (1985): 239-258.

Morton, J.E. *On Manpower Forecasting*. Kalamazoo, Mich.: W.E. Upjohn Institute for Employment Research, 1971.

Moss, Mitchell L. and Andrew Dunau. "Will the Cities Lose Their Back Offices?" *Real Estate Review* (Spring 1987): 62-68.

Mt. Auburn Associates. "How to Analyze the Local Financial Market." In *Design and Management of State and Local Revolving Loan Funds: A Handbook*. Washington, D.C.: Economic Development Administration, 1987.

Murdock, Steve H. et al. *Population Projections* Applied Community Research Monograph E2. Alexandria, Va.: American Chamber of Commerce Researchers Association, 1989.

National Council on Public Works Improvement. *Fragile Foundations: A Report on America's Public Works*. Washington, D.C.: U.S. Government Printing Office, February 1988.

NCI Research. *Data Needs for Regional Analysis and Economic Development Practice: Symposium Proceedings*. Evanston, Ill.: NCI Research, 1988.

NCI Research. *Northeast Michigan Economic Study*. Evanston, Ill.: NCI Research, 1990.

Neithercut, Mark E. et al. *Local Economic Development Research: A Guide to Data Sources*. Detroit, Mich.: Center for Urban Studies, Wayne State University, 1989.

North, Douglas. "Location Theory and Regional Economic Growth." *Journal of Political Economy*, Vol. 63, No. 3 (1955): 243-258.

Norton, R. D. and J. Rees. "The Product Cycle and the Spatial Decentralization of American Manufacturing." *Regional Studies* 13 (August 1979): 141-51.

Nourse, Hugh O. *Regional Economics*. New York: McGraw-Hill, 1968.

Ó hUallacháin, Breandán. "The Location and Growth of Business Services in U.S. Metropolitan Areas." In *Assessing the Development Status of Metropolitan Areas* by John F. McDonald, Breandán Ó hUallacháin, and Thomas M. Beam. Evanston, Ill.: NCI Research, 1989.

Ó hUallacháin, Breandán and Mark Satterthwaite. *Sectoral Growth Patterns at the Metropolitan Level: An Evaluation of Economic Development Incentives*. Evanston, Ill.: NCI Research, 1988.

Olsen, John B. and Douglas C. Eadie. *The Game Plan*. Washington, D.C.: Council of State Planning Agencies, 1982.

Ottensmann, John R. *Basic Microcomputer Programs for Urban Analysis and Planning*. New York: Chapman and Hall, 1986.

Pascal, Anthony and Aaron Gurwitz. *Picking Winners: Industrial Strategies for Local Economic Development*. Santa Monica, Calif.: The Rand Corporation, 1983.

Patton, Carl V. "Information for Planning." In *The Practice of Local Government Planning*, Frank S. So and Judith Getzels, eds. Washington: D.C.: International City Management Association, 1988.

_____ and David S. Sawicki. *Basic Methods of Policy Analysis and Planning*. Chicago: American Planning Association, 1985.

Planning Advisory Service. *Analyzing the Economic Feasibility of a Development Project*. PAS 380. Chicago: American Planning Association, 1984.

Porter, Michael E. "The Competitive Advantage of Nations." *Harvard Business Review*, March-April 1990, pp. 73-93.

Porter, Michael E. *The Competitive Advantage of Nations*. New York: Macmillan-The Free Press, 1990.

Reich, Robert C. *The Next American Frontier*. New York: Basic Books, 1983.

Reigeluth, George A. and Harold Wolman. *The Determinants and Implications of Communities' Changing Competitive Advantages: A Literature Review*. Washington, D.C.: The Urban Institute, 1981.

Richardson, Harry W. *Regional Economics*. Urbana, Ill.: The University of Illinois Press, 1979.

_____. *Regional and Urban Economics*. London: Penguin Books, 1978.

Satterthwaite, Mark A. "High Growth Industries and Uneven Metropolitan Growth." In *Sources of Metropolitan Growth*, Edwin S. Mills and John F. McDonald, eds. New Brunswick, N.J.: Center for Urban Policy Research, 1992.

_____. "Location Patterns of High-Growth Firms." *Economic Development Commentary* (Spring 1988), Washington, D.C.: National Council for Urban Economic Development.

Sawicki, David. "Microcomputer Applications in Planning." *American Planning Association Journal*, 50 (Spring 1985): 209-215.

Schmenner, Roger W. *Making Business Location Decisions*. Englewood Cliffs, N.J.: Prentice Hall, 1982.

Simpson, Jeff L. *Visual Display of Statistics*. Applied Community Research Monograph CS-5. Alexandria, Va.: American Chamber of Commerce Researchers Association, 1989.

Singlemann, Joachim. *From Agriculture to Services*. Beverly Hills, Calif.: Sage Publications, 1978.

So, Frank A. and Judith Getzels, eds. *The Practice of Local Government Planning*. Washington, D.C.: International City Management Association, 1988.

Sorkin, Donna L. et al. *Strategic Planning for Cities and Counties*. Washington, D.C.: Public Technology, Inc., 1982.

Stanback, T.M.; P. Bearse, T.J. Noyelle, and R. Karasek. *Services: The New Economy*. Totowa, N.J.: Allenheld, Osmun and Company, 1981.

Swanstrom, Todd. "The Limits of Strategic Planning for Cities." *Journal of Urban Affairs*, 9 (1987): 139-157.

Thompson, Phillip R. and Wilbur R. Thompson. "National Industries and Local Occupational Strengths: The Cross Hairs of Targeting." *Urban Studies*, Vol. 24, No. 4 (1985): 547-560.

Thompson, Wilbur R. "The Economic Basc of Urban Problems." in *Contemporary Economic Issues*, Neil W. Chamberlain, ed. Chicago: Richard D. Irwin, Inc., 1973.

_____. "Policy-Based Analysis for Local Economic Development." *Economic Development Quarterly*, Vol. 1, No. 4 (1987): 203-213.

Tiebout, Charles M. "Exports and Regional Economic Growth." *Journal of Political Economy*, Vol. 64 (1956) No. 2: 160-169.

Tufte, Edward R. *The Visual Display of Quantitative Information*. Chesire, Conn.: Graphics Press, 1983.

Ullman, Edward and Michael Dacey. "The Minimum Requirements Approach to the Urban Economic Base." *Papers and Proceedings of the Regional Science Association*, Vol. 6 (1960): 175-199.

U.S. Department of Commerce, Economic Development Administration. *Handbook for Economic Development District Organizations*. Washington, D.C.: Government Printing Office, 1968.

U.S. Department of Labor, Bureau of Labor Statistics. *BLS Handbook of Methods* (Bulletin No. 2285). Washington, D.C.: U.S. Government Printing Office, April 1988.

Vaughn, Roger J. *The Urban Impacts of Federal Policies*. Santa Monica, Calif.: The Rand Corporation, 1977.

Voytek, Kenneth P. "The Comparative Performance of Michigan's Substate Regions, 1979-1987." Paper presented at the Michigan Association of Regions' Annual Conference, 1989.

_____. "The Economic Performance and Condition of Michigan MSA's, 1979-88." *Business Outlook*, Vol. 5., No. 4 (1989): 1-7.

_____ and Harold Wolman. "Detroit: An Economy Still Driven by Automobiles." in *The Restructuring of the American Midwest*, Richard D. Bingham and Randall W. Eberts, eds. Norwell, Mass.: Kluwer Academic Publishers, 1990.

Watkins, Alfred J. *The Practice of Urban Economics*. Beverly Hills, Calif.: Sage Publications, 1980.

Wolman, Harold. "U.S. Urban Economic Performance: What Accounts for Success and Failure." *Journal of Urban Affairs*, Vol. 9, No. 1 (1987): 1-17.

APPENDIX A

METROPOLITAN AREA DEFINITIONS

- Bureau of the Census, Geographic Areas (Geographic subdivisions used in Census reporting, with illustration)

- List of Metropolitan Statistical Areas (As defined effective June 30, 1990)

- Revised Standards for Defining Metropolitan Areas in the 1990s (*Federal Register*, March 30, 1990)

Geographic Subdivisions in a Metropolitan County .... and in a Non-Metropolitan County

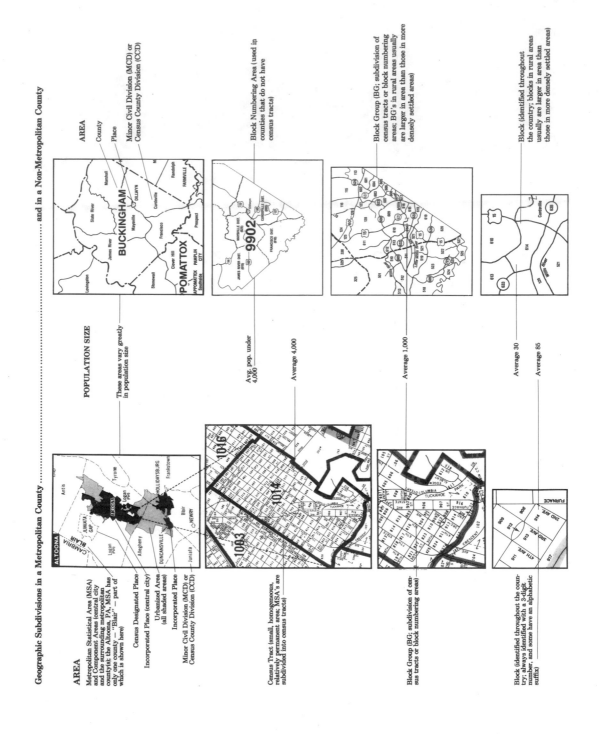

AREA

Metropolitan Statistical Area (MSA)
and Component Areas (central city
and the surrounding metropolitan
county(s); the Altoona, PA, MSA has
only one county — "Blair" — part of
which is shown here)

Census Designated Place

Incorporated Place (central city)

Urbanized Area
(all shaded areas)

Incorporated Place

Minor Civil Division (MCD) or
Census County Division (CCD)

AREA

County

Place

Minor Civil Division (MCD) or
Census County Division (CCD)

Block Numbering Area (used in
counties that do not have
census tracts)

Block Group (BG; subdivision of
census tracts or block numbering
areas; BG's in rural areas usually
are larger in area than those in more
densely settled areas)

Block (identified throughout
the country; blocks in rural areas
usually are larger in area than
those in more densely settled areas)

POPULATION SIZE

These areas vary greatly
in population size

Avg. pop. under
4,000

Average 4,000

Census Tract (small, homogeneous,
relatively permanent area; MSA's are
subdivided into census tracts)

Block Group (BG; subdivision of census tracts or block numbering areas)

Average 1,000

Block (identified throughout the country; always identified with a 3-digit
number, and some have an alphabetic
suffix)

Average 30

Average 85

- 184 -

BUREAU OF THE CENSUS

Geographic Areas[1]

Census data are provided for various political and statistical areas. Many are illustrated in the figure at left.

Political areas include the following:

- United States

- States, the District of Columbia, Puerto Rico, the Virgin Islands of the United States, Guam, the Commonwealth of the Northern Mariana Islands, American Samoa, and Palau

- Congressional districts

- Counties

- Minor civil divisions (MCDs; legal subdivisions of counties, called townships in many States)

- Incorporated places (cities, villages, and so forth)

- American Indian reservations and associated trust lands

- Alaska Native Regional Corporations (ANRCs)

Statistical areas include the following:

- *Census regions and divisions* — The 50 States and the District of Columbia have been grouped into four regions, each containing two or three divisions.

- *Metropolitan statistical areas (MSAs), formerly known as standard metropolitan statistical areas (SMSAs)* — Areas consisting of one or more counties (minor civil divisions in New England) including a large population nucleus and nearby communities that have a high degree of interaction. Primary metropolitan statistical areas (PMSAs) are MSAs that make up consolidated metropolitan statistical areas (CMSAs).

- *Urbanized areas (UAs)* — Defined by population density, each includes a central city and the surrounding closely settled urban fringe (suburbs) that together have a population of 50,000 or more with a population density generally exceeding 1,000 people per square mile.

- *Urban/rural* — All persons living in urbanized areas and in places of 2,500 or more population outside of UAs constitute the "urban" population; all others constitute the "rural" population.

---

[1]Excerpted from *Census '90 Basics*, Bureau of the Census, 1990, pp.5-6.

- *Census county divisions (CCDs)* — Statistical subdivisions of a county defined by the Census Bureau in cooperation with State officials in 21 States where minor civil divisions do not exist or are not adequate for producing subcounty statistics.

- *Census designated places (CDPs)* — Densely settled population centers without legally defined corporate limits or corporate powers.

- *Census tracts* — Small, locally defined statistical areas in metropolitan areas and some other counties. They generally have stable boundaris and an average population of 4,000.

- *Block numbering areas (BNAs)* — Areas defined, with State assistance, for grouping and numbering blocks and reporting statistics in counties without census tracts.

- *Block groups* — Groupings of census blocks within census tracts and BNAs. (These replace the enumeration districts (EDs) for which the Census Bureau provided data for many areas of the Nation in the 1980 census.)

- *Blocks* — The smallest census geographic areas, normally bounded by streets and other prominent physical features. County, MCD, and place limits also serve as block boundaries. Blocks may be as small as a typical city block bounded by four streets or as large as several square miles in rural areas. The 1990 census will be the first census in which data will be available by block for the entire Nation.

- *Alaska Native village statistical areas (ANVSAs)* — A 1990 census statistical area that delineates the settled area of each Alaska Native village (ANV). Officials of Alaska Native Regional Corporations (business and nonprofit corporate entities) outlined the ANVSAs for the Census Bureau for the sole purpose of presenting 1990 census data.

- *Tribal designated statistical areas (TDSAs)* — Geographic areas outlined for 1990 census tabulation purposes by American Indian tribal officials of recognized tribes that do not have a recognized land area.

- *Tribal jurisdiction statistical areas (TJSAs)* — Geographic areas delineated by tribal officials in Oklahoma for 1990 census tabulation purposes.

Metropolitan Area Definitions and Population Counts, 1980 and 1990

Metropolitan areas are defined for federal statistical use by the Office of Management and Budget, with technical assistance from the Census Bureau. Most individual metropolitan areas are designated as "metropolitan statistical areas" (MSAs). Metropolitan areas over one million may under specified circumstances be subdivided into component "primary metropolitan statistical areas" (PMSAs), in which case the area as a whole is designated a "consolidated metropolitan statistical area" (CMSA). In the main tables of this release, the 1980 and 1990 data refer to the areas as defined effective June 30, 1990. After detailed results of the census become available, OMB expects to issue revised definitions of all metropolitan areas in early 1993.

Source: Excerpted from Bureau of the Census "Half of the Nation's Population Lives in Large Metropolitan Areas," press release, February 21, 1991

POPULATION OF METROPOLITAN AREAS: 1990 AND 1980, BY 1990 POPULATION RANK

Areas defined by Office of Management and Budget, June 30, 1990. Primary MSAs (PMSAs) appear under their consolidated MSA (CMSA)

Metropolitan area	April 1, 1990 census	April 1, 1980 census	Change, 1980-90 Number	Change, 1980-90 Pct.	CMSA/MSA rank Population 1990	CMSA/MSA rank Population 1980	CMSA/MSA rank Percent change, 1980-90
New York-Northern New Jersey-Long Island, NY-NJ-CT CMSA ...	18,087,251	17,539,532	547,719	3.1	1	1	194
New York, NY PMSA	8,546,846	8,274,961	271,885	3.3			
Nassau-Suffolk, NY PMSA	2,609,212	2,605,813	3,399	0.1			
Newark, NJ PMSA	1,824,321	1,879,147	-54,826	-2.9			
Bergen-Passaic, NJ PMSA	1,278,440	1,292,970	-14,530	-1.1			
Middlesex-Somerset-Hunterdon, NJ PMSA	1,019,835	886,383	133,452	15.1			
Monmouth-Ocean, NJ PMSA	986,327	849,211	137,116	16.1			
Jersey City, NJ PMSA	553,099	556,972	-3,873	-0.7			
Bridgeport-Milford, CT PMSA	443,722	438,557	5,165	1.2			
Orange County, NY PMSA	307,647	259,603	48,044	18.5			
Stamford, CT PMSA	202,557	198,854	3,703	1.9			
Danbury, CT PMSA	187,867	170,369	17,498	10.3			
Norwalk, CT PMSA	127,378	126,692	686	0.5			
Los Angeles-Anaheim-Riverside, CA CMSA	14,531,529	11,497,549	3,033,980	26.4	2	2	42
Los Angeles-Long Beach, CA PMSA	8,863,164	7,477,239	1,385,925	18.5			
Riverside-San Bernardino, CA PMSA	2,588,793	1,558,215	1,030,578	66.1			
Anaheim-Santa Ana, CA PMSA	2,410,556	1,932,921	477,635	24.7			
Oxnard-Ventura, CA PMSA	669,016	529,174	139,842	26.4			
Chicago-Gary-Lake County, IL-IN-WI CMSA ...	8,065,633	7,937,290	128,343	1.6	3	3	210
Chicago, IL PMSA	6,069,974	6,060,383	9,591	0.2			
Gary-Hammond, IN PMSA	604,526	642,733	-38,207	-5.9			
Lake County, IL PMSA	516,418	440,388	76,030	17.3			
Joliet, IL PMSA	389,650	355,042	34,608	9.7			
Aurora-Elgin, IL PMSA	356,884	315,607	41,277	13.1			
Kenosha, WI PMSA	128,181	123,137	5,044	4.1			
San Francisco-Oakland-San Jose, CA CMSA ...	6,253,311	5,367,900	885,411	16.5	4	5	77
Oakland, CA PMSA	2,082,914	1,761,710	321,204	18.2			
San Francisco, CA PMSA	1,603,678	1,488,895	114,783	7.7			
San Jose, CA PMSA	1,497,577	1,295,071	202,506	15.6			
Vallejo-Fairfield-Napa, CA PMSA	451,186	334,402	116,784	34.9			
Santa Rosa-Petaluma, CA PMSA	388,222	299,681	88,541	29.5			
Santa Cruz, CA PMSA	229,734	188,141	41,593	22.1			
Philadelphia-Wilmington-Trenton, PA-NJ-DE-MD CMSA	5,899,345	5,680,509	218,836	3.9	5	4	188
Philadelphia, PA-NJ PMSA ...~..:.........................	4,856,881	4,716,559	140,322	3.0			
Wilmington, DE-NJ-MD PMSA	578,587	523,221	55,366	10.6			
Trenton, NJ PMSA	325,824	307,863	17,961	5.8			
Vineland-Millville-Bridgeton, NJ PMSA	138,053	132,866	5,187	3.9			
Detroit-Ann Arbor, MI CMSA	4,665,236	4,752,764	-87,528	-1.8	6	6	237
Detroit, MI PMSA	4,382,299	4,488,024	-105,725	-2.4			
Ann Arbor, MI PMSA	282,937	264,740	18,197	6.9			

POPULATION OF METROPOLITAN AREAS: 1990 AND 1980, BY 1990 POPULATION RANK

Areas defined by Office of Management and Budget, June 30, 1990. Primary MSAs (PMSAs) appear under their consolidated MSA (CMSA)

					CMSA/MSA rank		
					Population		Percent
	April 1, 1990	April 1, 1980	Change, 1980-90				change,
Metropolitan area	census	census	Number	Pct.	1990	1980	1980-90
Boston-Lawrence-Salem, MA-NH CMSA	4,171,643	3,971,792	199,851	5.0	7	7	181
Boston, MA PMSA	2,870,669	2,805,911	64,758	2.3			
Lawrence-Haverhill, MA-NH PMSA	393,516	339,090	54,426	16.1			
Lowell, MA-NH PMSA	273,067	243,142	29,925	12.3			
Salem-Gloucester, MA PMSA	264,356	258,231	6,125	2.4			
Brockton, MA PMSA	189,478	182,891	6,587	3.6			
Nashua, NH PMSA	180,557	142,527	38,030	26.7			
Washington, DC-MD-VA MSA	3,923,574	3,250,921	672,653	20.7	8	8	59
Dallas-Fort Worth, TX CMSA	3,885,415	2,930,568	954,847	32.6	9	10	25
Dallas, TX PMSA	2,553,362	1,957,430	595,932	30.4			
Fort Worth-Arlington, TX PMSA	1,332,053	973,138	358,915	36.9			
Houston-Galveston-Brazoria, TX CMSA	3,711,043	3,099,942	611,101	19.7	10	9	64
Houston, TX PMSA	3,301,937	2,734,617	567,320	20.7			
Galveston-Texas City, TX PMSA	217,399	195,738	21,661	11.1			
Brazoria, TX PMSA	191,707	169,587	22,120	13.0			
Miami-Fort Lauderdale, Fl CMSA	3,192,582	2,643,766	548,816	20.8	11	12	58
Miami-Hialeah, FL PMSA	1,937,094	1,625,509	311,585	19.2			
Fort Lauderdale-Hollywood-Pompano Beach, FL PMSA	1,255,488	1,018,257	237,231	23.3			
Atlanta, GA MSA	2,833,511	2,138,136	695,375	32.5	12	16	26
Cleveland-Akron-Lorain, OH CMSA	2,759,823	2,834,062	-74,239	-2.6	13	11	243
Cleveland, OH PMSA	1,831,122	1,898,825	-67,703	-3.6			
Akron, OH PMSA	657,575	660,328	-2,753	-0.4			
Lorain-Elyria, OH PMSA	271,126	274,909	-3,783	-1.4			
Seattle-Tacoma, WA CMSA	2,559,164	2,093,285	465,879	22.3	14	18	53
Seattle, WA PMSA	1,972,961	1,607,618	365,343	22.7			
Tacoma, WA PMSA	586,203	485,667	100,536	20.7			
San Diego, CA MSA	2,498,016	1,861,846	636,170	34.2	15	19	22
Minneapolis-St. Paul, MN-WI MSA	2,464,124	2,137,133	326,991	15.3	16	17	86
St. Louis, MO-IL MSA	2,444,099	2,376,968	67,131	2.8	17	14	198
Baltimore, MD MSA	2,382,172	2,199,497	182,675	8.3	18	15	134
Pittsburgh-Beaver Valley, PA CMSA	2,242,798	2,423,311	-180,513	-7.4	19	13	274
Pittsburgh, PA PMSA	2,056,705	2,218,870	-162,165	-7.3			
Beaver County, PA PMSA	186,093	204,441	-18,348	-9.0			
Phoenix, AZ MSA	2,122,101	1,509,175	612,926	40.6	20	24	13
Tampa-St. Petersburg-Clearwater, FL MSA	2,067,959	1,613,600	454,359	28.2	21	22	38

POPULATION OF METROPOLITAN AREAS: 1990 AND 1980, BY 1990 POPULATION RANK

Areas defined by Office of Management and Budget, June 30, 1990. Primary MSAs (PMSAs) appear under their consolidated MSA (CMSA)

Metropolitan area	April 1, 1990 census	April 1, 1980 census	Change, 1980-90 Number	Change, 1980-90 Pct.	CMSA/MSA rank Population 1990	CMSA/MSA rank Population 1980	CMSA/MSA rank Percent change, 1980-90
Denver-Boulder, CO CMSA	1,848,319	1,618,461	229,858	14.2	22	21	91
Denver, CO PMSA	1,622,980	1,428,836	194,144	13.6			
Boulder-Longmont, CO PMSA	225,339	189,625	35,714	18.8			
Cincinnati-Hamilton, OH-KY-IN CMSA	1,744,124	1,660,257	83,867	5.1	23	20	179
Cincinnati, OH-KY-IN PMSA	1,452,645	1,401,470	51,175	3.7			
Hamilton-Middletown, OH PMSA	291,479	258,787	32,692	12.6			
Milwaukee-Racine, WI CMSA	1,607,183	1,570,152	37,031	2.4	24	23	205
Milwaukee, WI PMSA	1,432,149	1,397,020	35,129	2.5			
Racine, WI PMSA	175,034	173,132	1,902	1.1			
Kansas City, MO-KS MSA	1,566,280	1,433,464	132,816	9.3	25	25	126
Sacramento, CA MSA	1,481,102	1,099,814	381,288	34.7	26	32	20
Portland-Vancouver, OR-WA CMSA	1,477,895	1,297,977	179,918	13.9	27	26	93
Portland, OR PMSA	1,239,842	1,105,750	134,092	12.1			
Vancouver, WA PMSA	238,053	192,227	45,826	23.8			
Norfolk-Virginia Beach-Newport News, VA MSA	1,396,107	1,160,311	235,796	20.3	28	31	60
Columbus, OH MSA	1,377,419	1,243,827	133,592	10.7	29	28	110
San Antonio, TX MSA	1,302,099	1,072,125	229,974	21.5	30	34	54
Indianapolis, IN MSA	1,249,822	1,166,575	83,247	7.1	31	30	155
New Orleans, LA MSA	1,238,816	1,256,668	-17,852	-1.4	32	27	235
Buffalo-Niagara Falls, NY CMSA	1,189,288	1,242,826	-53,538	-4.3	33	29	254
Buffalo, NY PMSA	968,532	1,015,472	-46,940	-4.6			
Niagara Falls, NY PMSA	220,756	227,354	-6,598	-2.9			
Charlotte-Gastonia-Rock Hill, NC-SC MSA	1,162,093	971,447	190,646	19.6	34	36	65
Providence-Pawtucket-Fall River, RI-MA CMSA	1,141,510	1,083,139	58,371	5.4	35	33	175
Providence, RI PMSA	654,854	618,514	36,340	5.9			
Pawtucket-Woonsocket-Attleboro, RI-MA PMSA	329,384	307,403	21,981	7.2			
Fall River, MA-RI PMSA	157,272	157,222	50	0.0			
Hartford-New Britain-Middletown, CT CMSA	1,085,837	1,013,508	72,329	7.1	36	35	154
Hartford, CT PMSA	767,841	715,923	51,918	7.3			
New Britain, CT PMSA	148,188	142,241	5,947	4.2			
Middletown, CT PMSA	90,320	81,582	8,738	10.7			
Bristol, CT PMSA	79,488	73,762	5,726	7.8			
Orlando, FL MSA	1,072,748	699,904	372,844	53.3	37	51	6
Salt Lake City-Ogden, UT MSA	1,072,227	910,222	162,005	17.8	38	41	71
Rochester, NY MSA	1,002,410	971,230	31,180	3.2	39	37	193
Nashville, TN MSA	985,026	850,505	134,521	15.8	40	45	81

POPULATION OF METROPOLITAN AREAS: 1990 AND 1980, BY 1990 POPULATION RANK

Areas defined by Office of Management and Budget, June 30, 1990. Primary MSAs (PMSAs) appear under their consolidated MSA (CMSA)

Metropolitan area	April 1, 1990 census	April 1, 1980 census	Change, 1980-90 Number	Pct.	CMSA/MSA rank Population 1990	1980	Percent change, 1980-90
Memphis, TN-AR-MS MSA	981,747	913,472	68,275	7.5	41	40	149
Oklahoma City, OK MSA	958,839	860,969	97,870	11.4	42	43	103
Louisville, KY-IN MSA	952,662	956,426	-3,764	-0.4	43	38	229
Dayton-Springfield, OH MSA	951,270	942,083	9,187	1.0	44	39	216
Greensboro--Winston-Salem--High Point, NC MSA	942,091	851,444	90,647	10.6	45	44	111
Birmingham, AL MSA	907,810	883,993	23,817	2.7	46	42	203
Jacksonville, FL MSA	906,727	722,252	184,475	25.5	47	50	45
Albany-Schenectady-Troy, NY MSA	874,304	835,880	38,424	4.6	48	46	185
Richmond-Petersburg, VA MSA	865,640	761,311	104,329	13.7	49	48	95
West Palm Beach-Boca Raton-Delray Beach, FL MSA	863,518	576,758	286,760	49.7	50	58	7
Honolulu, HI MSA	836,231	762,565	73,666	9.7	51	47	120
Austin, TX MSA	781,572	536,688	244,884	45.6	52	63	9
Las Vegas, NV MSA	741,459	463,087	278,372	60.1	53	72	4
Raleigh-Durham, NC MSA	735,480	560,774	174,706	31.2	54	61	28
Scranton--Wilkes-Barre, PA MSA	734,175	728,796	5,379	0.7	55	49	219
Tulsa, OK MSA	708,954	657,173	51,781	7.9	56	52	144
Grand Rapids, MI MSA	688,399	601,680	86,719	14.4	57	56	88
Allentown-Bethlehem-Easton, PA-NJ MSA	686,688	635,481	51,207	8.1	58	54	141
Fresno, CA MSA	667,490	514,621	152,869	29.7	59	67	34
Tucson, AZ MSA	666,880	531,443	135,437	25.5	60	64	46
Syracuse, NY MSA	659,864	642,971	16,893	2.6	61	53	204
Greenville-Spartanburg, SC MSA	640,861	570,210	70,651	12.4	62	59	100
Omaha, NE-IA MSA	618,262	585,122	33,140	5.7	63	57	174
Toledo, OH MSA	614,128	616,864	-2,736	-0.4	64	55	230
Knoxville, TN MSA	604,816	565,970	38,846	6.9	65	60	161
El Paso, TX MSA	591,610	479,899	111,711	23.3	66	70	50
Harrisburg-Lebanon-Carlisle, PA MSA	587,986	556,242	31,744	5.7	67	62	173
Bakersfield, CA MSA	543,477	403,089	140,388	34.8	68	84	19
New Haven-Meriden, CT MSA	530,180	500,462	29,718	5.9	69	68	167
Springfield, MA MSA	529,519	515,259	14,260	2.8	70	66	200
Baton Rouge, LA MSA	528,264	494,151	34,113	6.9	71	69	159
Little Rock-North Little Rock, AR MSA	513,117	474,463	38,654	8.1	72	71	137
Charleston, SC MSA	506,875	430,346	76,529	17.8	73	77	72
Youngstown-Warren, OH MSA	492,619	531,350	-38,731	-7.3	74	65	272
Wichita, KS MSA	485,270	442,401	42,869	9.7	75	75	119
Stockton, CA MSA	480,628	347,342	133,286	38.4	76	94	16
Albuquerque, NM MSA	480,577	420,261	60,316	14.4	77	80	89
Mobile, AL MSA	476,923	443,536	33,387	7.5	78	74	147

POPULATION OF METROPOLITAN AREAS: 1990 AND 1980, BY 1990 POPULATION RANK

Areas defined by Office of Management and Budget, June 30, 1990. Primary MSAs (PMSAs) appear under their consolidated MSA (CMSA).

Metropolitan area	April 1, 1990 census	April 1, 1980 census	Change, 1980-90 Number	Change, 1980-90 Pct.	CMSA/MSA rank Population 1990	CMSA/MSA rank Population 1980	CMSA/MSA rank Percent change, 1980-90
Columbia, SC MSA	453,331	409,953	43,378	10.6	79	82	112
Worcester, MA MSA	436,905	402,918	33,987	8.4	80	85	132
Johnson City-Kingsport-Bristol, TN-VA MSA	436,047	433,638	2,409	0.6	81	76	221
Chattanooga, TN-GA MSA	433,210	426,443	6,767	1.6	82	78	211
Lansing-East Lansing, MI MSA	432,674	419,750	12,924	3.1	83	81	196
Flint, MI MSA	430,459	450,449	-19,990	-4.4	84	73	255
Lancaster, PA MSA	422,822	362,346	60,476	16.7	85	91	76
York, PA MSA	417,848	381,255	36,593	9.6	86	87	121
Lakeland-Winter Haven, FL MSA	405,382	321,652	83,730	26.0	87	101	43
Saginaw-Bay City-Midland, MI MSA	399,320	421,518	-22,198	-5.3	88	79	259
Melbourne-Titusville-Palm Bay, FL MSA	398,978	272,959	126,019	46.2	89	116	8
Colorado Springs, CO MSA	397,014	309,424	87,590	28.3	90	105	37
Augusta, GA-SC MSA	396,809	345,923	50,886	14.7	91	95	87
Jackson, MS MSA	395,396	362,038	33,358	9.2	92	92	128
Canton, OH MSA	394,106	404,421	-10,315	-2.6	93	83	242
Des Moines, IA MSA	392,928	367,561	25,367	6.9	94	89	160
McAllen-Edinburg-Mission, TX MSA	383,545	283,323	100,222	35.4	95	110	18
Daytona Beach, FL MSA	370,712	258,762	111,950	43.3	96	124	10
Modesto, CA MSA	370,522	265,900	104,622	39.3	97	120	15
Santa Barbara-Santa Maria-Lompoc, CA MSA	369,608	298,694	70,914	23.7	98	106	49
Madison, WI MSA	367,085	323,545	43,540	13.5	99	100	96
Fort Wayne, IN MSA	363,811	354,156	9,655	2.7	100	93	202
Spokane, WA MSA	361,364	341,835	19,529	5.7	101	96	172
Beaumont-Port Arthur, TX MSA	361,226	373,211	-11,985	-3.2	102	88	249
Salinas-Seaside-Monterey, CA MSA	355,660	290,444	65,216	22.5	103	108	52
Davenport-Rock Island-Moline, IA-IL MSA	350,861	384,749	-33,888	-8.8	104	86	277
Corpus Christi, TX MSA	349,894	326,228	23,666	7.3	105	99	153
Lexington-Fayette, KY MSA	348,428	317,548	30,880	9.7	106	103	118
Pensacola, FL MSA	344,406	289,782	54,624	18.9	107	109	69
Peoria, IL MSA	339,172	365,864	-26,692	-7.3	108	90	273
Reading, PA MSA	336,523	312,509	24,014	7.7	109	104	146
Fort Myers-Cape Coral, FL MSA	335,113	205,266	129,847	63.3	110	140	3
Shreveport, LA MSA	334,341	333,158	1,183	0.4	111	98	224
Atlantic City, NJ MSA	319,416	276,385	43,031	15.6	112	113	84
Utica-Rome, NY MSA	316,633	320,180	-3,547	-1.1	113	102	233
Appleton-Oshkosh-Neenah, WI MSA	315,121	291,369	23,752	8.2	114	107	136
Huntington-Ashland, WV-KY-OH MSA	312,529	336,410	-23,881	-7.1	115	97	270
Visalia-Tulare-Porterville, CA MSA ...	311,921	245,738	66,183	26.9	116	128	40

POPULATION OF METROPOLITAN AREAS: 1990 AND 1980, BY 1990 POPULATION RANK

Areas defined by Office of Management and Budget, June 30, 1990. Primary MSAs (PMSAs) appear under their consolidated MSA (CMSA)

| | | | | | CMSA/MSA rank | | |
| Metropolitan area | April 1, 1990 census | April 1, 1980 census | Change, 1980-90 | | Population | | Percent change, 1980-90 |
			Number	Pct.	1990	1980	
Montgomery, AL MSA	292,517	272,687	19,830	7.3	117	117	152
Rockford, IL MSA	283,719	279,514	4,205	1.5	118	112	212
Eugene-Springfield, OR MSA	282,912	275,226	7,686	2.8	119	115	199
Macon-Warner Robins, GA MSA	281,103	263,591	17,512	6.6	120	122	163
Evansville, IN-KY MSA	278,990	276,252	2,738	1.0	121	114	215
Salem, OR MSA	278,024	249,895	28,129	11.3	122	126	104
Sarasota, FL MSA	277,776	202,251	75,525	37.3	123	143	17
Erie, PA MSA	275,572	279,780	-4,208	-1.5	124	111	236
Fayetteville, NC MSA	274,566	247,160	27,406	11.1	125	127	105
New London-Norwich, CT-RI MSA	266,819	250,839	15,980	6.4	126	125	165
Binghamton, NY MSA	264,497	263,460	1,037	0.4	127	123	223
Provo-Orem, UT MSA	263,590	218,106	45,484	20.9	128	134	57
Brownsville-Harlingen, TX MSA	260,120	209,727	50,393	24.0	129	138	48
Poughkeepsie, NY MSA	259,462	245,055	14,407	5.9	130	129	168
Killeen-Temple, TX MSA	255,301	214,587	40,714	19.0	131	135	67
Reno, NV MSA	254,667	193,623	61,044	31.5	132	146	27
Fort Pierce, FL MSA	251,071	151,196	99,875	66.1	133	178	2
Charleston, WV MSA	250,454	269,595	-19,141	-7.1	134	118	271
South Bend-Mishawaka, IN MSA	247,052	241,617	5,435	2.2	135	130	206
Columbus, GA-AL MSA	243,072	239,196	3,876	1.6	136	131	209
Savannah, GA MSA	242,622	220,553	22,069	10.0	137	132	115
Johnstown, PA MSA	241,247	264,506	-23,259	-8.8	138	121	276
Springfield, MO MSA	240,593	207,704	32,889	15.8	139	139	80
Duluth, MN-WI MSA	239,971	266,650	-26,679	-10.0	140	119	280
Huntsville, AL MSA	238,912	196,966	41,946	21.3	141	144	55
Tallahassee, FL MSA	233,598	190,329	43,269	22.7	142	149	51
Anchorage, AK MSA	226,338	174,431	51,907	29.8	143	156	32
Roanoke, VA MSA	224,477	220,393	4,084	1.9	144	133	208
Portsmouth-Dover-Rochester, NH-ME MSA	223,578	190,938	32,640	17.1	145	148	74
Kalamazoo, MI MSA	223,411	212,378	11,033	5.2	146	136	177
Lubbock, TX MSA	222,636	211,651	10,985	5.2	147	137	178
Hickory-Morganton, NC MSA	221,700	202,711	18,989	9.4	148	142	124
Waterbury, CT MSA	221,629	204,968	16,661	8.1	149	141	138
Portland, ME MSA	215,281	193,831	21,450	11.1	150	145	106
Lincoln, NE MSA	213,641	192,884	20,757	10.8	151	147	108
Bradenton, FL MSA	211,707	148,445	63,262	42.6	152	181	11
Lafayette, LA MSA	208,740	190,231	18,509	9.7	153	150	117
Boise City, ID MSA	205,775	173,125	32,650	18.9	154	158	68

POPULATION OF METROPOLITAN AREAS: 1990 AND 1980, BY 1990 POPULATION RANK

Areas defined by Office of Management and Budget, June 30, 1990. Primary MSAs (PMSAs) appear under their consolidated MSA (CMSA)

Metropolitan area	April 1, 1990 census	April 1, 1980 census	Change, 1980-90 Number	Pct.	Population 1990	CMSA/MSA rank Population 1980	Percent change, 1980-90
Gainesville, FL MSA	204,111	171,392	32,719	19.1	155	160	66
Biloxi-Gulfport, MS MSA	197,125	182,161	14,964	8.2	156	153	135
Ocala, FL MSA	194,833	122,488	72,345	59.1	157	213	5
Green Bay, WI MSA	194,594	175,280	19,314	11.0	158	155	107
St. Cloud, MN MSA	190,921	163,256	27,665	16.9	159	168	75
Bremerton, WA MSA	189,731	147,152	42,579	28.9	160	182	36
Springfield, IL MSA	189,550	187,770	1,780	0.9	161	151	217
Waco, TX MSA	189,123	170,755	18,368	10.8	162	162	109
Yakima, WA MSA	188,823	172,508	16,315	9.5	163	159	122
Amarillo, TX MSA	187,547	173,699	13,848	8.0	164	157	143
Fort Collins-Loveland, CO MSA	186,136	149,184	36,952	24.8	165	180	47
Houma-Thibodaux, LA MSA	182,842	176,876	5,966	3.4	166	154	192
Chico, CA MSA	182,120	143,851	38,269	26.6	167	185	41
Merced, CA MSA	178,403	134,558	43,845	32.6	168	198	24
Fort Smith, AR-OK MSA	175,911	162,813	13,098	8.0	169	169	142
New Bedford, MA MSA	175,641	166,699	8,942	5.4	170	166	176
Asheville, NC MSA	174,821	160,934	13,887	8.6	171	171	131
Champaign-Urbana-Rantoul, IL MSA	173,025	168,392	4,633	2.8	172	164	201
Clarksville-Hopkinsville, TN-KY MSA	169,439	150,220	19,219	12.8	173	179	99
Cedar Rapids, IA MSA	168,767	169,775	-1,008	-0.6	174	163	231
Lake Charles, LA MSA	168,134	167,223	911	0.5	175	165	222
Longview-Marshall, TX MSA	162,431	151,760	10,671	7.0	176	176	156
Benton Harbor, MI MSA	161,378	171,276	-9,898	-5.8	177	161	265
Olympia, WA MSA	161,238	124,264	36,974	29.8	178	211	33
Topeka, KS MSA	160,976	154,916	6,060	3.9	179	174	186
Wheeling, WV-OH MSA	159,301	185,566	-26,265	-14.2	180	152	283
Muskegon, MI MSA	158,983	157,589	1,394	0.9	181	173	218
Athens, GA MSA	156,267	130,015	26,252	20.2	182	204	62
Elkhart-Goshen, IN MSA	156,198	137,330	18,868	13.7	183	193	94
Lima, OH MSA	154,340	154,795	-455	-0.3	184	175	228
Fargo-Moorhead, ND-MN MSA	153,296	137,574	15,722	11.4	185	191	102
Naples, FL MSA	152,099	85,971	66,128	76.9	186	266	1
Tyler, TX MSA	151,309	128,366	22,943	17.9	187	207	70
Tuscaloosa, AL MSA	150,522	137,541	12,981	9.4	188	192	123
Richland-Kennewick-Pasco, WA MSA	150,033	144,469	5,564	3.9	189	184	189
Jacksonville, NC MSA	149,838	112,784	37,054	32.9	190	229	23
Jackson, MI MSA	149,756	151,495	-1,739	-1.1	191	177	234
Parkersburg-Marietta, WV-OH MSA	149,169	157,893	-8,724	-5.5	192	172	261

POPULATION OF METROPOLITAN AREAS: 1990 AND 1980, BY 1990 POPULATION RANK

Areas defined by Office of Management and Budget, June 30, 1990. Primary MSAs (PMSAs) appear under their consolidated MSA (CMSA)

| Metropolitan area | April 1, 1990 census | April 1, 1980 census | Change, 1980-90 | | CMSA/MSA rank | | Percent change, 1980-90 |
| | | | Number | Pct. | Population | | |
					1990	1980	
Manchester, NH MSA	147,809	129,305	18,504	14.3	193	205	90
Redding, CA MSA	147,036	115,613	31,423	27.2	194	223	39
Waterloo-Cedar Falls, IA MSA	146,611	162,781	-16,170	-9.9	195	170	279
Medford, OR MSA	146,389	132,456	13,933	10.5	196	200	113
Anderson, SC MSA	145,196	133,235	11,961	9.0	197	199	129
Fort Walton Beach, FL MSA	143,776	109,920	33,856	30.8	198	237	29
Steubenville-Weirton, OH-WV MSA	142,523	163,734	-21,211	-13.0	199	167	282
Lynchburg, VA MSA	142,199	141,289	910	0.6	200	187	220
Monroe, LA MSA	142,191	139,241	2,950	2.1	201	190	207
Jamestown-Dunkirk, NY MSA	141,895	146,925	-5,030	-3.4	202	183	250
Janesville-Beloit, WI MSA	139,510	139,420	90	0.1	203	188	227
Eau Claire, WI MSA	137,543	130,932	6,611	5.0	204	203	180
Battle Creek, MI MSA	135,982	141,579	-5,597	-4.0	205	186	253
Las Cruces, NM MSA	135,510	96,340	39,170	40.7	206	256	12
Joplin, MO MSA	134,910	127,513	7,397	5.8	207	209	170
Laredo, TX MSA	133,239	99,258	33,981	34.2	208	252	21
Greeley, CO MSA	131,821	123,438	8,383	6.8	209	212	162
Alexandria, LA MSA	131,556	135,282	-3,726	-2.8	210	196	245
Decatur, AL MSA	131,556	120,401	11,155	9.3	211	217	127
Burlington, VT MSA	131,439	115,308	16,131	14.0	212	225	92
Florence, AL MSA	131,327	135,065	-3,738	-2.8	213	197	246
Charlottesville, VA MSA	131,107	113,568	17,539	15.4	214	226	85
Dothan, AL MSA	130,964	122,453	8,511	7.0	215	214	157
Terre Haute, IN MSA	130,812	137,247	-6,435	-4.7	216	194	257
Anderson, IN MSA	130,669	139,336	-8,667	-6.2	217	189	266
Lafayette-West Lafayette, IN MSA	130,598	121,702	8,896	7.3	218	215	151
Altoona, PA MSA	130,542	136,621	-6,079	-4.4	219	195	256
Bloomington-Normal, IL MSA	129,180	119,149	10,031	8.4	220	219	133
Bellingham, WA MSA	127,780	106,701	21,079	19.8	221	242	63
Panama City, FL MSA	126,994	97,740	29,254	29.9	222	254	31
Mansfield, OH MSA	126,137	131,205	-5,068	-3.9	223	202	252
Sioux Falls, SD MSA	123,809	109,435	14,374	13.1	224	239	97
State College, PA MSA	123,786	112,760	11,026	9.8	225	230	116
Pueblo, CO MSA	123,051	125,972	-2,921	-2.3	226	210	239
Yuba City, CA MSA	122,643	101,979	20,664	20.3	227	247	61
Wichita Falls, TX MSA	122,378	121,082	1,296	1.1	228	216	214
Bryan-College Station, TX MSA	121,862	93,588	28,274	30.2	229	259	30
Hagerstown, MD MSA	121,393	113,086	8,307	7.3	230	227	150

POPULATION OF METROPOLITAN AREAS: 1990 AND 1980, BY 1990 POPULATION RANK

Areas defined by Office of Management and Budget, June 30, 1990. Primary MSAs (PMSAs) appear under their consolidated MSA (CMSA)

| | | | | | CMSA/MSA rank | | |
Metropolitan area	April 1, 1990 census	April 1, 1980 census	Change, 1980-90 Number	Pct.	Population 1990	1980	Percent change, 1980-90
Sharon, PA MSA	121,003	128,299	-7,296	-5.7	231	208	262
Wilmington, NC MSA	120,284	103,471	16,813	16.2	232	244	78
Texarkana, TX-Texarkana, AR MSA	120,132	113,067	7,065	6.2	233	228	166
Muncie, IN MSA	119,659	128,587	-8,928	-6.9	234	206	269
Abilene, TX MSA	119,655	110,932	8,723	7.9	235	235	145
Odessa, TX MSA	118,934	115,374	3,560	3.1	236	224	195
Williamsport, PA MSA	118,710	118,416	294	0.2	237	220	225
Glens Falls, NY MSA	118,539	109,649	8,890	8.1	238	238	139
Decatur, IL MSA	117,206	131,375	-14,169	-10.8	239	201	281
Santa Fe, NM MSA	117,043	93,118	23,925	25.7	240	260	44
Anniston, AL MSA	116,034	119,761	-3,727	-3.1	241	218	247
Wausau, WI MSA	115,400	111,270	4,130	3.7	242	234	191
Pascagoula, MS MSA	115,243	118,015	-2,772	-2.3	243	221	240
Sioux City, IA-NE MSA	115,018	117,457	-2,439	-2.1	244	222	238
Florence, SC MSA	114,344	110,163	4,181	3.8	245	236	190
Billings, MT MSA	113,419	108,035	5,384	5.0	246	240	182
Fayetteville-Springdale, AR MSA	113,409	100,494	12,915	12.9	247	249	98
Albany, GA MSA	112,561	112,394	167	0.1	248	232	226
Columbia, MO MSA	112,379	100,376	12,003	12.0	249	250	101
Lawton, OK MSA	111,486	112,456	-970	-0.9	250	231	232
Bloomington, IN MSA	108,978	98,787	10,191	10.3	251	253	114
Danville, VA MSA	108,711	111,789	-3,078	-2.8	252	233	244
Burlington, NC MSA	108,213	99,319	8,894	9.0	253	251	130
Yuma, AZ MSA	106,895	76,205	30,690	40.3	254	276	14
Midland, TX MSA	106,611	82,636	23,975	29.0	255	272	35
Rochester, MN MSA	106,470	92,006	14,464	15.7	256	261	82
Sheboygan, WI MSA	103,877	100,935	2,942	2.9	257	248	197
Fitchburg-Leominster, MA MSA	102,797	94,018	8,779	9.3	258	257	125
Cumberland, MD-WV MSA	101,643	107,782	-6,139	-5.7	259	241	263
Gadsden, AL MSA	99,840	103,057	-3,217	-3.1	260	245	248
San Angelo, TX MSA	98,458	84,784	13,674	16.1	261	269	79
La Crosse, WI MSA	97,904	91,056	6,848	7.5	262	262	148
Kokomo, IN MSA	96,946	103,715	-6,769	-6.5	263	243	268
Kankakee, IL MSA	96,255	102,926	-6,671	-6.5	264	246	267
Iowa City, IA MSA	96,119	81,717	14,402	17.6	265	273	73
Elmira, NY MSA	95,195	97,656	-2,461	-2.5	266	255	241
Sherman-Denison, TX MSA	95,021	89,796	5,225	5.8	267	264	169
Bangor, ME MSA	88,745	83,919	4,826	5.8	268	270	171

POPULATION OF METROPOLITAN AREAS: 1990 AND 1980, BY 1990 POPULATION RANK

Areas defined by Office of Management and Budget, June 30, 1990. Primary MSAs (PMSAs) appear under their consolidated MSA (CMSA)

Metropolitan area	April 1, 1990 census	April 1, 1980 census	Change, 1980-90		CMSA/MSA rank		
			Number	Pct.	Population		Percent change,
					1990	1980	1980-90
Lewiston-Auburn, ME MSA	88,141	84,864	3,277	3.9	269	268	187
Owensboro, KY MSA	87,189	85,949	1,240	1.4	270	267	213
Dubuque, IA MSA	86,403	93,745	-7,342	-7.8	271	258	275
Pine Bluff, AR MSA	85,487	90,718	-5,231	-5.8	272	263	264
Bismarck, ND MSA	83,831	79,988	3,843	4.8	273	275	183
St. Joseph, MO MSA	83,083	87,888	-4,805	-5.5	274	265	260
Lawrence, KS MSA	81,798	67,640	14,158	20.9	275	282	56
Rapid City, SD MSA	81,343	70,361	10,982	15.6	276	279	83
Pittsfield, MA MSA	79,250	83,490	-4,240	-5.1	277	271	258
Jackson, TN MSA	77,982	74,546	3,436	4.6	278	277	184
Great Falls, MT MSA	77,691	80,696	-3,005	-3.7	279	274	251
Victoria, TX MSA	74,361	68,807	5,554	8.1	280	280	140
Cheyenne, WY MSA	73,142	68,649	4,493	6.5	281	281	164
Grand Forks, ND MSA	70,683	66,100	4,583	6.9	282	283	158
Casper, WY MSA	61,226	71,856	-10,630	-14.8	283	278	284
Enid, OK MSA	56,735	62,820	-6,085	-9.7	284	284	278

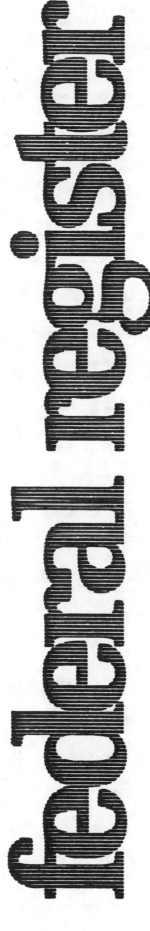

Friday
March 30, 1990

Part VI

Office of Management and Budget

Revised Standards for Defining
Metropolitan Areas in the 1990's; Notice

This reprint incorporates corrections
published in the *Federal Register* on
April 10, 1990, April 30, 1990, and
May 10, 1990.

OFFICE OF MANAGEMENT AND BUDGET

Revised Standards for Defining Metropolitan Areas in the 1990's

AGENCY: Statistical Policy Office, Office of Information and Regulatory Affairs, Office of Management and Budget (OMB).

ACTION: Revised standards for defining metropolitan areas in the 1990's.

SUMMARY: Under the authority of the Paperwork Reduction Act of 1980 (44 U.S.C. 3504), the Office of Management and Budget (OMB) defines Metropolitan Areas (MAs) for statistical purposes in accordance with a set of official published standards. Attached are revised standards to be used in the 1990's. These standards have been developed with comments received directly from the public, from a public hearing, and from the interagency Federal Executive Committee on Metropolitan Areas. Federal agencies use MAs for collecting, tabulating, and publishing data by geographic areas.

In addition to the standards this notice includes an overview; a description of the changes from the previous standards; and a list of definitions of key terms and guidelines used in the standards.

EFFECTIVE DATES: These standards will be used to define metropolitan areas after the data from the 1990 decennial census become available. We expect to issue the list of metropolitan areas based on the 1990 decennial census data in June 1992. The standards published in the **Federal Register** on January 3, 1980, (45 FR 956), remain in effect until the list of metropolitan areas is issued in June 1992.

FOR FURTHER INFORMATION CONTACT:
Maria E. Gonzalez, Statistical Policy Office, Office of Information and Regulatory Affairs, New Executive Office Building, Room 3228, Office of Management and Budget, Washington, DC 20503, telephone (202) 395-7313.
Richard G. Darman,
Director.

Part I. Overview

Part I gives the structure of this document. Part II describes the changes from the previous standards and the reasons for the changes. Part III gives the official metropolitan area standards for the 1990's. Part IV gives a list of definitions of key terms and guidelines used in the standards. The terms in Part IV are listed in alphabetical order.

In part III, sections 1 through 7 contain the basic standards for defining metropolitan statistical areas in all

States except the New England States: They specify standards for determining: how large a population nucleus must be to qualify as an MSA (section 1); the central county/counties of the MSA (section 2); additional outlying counties with sufficient metropolitan character and integration to the central county/counties to qualify for inclusion in the MSA (section 3); the central city or cities of each MSA (section 4); whether two adjacent MSAs qualify to be combined (section 5); four categories or levels of MSAs, based on the total population of each area (section 6); and the title of each MSA (section 7).

Sections 8 through 10 provide a framework for identifying PMSAs within an MSA of at least one million population. If such PMSAs are identified, the larger area of which they are components is designated a CMSA.

Sections 11 through 15 apply only to the New England States. In these States, metropolitan areas are composed of cities and towns rather than whole counties. Sections 11, 12, and 13 specify how New England MSAs are defined and titled. Sections 14 and 15 show how CMSAs and PMSAs are defined and titled.

Section 16 sets forth the standards for updating definitions between decennial censuses.

Part II. Changes in the Standards for the 1990's

The metropolitan area standards for the 1990's generally reflect a continuity with those adopted for the 1980's, and they maintain the basic concepts originally developed in 1950. The substantive modifications of the standards are specified below. Some other modifications have been made that involve word changes but not substance.

1. Effective April 1, 1990, the set of areas known as Metropolitan Statistical Areas (MSAs), Primary Metropolitan Statistical Areas (PMSAs), and Consolidated Metropolitan Statistical Areas (CMSAs) will be designated collectively as Metropolitan Areas (MAs). The reason for this change is to distinguish between the individual areas known as MSAs and the set of all areas.

2. A small group of counties containing a portion of a city's urbanized area will now qualify as outlying, even though their population density is relatively low. This change allows the inclusion in metropolitan areas of entire urbanized areas.

3. Counties included solely because they contain at least 2,500 population in a central city now will be assigned outlying county rather than central county status (section 3A(6)). This will

ensure that additional outlying counties will not be designated solely because of commuting with a county including a small portion of the central city.

4. The largest city, and other cities of at least 15,000 in a secondary noncontiguous urbanized area within a metropolitan statistical area, now may be identified as central cities, provided that the other requirements for central cities are met (sections 4E and 4F). This allows cities that perform as central cities in secondary noncontiguous urbanized areas to be designated as central cities.

5. The employment criterion for inclusion in an area title is deleted; only the population criteria remain (section 7). This change was made because in 1980 only one area qualified based on employment.

6. A place qualifying as a central city but with less than one-third the population of the largest city may now be included in the metropolitan statistical area title if strongly supported by local opinion (section 7A(3)). Communities often have strong views on the way their MSAs are titled. This change allows taking these views into account.

7. The presence of a small portion (less than 2,500 population) of the largest city of a CMSA in a county no longer precludes consideration of that county as a PMSA (section 8B(4)). Such a small portion of a city does not alter the characteristics of the PMSA.

8. We have added standards for intercensal updating of metropolitan areas (section 16). These standards existed separately, but we felt they should be incorporated into the published standards.

9. Qualifying percentages and ratios are considered to one decimal and ratios on the basis of two decimals (in each case, one less decimal than previously) (part IV). The previous standards implied a level of accuracy that was not justified.

10. Several technical adjustments were made (part IV). For example, localities in Puerto Rico officially known as *aldeas* in 1980, are now termed *comunidades*.

Part III. Official Standards For Metropolitan Areas

Basic Standards. Sections 1 through 7 apply to all States except the six New England States, that is, Connecticut, Maine, Massachusetts, New Hampshire, Rhode Island, and Vermont. They also apply to Puerto Rico.[1]

---

[1] Those provisions of sections 1 through 7 that are applicable to New England are specified in the
Continued

Section 1. Population Size Requirements for Qualification

Each metropolitan statistical area must include:

A. A city of 50,000 or more population, or [2]

B. A Census Bureau defined urbanized area of at least 50,000 population, provided that the component county/counties of the metropolitan statistical area have a total population of at least 100,000.[3]

Section 2. Central Counties

The central county/counties of the MSA are:

A. Those counties that include a central city (see section 4) of the MSA, or at least 50 percent of the population of such a city, provided the city is located in a qualifier urbanized area; and

B. Those counties in which at least 50 percent of the population lives in the qualifier urbanized area(s).

Section 3. Outlying Counties

A. An outlying county is included in an MSA if any one of the six following conditions is met:

(1) At least 50 percent of the employed workers residing in the county commute to the central county/counties, and either

(a) The population density of the county is at least 25 persons per square mile, or

(b) At least 10 percent, or at least 5,000, of the population lives in the qualifier urbanized area(s);

(2) From 40 to 50 percent of the employed workers commute to the central county/counties, and either

(a) the population density is at least 35 persons per square mile, or

(b) At least 10 percent, or at least 5,000, of the population lives in the qualifier urbanized area(s);

(3) From 25 to 40 percent of the employed workers commute to the central county/counties and either the population density of the county is at least 50 persons per square mile, or any two of the following conditions' exists:

(a) Population density is at least 35 persons per square mile,

(b) At least 35 percent of the population is urban,

(c) At least 10 percent, or at least 5,000, of the population lives in the qualifier urbanized area(s);

(4) From 15 to 25 percent of the employed workers commute to the central county/counties,[4] the population density of the county is at least 50 persons per square mile, and any two of the following conditions also exist:

(a) Population density is at least 60 persons per square mile,

(b) At least 35 percent of the population is urban,

(c) Population growth between the last two decennial censuses is at least 20 percent,

(d) At least 10 percent, or at least 5,000, of the population lives in the qualifier urbanized area(s);

(5) From 15 to 25 percent of the employed workers commute to the central county/counties,[4] the population density of the county is less than 50 persons per square mile, and any two of the following conditions also exist:

(a) At least 35 percent of the population is urban,

(b) Population growth between the last two decennial censuses is at least 20 percent,

(c) At least 10 percent, or at least 5,000, of the population lives in the qualifier urbanized area(s);

(6) at least 2,500 of the population lives in a central city of the MSA located in the qualifier urbanized area(s).[5]

B. If a county qualifies on the basis of commuting to the central county/counties of two different MSAs, it is assigned to the area to which commuting is greatest, unless the relevant commuting percentages are within 5 points of each other, in which case local opinion about the most appropriate assignment will be considered.

(c) If a county qualifies as a central county under section 2 and also qualifies as an outlying county of another metropolitan area under section 3A on the basis of commuting to (or from) another central county, both counties become central counties of a single merged MSA.

Section 4. Central Cities

The central city/cities of the MSA are:

A. The city with the largest population in the MSA;

B. Each additional city with a population of at least 250,000 or with at least 100,000 persons working within its limits;

C. Each additional city with a population of at least 25,000, an employment/residence ratio of at least 0.75, and at least 40 percent of its employed residents working in the city;

D. Each city of 15,000 to 24,999 population that is at least one-third as large as the largest central city, has an employment/residence ratio of at least 0.75, and has at least 40 percent of its employed residents working in the city;

E. The largest city in a secondary noncontiguous urbanized area, provided it has at least 15,000 population, an employment/residence ratio of at least 0.75, and has at least 40 percent of its employed residents working in the city;

F. Each additional city in a secondary noncontiguous urbanized area that is at least one-third as large as the largest central city of that urbanized area, that has at least 15,000 population and an employment/residence ratio of at least 0.75, and that has at least 40 percent of its employed residents working in the city.

Section 5. Combining Adjacent Metropolitan Statistical Areas

Two adjacent MSAs defined by sections 1 through 4 are combined as a single MSA provided:

A. The total population of the combination is at least one million, and:

(1) The commuting interchange between the two MSAs is equal to:

(a) At least 15 percent of the employed workers residing in the smaller MSA, or

(b) At least 10 percent of the employed workers residing in the smaller MSA, and

(i) The urbanized area of a central city of one MSA is contiguous with the urbanized area of a central city of the other MSA, or

(ii) A central city in one MSA is included in the same urbanized area as a central city in the other MSA; and

(2) At least 60 percent of the population of each MSA is urban.

B. The total population of the combination is less than one million and:

(1) Their largest central cities are within 25 miles of one another, or their urbanized areas are continguous; and

(2) There is definite evidence that the two areas are closely integrated with each other economically and socially; and

---

standards relating to New England (sections 11 through 15).

[2] An MSA designated on the basis of census data according to standards in effect at the time of designation will not be disqualified on the basis of lacking a city of at least 50,000 population.

[3] An MSA designated on the basis of census data according to standards in effect at the time of designation will not be disqualified on the basis of lacking an urbanized area of at least 50,000 or a total MSA population of at least 100,000.

---

[4] Also accepted as meeting this commuting requirement are:

(a) the number of persons working in the county who live in the central county/counties is equal to at least 15 percent of the number of employed workers living in the county; or

(b) the sum of the number of workers commuting to and from the central county/counties is equal to at least 20 percent of the number of employed workers living in the county.

[5] See section 4 for the standards for identifying central cities.

(3) Local opinion in both areas supports the combination.

Section 6. Levels

A. Each MSA defined by sections 1 through 5 is categorized in one of the following levels based on total population:

Level A—MSAs of 1 million or more;
Level B—MSAs of 250,000 to 999,999;
Level C—MSAs of 100,000 to 249,999; and
Level D—MSAs of less than 100,000.

B. Areas assigned to Level B, C, or D are designated as MSAs. Areas assigned to Level A are not finally designated or titled until they have been reviewed under sections 8 and 9.

Section 7. Titles of Metropolitan Statistical Areas (MSAs)

A. The title of a MSA assigned to Level B, C, or D includes the name of the largest central city, and up to two additional city names, as follows:

(1) The name of each additional city with a population of at least 250,000;

(2) The names of the additional cities qualified as central cities by section 4, provided each is at least one-third as large as the largest central city; and

(3) The names of other central cities (up to the maximum of two additional names) if local opinion supports the resulting title.

B. An area title that includes the names of more than one city begins with the name of the largest city and lists the other cities in order of their population according to the most recent national census.[6]

C. In addition to city names, the title contains the name of each State in which the MSA is located.

Standards for Primary and Consolidated Metropolitan Statistical Areas (PMSAs and CMSAs). Sections 8 through 10 apply to Level A metropolitan statistical areas outside New England.

Section 8. Qualifications for Designation of Primary Metropolitan Statistical Areas (PMSAs)

Within a Level A MSA:

A. Any county or group of counties that was designated an SMSA on January 1, 1980, will be designated a PMSA, unless local opinion does not support its continued separate designation for statistical purposes.

B. Any additional county/counties for which local opinion strongly supports

separate designation will be considered for identification as a PMSA, provided one county is included that has:

(1) At least 100,000 population;

(2) At least 60 percent of its population urban;

(3) Less than 35 percent of its resident workers working outside the county; and

(4) Less than 2,500 population of the largest central city of the Level A MSA.

C. A set of two or more contiguous counties for which local opinion strongly supports separate designation, and that may include a county or counties that also could qualify as a PMSA under section 8B, also will be considered for designation as a PMSA, provided:

(1) Each county meets requirements (1), (2), and (4) of section 8B, and has less than 50 percent of its resident workers working outside the county;

(2) Each county in the set has a commuting interchange of at least 20 percent with the other counties in the set; and

(3) The set of two or more contiguous counties has less than 35 percent of its resident workers working outside its area.

D. Each county in the interim Level A MSA, not included within a central core under sections 8A through C, is assigned to the contiguous PMSA to whose central core commuting is greatest, provided this commuting is:

(1) At least 15 percent of the county's resident workers;

(2) At least 5 percentage points higher than the commuting flow to any other PMSA central core that exceeds 15 percent; and

(3) Larger than the flow to the county containing the Level A MSA's largest central city.

E. If a county has qualifying commuting ties to two or more PMSA central cores and the relevant values are within 5 percentage points of each other, local opinion is considered before the county is assigned to any PMSA.

F. The interim PMSA definitions resulting from these procedures (including possible alternative definitions, where appropriate) are submitted to local opinion. Final definitions of PMSAs are made based on these standards, and a review of local opinion.

G. If any primary metropolitan statistical area or areas have been recognized under sections 8A through F, the balance of the Level A metropolitan statistical area, which includes its largest central city, also is recognized as a primary metropolitan statistical area.[7]

Section 9. Levels and Titles of Primary Metropolitan Statistical Areas

A. PMSAs are categorized in one of four levels according to total population, following the standards of Section 6A.

B. PMSAs are titled in either of two ways:

(1) Using the names of up to three cities in the primary metropolitan statistical area that have qualified as central cities of the Level A MSA under section 4, following the standards of section 7 for selection and sequencing; or

(2) Using the names of up to three counties in the PMSA, sequenced in order from largest to smallest population.

c. Local opinion on the most appropriate title will be considered.

Section 10. Designation and titles of Consolidated Metropolitan Statistical Areas

A. A Level A metropolitan statistical area in which two or more primary metropolitan statistical areas are identified by section 8 is designated a consolidated metropolitan statistical area. If no primary metropolitan statistical areas are defined, the Level A area remains a metropolitan statistical area, and is titled according to section 7.

B. Consolidated metropolitan statistical areas are titled according to the following guidelines. Local opinion is always sought before determining the title of a consolidated metropolitan statistical area.

(1) The title of each area includes up to three names, the first of which is always the name of the largest central city in the area. A change in the first-named city in the title will not be made until both its population and the number of persons working within its limits are exceeded by those of another city in the consolidated area.

(2) The preferred basis for determining the two remaining names is:

(a) The first city (or county) name that appears in the title of the remaining primary metropolitan statistical area with the largest total population; and

(b) The first city (or county) name that appears in the title of the primary metropolitan statistical area with the next largest total population.

(3) A regional designation may be substituted for the second and/or third names in the title if there is strong local support and the proposed designation is unambiguous and suitable for inclusion in a national standard.

---

[6] The largest central city included in an existing metropolitan area title will not be resequenced in or displaced from that title until both its population and the number of persons working within its limits are exceeded by those of another city qualifying for the area title.

---

[7] If section 8G would result in the balance of the Level A metropolitan statistical area including a

noncontiguous county, this county will be added to the contiguous primary metropolitan statistical area to which the county has the greatest commuting.

Standards for New England

In the six New England States of Connecticut, Maine, Massachusetts, New Hampshire, Rhode Island, and Vermont, the cities and towns are administratively more important than the counties, and a wide range of data is compiled locally for these entities. Therefore, the cities and towns are the units used to define metropolitan areas in these States. The New England standards are based primarily on population density and commuting. As a basis for measuring commuting, a central core is first defined for each New England urbanized area.

In New England, there is an alternative county-based definition of MSAs known as the New England County Metropolitan Areas (NECMAs) (See part IV).

Section 11. New England Central Cores

A central core is determined in each New England urbanized area through the definition of two zones.

A. Zone A comprises:

(1) The largest city in the urbanized area;

(2) Each additional place in the urbanized area or in a contiguous urbanized area that qualifies as a central city under section 4, provided at least 15 percent of its resident employed workers work in the largest city in the urbanized area; [8]

(3) Each additional city or town at least 50 percent of whose population lives in the urbanized area or a contiguous urbanized area, provided at least 15 percent of its resident employed workers work in the largest city in the urbanized area plus any additional central cities qualified by section 11A(2). [8]

B. Zone B Comprises each city or town that has:

(1) At least 50 percent of its population living in the urbanized area or in a contiguous urbanized area; and

(2) At least 15 percent of its resident employed workers working in Zone A. [8]

C. The central core comprises Zone A, Zone B, and any city or town that is physically surrounded by Zones A or B, except that cities or towns that are not contiguous with the main portion of the central core are not included.

___

[8] Also accepted as meeting this commuting requirement are:

(a) The number of persons working in the subject city or town who live in the specified city or area is equal to at least 15 percent of the employed workers living in the subject city or town; or

(b) The sum of the number of workers commuting to and from the specified city or area is equal to at least 20 percent of the employed workers living in the subject city or town.

D. If a city or town qualifies under sections 11A through C for more than one central core, it is assigned to the core to which commuting is greatest, unless the relevant commuting percentages are within 5 points of each other, in which case local opinion as to the most appropriate assignment also is considered.

Section 12. Outlying Cities and Towns

A. A city or town contiguous to a central core as defined by section 11 is included in its metropolitan statistical area if:

(1) It has a population density of at least 60 persons per square mile and at least 30 percent of its resident employed workers work in the central core; or

(2) It has a population density of at least 100 persons per square mile and at least 15 percent of the employed workers living in the city or town work in the central core. [9]

B. If a city or town has the qualifying level of commuting to two different central cores, it is assigned to the metropolitan statistical area to which commuting is greatest, unless the relevant commuting percentages are within 5 points of each other, in which case local opinion as to the most appropriate assignment also is considered.

C. If a city or town has the qualifying level of commuting to a central core, but has greater commuting to a nonmetropolitan city or town, it will not be assigned to any metropolitan statistical area unless the relevant commuting percentages are within 5 points of each other, in which case local opinion as to the most appropriate assignment will also be considered.

Section 13. Applicability of Basic Standards to New England Metropolitan Statistical Areas

A. An area defined by sections 11 and 12 qualifies as a metropolitan statistical area if it contains a city of at least 50,000 population or has a total population of at least 75,000. [10]

___

[9] This commuting requirement is also considered to have been met if:

(a) The number of persons working in the city or town who live in the central core is equal to at least 15 percent of the employed workers living in the city or town; or

(b) The sum of the number of workers commuting to and from the central core is equal to at least 20 percent of the employed workers living in the city or town.

[10] A New England metropolitan statistical area designated on the basis of census data according to standards in effect at the time of designation will not be disqualified on the basis of lacking a total population of at least 75,000.

B. The area's central cities are determined according to the standards of section 4.

C. Two adjacent New England metropolitan statistical areas are combined as a single metropolitan statistical area provided the conditions of section 5A are met. Section 5B is not applied in New England.

D. Each New England metropolitan statistical area defined by sections 13A through C is categorized in one of the four levels specified in section 6A. Areas assigned to Level B, C, or D are designated as metropolitan statistical areas. Areas assigned to Level A are not finally designated until they have been reviewed under sections 14 and 15.

E. New England metropolitan statistical areas are titled according to the standards of section 7.

Section 14. Qualification for Designation of Primary Metropolitan Statistical Areas (PMSAs)

The following are qualifications within a Level A metropolitan statistical area in New England:

A. Any group of cities and towns that was recognized as a standard metropolitan statistical area on January 1, 1980, will be recognized as a primary metropolitan statistical area, unless local opinion does not support its continued separate recognition for statistical purposes.

B. Any additional group of cities and/or towns for which local opinion strongly supports separate recognition will be considered for designation as a primary metropolitan statistical area, if:

(1) The total population of the group is at least 75,000;

(2) It includes at least one city with a population of 15,000 or more, an employment/residence ratio of at least 0.75, and at least 40 percent of its employed residents working in the city;

(3) It contains a core of communities, each of which has at least 50 percent of its population living in the urbanized area, and which together have less than 40 percent of their resident workers commuting to jobs outside the core; and

(4) Each community in the core also has:

(a) At least 5 percent of its resident workers working in the component core city identified in section 14B(2), or at least 10 percent working in the component core city or in places already qualified for this core; this percentage also must be greater than that to any other core or to the largest city of the Level A MSA; and

(b) At least 20 percent commuting interchange with the component core city together with other cities and towns already qualified for the core; this interchange also must be greater than with any other core or with the largest city of the Level A MSA.

C. Contiguous component central cores may be merged as a single core if:

(1) Section 14B would qualify the component core city of one core for inclusion in the other core; and

(2) There is substantial local support for treating the two as a single core.

D. Each city or town in the interim Level A MSA not included in a core under sections 14A through C is assigned to the contiguous PMSA to whose core its commuting is greatest, if:

(1) This commuting is at least 15 percent of the place's resident workers; and

(2) The commuting interchange with the core is greater than with the Level A MSA's largest city.

E. If a city or town has qualifying commuting ties to two or more cores and the relevant values are within 5 percentage points of each other, local opinion is considered before the place is assigned to any PMSA.

F. The interim PMSA definitions resulting from these procedures (including possible alternative definitions, where appropriate) are submitted to local opinion. Final definitions of PMSAs are made based on these standards, and a review of local opinion.

G. If any primary metropolitan statistical area or areas have been recognized under sections 14A through F, the balance of the Level A metropolitan statistical area, which includes its largest city, also is recognized as a primary metropolitan statistical area.[11]

Section 15. Levels and Titles of Primary Metropolitan Statistical Areas and Consolidated Metropolitan Statistical Areas in New England

A. New England primary metropolitan statistical areas are categorized in one of four levels according to total population, following section 6A.

B. New England primary metropolitan statistical areas are titled using the names of up to three cities in the primary area that have qualified as central cities under section 4, following the standards of section 7 for selection and sequencing.

C. Each Level A metropolitan statistical area in New England in which primary metropolitan statistical areas

---

[11] If section 14G results in the balance of the Level A metropolitan statistical area including a noncontiguous city or town, this place will be added to the contiguous primary metropolitan statistical area to which it has the greatest commuting.

---

have been identified and supported by local opinion (according to section 14) is designated a consolidated metropolitan statistical area. Titles of New England consolidated metropolitan statistical areas are determined following the standards of section 10. A Level A metropolitan statistical area in which no primary metropolitan statistical areas have been defined is designated a metropolitan statistical area, and is titled according to the rules of section 7.

Section 16. Intercensal Metropolitan Area Changes

A. *Definitions.*

(1) A *Census Count* is a special census conducted by the U.S. Bureau of the Census or a decennial census count updated to reflect annexations and boundary changes since the census.

(2) A *Census Bureau Estimate* is a population estimate issued by the U.S. Bureau of the Census for an intercensal year.

B. *Qualification for Designation of a Metropolitan Statistical Area.* The qualification for designation are as follows:

(1) A city reaches 50,000 population according to a Census Count or Census Bureau Estimate.

(2) A nonmetropolitan county containing an urbanized area (UA) defined by the Bureau of the Census at the most recent decennial census reaches 100,000 population according to a Census Count or Census Bureau Estimate. If the potential metropolitan statistical area centered on the urbanized area consists of two or more counties, their total population must reach 100,000. In New England, the cities and towns qualifying for the potential metropolitan statistical area must reach a total population of 75,000.

(3) The Census Bureau defines a new urbanized area based on a Census Count after the decennial census, and the potential metropolitan statistical area containing the urbanized area meets the population requirements of section 16B(2).

If a metropolitan statistical area is qualified intercensally by a Census Bureau Estimate, the qualification must be confirmed by the next decennial census, or the area is disqualified.

C. *Addition of Counties.* Counties are not added to metropolitan statistical areas between censuses, except as follows:

(1) If a central city located in a qualifier urbanized area extends into a county not included in the metropolitan statistical area and the population of the portion of the city in the county reaches 2,500 according to a Census Count, then the county qualifies as an outlying

county and is added to the metropolitan statistical area.

(2) If a metropolitan statistical area qualified intercensally under section 16B meets the requirements of section 5B for combination with a metropolitan statistical area already recognized, that combination may take place and thereby alter the definition of the existing metropolitan statistical area.

D. *Qualification for Designation of a Central City.* A Census Count serves to qualify a central city (section 4) that has failed to qualify solely because its population was smaller than required—for example, it did not qualify as the largest city of the metropolitan statistical area (section 4A), or was below 250,000 (4B), below 25,000 (4C), or below 15,000 (4D–F). If qualification requires comparison with the population of another city, comparison is made with the latest available Census Bureau Estimate or Census Count of the population of the other city.

E. *Area Titles.* The title of a metropolitan statistical area, primary metropolitan statistical area, or consolidated metropolitan statistical area may be altered to include the name of a place that has newly qualified as a central city on the basis described in section 16D and that also meets the requirements of section 7. Such a change is made by adding the new name at the end of the existing title, but cannot be made if the title already contains three names. Names in area titles are not resequenced except on the basis of a decennial census.

F. Other aspects of the metropolitan area definitions are not subject to change between censuses.

Part IV—General Procedures and Definitions

This part specifies certain important guidelines regarding the data and procedures used in implementing the standards. It also gives definitions for "city," "urbanized area," and other key terms.

General Procedures

Local Opinion. Local opinion is the reflection of the views of the public on specified matters relating to the application of the standards for defining metropolitan areas, obtained through the appropriate congressional delegation, and considered after the thresholds in the statistical standards have been met. Members of the congressional delegation will be urged to contact a wide range of groups in their communities, including business or other leaders, Chambers of Commerce, planning commissions, and local officials, to solicit comments on specified issues. OMB will consider all pertinent local opinion material on these matters in determining the final definition and title of the area. After a decision has been made on a particular matter, OMB will not again request local opinion on the same question until after the next national census.

Local opinion is considered for:

(a) Combining two adjacent metropolitan statistical areas (of less than one million population) whose central cities are within 25 miles of each other (section 5B).

(b) Metropolitan statistical area titles (section 7A(3)).

(c) Identifying primary metropolitan statistical areas within consolidated metropolitan statistical areas (sections 8 and 14).

(d) Titling primary metropolitan statistical areas (sections 9 and 15).

(e) Titling consolidated metropolitan statistical areas after identification of the largest city (section 10 and 15).

(f) Assignment of a county or place that, based on commuting, is eligible for inclusion in more than one area (section 3B, 8E, 11D, 12B and 12C, and 14E).

New England County Metropolitan Areas (NECMAs). The New England County Metropolitan Areas (NECMAs) provide an alternative to the official city-and-town-based metropolitan statistical areas in that region for the convenience of data users who desire a county-defined set of areas.

The NECMA for a metropolitan statistical area includes:

1. The county containing the first-named city in the metropolitan statistical area title. In some cases, this county will contain the first-named city of one or more additional metropolitan statistical areas.

2. Each other county which has at least half of its population in the metropolitan statistical area(s) whose first-named cities are in the county identified in step 1.

The NECMA for a consolidated metropolitan statistical area also is defined by the above rules, except that the New England portion of the consolidated metropolitan statistical area which includes New York City is used as the basis for defining a separate NECMA. No NECMAs are defined for individual primary metropolitan statistical areas.

The central cities of a NECMA are those cities in the NECMA that qualify as central cities of a metropolitan statistical area or consolidated metropolitan statistical area; some central cities may not be included in any NECMA title.

The title of the NECMA includes each city in the NECMA that is the first-named title city of a metropolitan area, in descending order of metropolitan statistical area (or primary metropolitan statistical area) total population. Other cities that appear in metropolitan area titles are included only if the resulting NECMA title would consist of no more than three names.

Levels for NECMAs are determined following section 6A of the official metropolitan area standards.

Percentages, Densities, and Ratios. Percentages and densities are computed to the nearest tenth (one decimal); ratios are computed to the nearest one hundredth (two decimals); and comparisons between them are made on that basis.

Populations. In general, the population data required by the standards are taken from the most recent national census. However, in certain situations either (1) the results of a special census taken by the Bureau of the Census, or (2) a population estimate published by the Bureau of the Census may be used to meet the requirements of the standards. (section 16)

Review of Cutoffs and Values. OMB has promulgated these standards with the advice of the Federal Executive Committee on Metropolitan Areas, following an open period of public comment. After the 1990 decennial census data become available, the Federal Executive Committee will review the census data and their implications for the cutoffs and values used in the standards, and will report to OMB the results of its review.

Definitions of Key Terms

Central Core—The counties (or cities and towns in New England) that are eligible for initial delineation as primary metropolitan statistical areas because they meet specified population and commuting criteria.

City—The term "city" includes:

(a) Any place incorporated under the laws of its State as a city, village, borough (except in Alaska), or town (except in the New England States, New York, and Wisconsin). These comprise the category of incorporated places recognized in Bureau of the Census publications.

(b) In Hawaii, any place recognized as a census designated place by the Bureau of the Census in consultation with the State government; in Puerto Rico, any place recognized as a *zona urbana* or a *comunidad* by the Bureau of the Census in consultation with the Commonwealth government. (Hawaii and Puerto Rico, do not have legally defined cities corresponding to those of most States.)

(c) Any township in Michigan, Minnesota, New Jersey, or Pennsylvania, and any town in the New England States, New York, or Wisconsin, at least 90 percent of whose population is classified by the Bureau of the Census as urban, provided it does not contain any part of a dependent incorporated place.

Commuting Interchange—The commuting interchange between two areas is the sum of the number of workers who live in either of the areas but work in the other.

County—For purposes of the standards, the term "county" includes county equivalents, such as parishes in Louisiana and boroughs and census areas (formerly census divisions) in Alaska. Certain States contain cities that are independent of any county; such independent cities in Maryland, Missouri, and Nevada are treated as county equivalents for purposes of the standards.

In Virginia, where most incorporated places of more than 15,000 are independent of counties, the standards usually regard each such city as included in the county for which it was originally formed, or primarily formed. In certain exceptional cases, the city itself is treated as a county equivalent, as follows:

(a) An independent city that has absorbed its parent county (Chesapeake, Hampton, Newport News, Suffolk, Virginia Beach); and

(b) An independent city associated with an urbanized area other than the one with which its parent county is primarily associated (for example, Colonial Heights).

A county included in a metropolitan area is either a central (section 2), or an outlying (section 3) county. An outlying county must be contiguous with a central county or with an outlying county that has already qualified for inclusion.

Employment/Residence Ratio—This ratio is computed by dividing the number of persons working in the city by the number of resident workers with place of work reported. (These items are taken from the most recent national census.) For example, a city with an equal number of jobs and working residents has an employment/residence ratio of 1.00.

Interim Area—An area that meets the requirements of sections 1 through 4, or sections 11 through 13, for metropolitan statistical area qualification, which needs to be further examined to determine: (1) if it qualifies for combination with any adjacent interim area, (2) its final level, based on population; and (3) if the area has 1 million or more population, the identification of primary metropolitan statistical areas, if any, and the preferences, expressed through local opinion, for consolidated or individual identity.

Largest Central City—The largest central city of a metropolitan area is the central city with the greatest population at the time of the initial metropolitan area designation. Once determined, the largest central city will not be replaced until both its population and the number of persons working within its limits are exceeded by those of another city in the area.

Outcommuting—The number (or percent) or workers living in a specified area, such as a city or a county, whose place of work is located outside that area.

Qualifier Urbanized Area—The qualifier urbanized area(s) for a metropolitan statistical area are:

1. The urbanized area that resulted in qualification under section 1B or the urbanized area containing the city that resulted in qualification under section 1A.

2. Any other urbanized area whose largest city is located in the same county as the largest city of the urbanized area identified in paragraph one above, or has at least 50 percent of its population in that county.

Secondary Noncontiguous Urbanized Area—An additional urbanized area within a metropolitan statistical area that has no common boundary of more than a mile with the main urbanized area around which the metropolitan statistical area is defined.

Standard Metropolitan Statistical Area—The term used from 1959 to 1983 to describe the statistical system of metropolitan areas, and the areas as individually defined. It was preceded by Standard Metropolitan Area (SMA) from 1950 to 1959, and superseded by Metropolitan Statistical Area in 1983. That term was adopted when the current system formally recognizing consolidated metropolitan statistical areas and their component primary metropolitan statistical areas was put in place. The term Metropolitan Area (MA) is used to describe the system and the areas collectively, but the individual areas will retain the MSA, CMSA, and PMSA nomenclature.

Urban—The Bureau of the Census classifies as urban:

(a) The population living in urbanized areas; plus

(b) The population in other incorporated or census designated places of at least 2,500 population at the most recent national census.

Urbanized Area—An area defined by the Bureau of the Census according to specific criteria, designed to include the densely settled area around a large place. The definition is based primarily on density rather than governmental unit boundaries. An urbanized area must have a total population of at least 50,000. (See qualifier urbanized area and secondary noncontiguous urbanized area.)

[FR Doc. 90–7425 Filed 3–29–90; 8:45 am]
BILLING CODE 3110–01–M

- 204 -

APPENDIX B

DATA SOURCES

- Major Federal Data Sources (overview)

- Bureau of the Census
  — Obtaining Products and Services

- Bureau of Labor Statistics
  — "Program Highlights" (Fact Sheet
    No. BLS 91-1)
  — Regional Offices
  — Products and Services for
    Local Area Analysis

MAJOR FEDERAL DATA SOURCES

Agency or Data Service

Relevant Series

Customer Services
Data User Services Division
Bureau of the Census
Washington, D.C. 20230
202/763-4100

County Business Patterns (annual)
Employment, payroll, establishments by industry for counties

Quinquennial Economic Censuses of Business, Manufacturing
Employment, payroll, sales data by industry for municipalities

Decennial Census of Population and Housing
Population counts with demographic breakdowns, occupations and educational attainment with demographic breakdowns, county-to-county migration

Current Population Reports (continuous, based on Current Population Survey of 60,000 households nationwide)
Interim survey statistics on population and income, including Series P-26 (Local Population Estimates) and P-28 (Special Censuses, conducted at the request of cities or other local governments)

Regional Economic Information System
BE-55
Bureau of Economic Analysis
Washington, D.C. 20230
202/254-6630

BEA Local Area Personal Income, County Series (Available for counties and metropolitan areas)
Personal income by source, population estimates, per capita income, earnings by industry, employment by industry, commuting flows (decennial Census Journey-to-Work data)

Office of Employment and Unemployment
  Statistics
Bureau of Labor Statistics
2 Massachusetts Ave. N.E.
Washington, D.C. 20212
202/606-7828 (BLS Directory)
202/606-6373 (Data & Publications Svcs.)
202/606-6559 (LAUS)

Local Area Unemployment Statistics (LAUS)
Monthly estimates of the labor force, employment (by place of residence), unemployment, and unemployment rates are available for States, Metropolitan Statistical Areas, small labor market areas, counties, and cities with populations of 25,000 or more.

Industry Employment, Hours, Earnings: States and Areas monthly data on payroll employment (by place of work) covering each state and 274 major labor areas, most of which are MSAs. Derived from Current Employment Statistics Survey of establishments.

Employment and Wages Survey: States and Metropolitan Areas
Annual pay in states and metropolitan areas, area wage studies (by request)

U.S. Department of Commerce
National Technical Information Service
5285 Port Royal Road
Springfield, VA 22161
703/487-4630

Economic Bulletin Board
Subscription-based electronic data service offering access to data files and information on the latest statistical releases from the Bureau of Economic Analysis, the Bureau of the Census, the Bureau of Labor Statistics, the Federal Reserve Board, the Department of the Treasury and other Federal agencies. Annual subscription, including two hours of connect time, $35; additional connect time billed at $0.05-$0.20 per minute depending on time of use (9600 modem service somewhat more).

Historical Data

U.S. Bureau of the Census. *Historical Statistics of the United States, Colonial Times to 1970*. Washington, D.C., 1975.

U.S. Bureau of Economic Analysis. *Regional Employment by Industry, 1940-1970*. Washington, D.C., n.d.

U.S. Bureau of Labor Statistics. *Employment, Hours, and Earnings, State and Area, 1939-82*. Washington, D.C., 1984.

General References
(See also by agency, below)

Executive Office of the President, Office of Management and Budget. *Standard Industrial Classification Manual, 1987*. Washington, D.C.: U.S. Government Printing Office. $24.

U.S. Department of Commerce, International Trade Administration. *U.S. Industrial Outlook*. (Annual, published in January for the current year). Washington, D.C.: U.S. Government Printing Office. Also available through the National Technical Information Service, Springfield, Va., 703/487-4600, $25-$32 depending on number of pages.

BUREAU OF THE CENSUS

Obtaining Products and Services

Census Regional Offices — Information requests can be directed to Data User Services in Washington, D.C. (301/763-4100) or one of the 12 regional offices listed below. The regional offices are often knowledgeable about other sources of data or research in the region.

Atlanta, GA 404/347-2274	Dallas, TX 214/767-7105	Los Angeles, CA 818/892-6674
Boston, MA 617/565-7078	Denver, CO 303/969-7750	New York, NY 212/264-4730
Charlotte, NC 704/371-6144	Detroit, MI 313-354-4654	Philadelphia, PA 215-597-8313
Chicago, IL 312/353-0980	Kansas City, KS 816/891-7562	Seattle, WA 206/728-5314

State Data Centers — These 1,400 organizations include lead agencies in each state plus affiliates (see *Hidden Treasures! Census Bureau Data and Where to Find It* for a list of lead agencies and *Census Catalog and Guide* for a complete list of affiliates). Some of these centers produce statistical abstracts for a particular state, similar to the *Statistical Abstract of the United States* produced by the Census Bureau for the country as a whole.

Business and Industry Data Centers — An outgrowth of the State Data Center program, these centers provide information useful in business planning. Centers were operating in 16 states as of 1990, including Connecticut, Delaware, Florida, Indiana, Kentucky, Maryland, Massachusetts, Minnesota, Montana, New Jersey, New Mexico, North Carolina, Pennsylvania, Washington, West Virginia, Wisconsin (see list in *Hidden Treasures! Census Bureau Data and Where to Find It*).

National Clearinghouse for Census Data Services — The Census Bureau maintains a list of private companies that provide products and services involving Census Bureau data (e.g., customized tabulations, development of applications software). The list includes a few government and academic organizations that also provide such services. (See listing in *Hidden Treasures!*) Proprietary data services companies are expected to play an important role in user support for the geographic TIGER/Line files, which contain latitude and longitude coordinates for the line segments of every block in the United States.

National Services Information Center — A pilot program to improve access to relevant data for nonprofit organizations with a focus on minority concerns (conducted in cooperation with the National Council of La Raza and the National Urban League, both in Washington, D.C., and the Southwest Voter Research Institute, San Antonio). For more information call the Census Bureau (301/763-1384).

Federal Depository Libraries — Some 1,500 libraries—including State appellate court libraries, government agency libraries, academic libraries, and public libraries—receive and make available publications from the Federal government. Participating libraries choose the publications they want, so collections vary. Contact a census regional office or Customer Services at Census Bureau headquarters for the name and address of a depository library in your area.

User Guides and References

Hidden Treasures! Census Bureau Data and Where to Find It. 1990. 20 pages, no charge.

Census '90 Basics. 1990. Overview of content and methods used for the 1990 Census, with listings of expected products and release dates. 19 pages, no charge.

Monthly Product Announcement. Monthly publication listing all Census Bureau products released in the past month. No charge.

Census and You. Monthly newsletter on Census products and services. Annual subscription, $18.

Census Catalog and Guide. Annual publication that describes the available reports, tapes, compact discs, and maps of the Census Bureau, $17.

County and City Data Book. Compendium of statistics for all U.S. counties and most U.S. cities. Published every five years. The current edition is 1988, $36; the next edition is due in 1993. Also available on computer tape, compact disc, and flexible disk.

State and Metropolitan Area Data Book. Statistical compendium similar to *County and City Data Book* but covering metropolitan areas, central cities, and component counties. Published every five years. The current edition is 1991, $26. Also available on computer tape, compact disc, and flexible disk.

Statistical Abstract of the United States. Statistics from numerous sources, government and private, published every five years. The current edition is 1992, $29 paper/$34 cloth.

BUREAU OF LABOR STATISTICS

Program Highlights

Fact Sheet No. BLS 91-1

Each month, millions of Americans look to the U.S. Department of Labor Statistics (BLS) for answers to questions like these: Is unemployment going up or down? How much have prices changed since last month? What's happening to wages? BLS also traces national trends in productivity, employment costs, and other labor-related measures.

Besides monitoring the economy's pulse, BLS national economic statistics serve as guides when wages, pensions, and other payments are adjusted for changing prices—as required by escalator clauses in contracts and by provisions of law.

People interested in State and local economies use the Bureau's area statistics—State unemployment rates, the Consumer Price Indexes (CPI) for metropolitan areas, and wage rates for occupations common to regional industries.

BLS industry statistics cover employment, earnings, prices, productivity, and technology and include data on major industry sectors such as mining and manufacturing, on specific industries such as clothing and textiles, or on State and local areas. The numbers are used to measure the performance of an industry from one month or one year to the next, to compare performance among industries, and to adjust contracts for changes in industry prices, wages, and other conditions.

The Bureau also looks at the people behind the statistics. It examines the racial composition of the labor force, the kinds of jobs held by men and women, the level of education of those working and not working, and the unemployment problems of worker groups including teenagers, blacks, Hispanics, and women.

The Bureau gathers data on how people spend their money. BLS consumer expenditure studies provide not only a fixed market basket for computing the Consumer Price Indexes, but also insight into patterns of consumer spending. Market researchers and merchandisers use the Bureau's consumer expenditure data, classified by family characteristics such as size, income, and place of residence.

The Bureau develops long-term economic projections, based upon certain specific assumptions that include projections of aggregate labor force, potential demand, industrial output, and employment in 226 industry sectors. Government officials use this information to evaluate alternative economic policy options, to analyze the implications of likely economic growth trends for the national economy, and to identify potential problems of labor utilization.

BLS analyzes changes in the occupational structure of industries resulting from changes in technology, product mix, and other factors, and translates projections of industry employment into future occupational employment demands. This job outlook information is used by persons planning careers, jobseekers, training officials, education planners, and employment counselors.

BLS conducts annual surveys which measure the number, incidence, and severity of job-related injuries and illnesses by industry. Through supplementary surveys, BLS helps to identify specific safety hazards on the job. The findings are used by the Occupational Safety and Health Administration (OSHA) and State safety agencies, as well as by management and labor. The Bureau collects information on wage and benefit changes in major collective bargaining agreements and on work stoppages involving 1,000 workers or more. The Bureau's file of collective bargaining agreements—open to the public—is a source of information about industry wage practices, supplementary benefits, and union security provisions. Negotiators for both labor and management use these BLS data. The Bureau also gathers international statistics. Comparisons of prices, wages, employment, unemployment, and unit labor costs show the competitiveness of U.S. industries and products in the world market.

The Bureau's sales publications are available from its Publications Sales Center, P.O. Box 2145, Chicago, IL 60690, or from the Superintendent of Documents, U.S. Government Printing Office, Washington, D.C. 20402. Single copies of other publications are available while supplies last from any of the Bureau's regional offices or from Data Users and Publications Services, 2 Massachusetts Ave. N.E., Washington, D.C. 20212.

BLS Regional Offices

Region I
10th Floor
1 Congress Street
Boston, MA 02114
(CT ME MA NH RI VT)

Region II
Room 808
201 Varick Street
New York, NY 10014
(NJ NY PR VI)

Region III
3535 Market Street
P.O. Box 13309
Philadelphia, PA 19101
(DE DC MD PA VA WV)

Region IV
1371 Peachtree St. N.E.
Atlanta, GA 30367
(AL FL GA KY MS NC SC TN)

Region V
9th Floor
Federal Office Building
230 S. Dearborn Street
Chicago, IL 60604
(IL IN MI MN OH WI)

Region VI
Room 221
Federal Building
525 Griffin Street
Dallas, TX 75202
(AR LA NM OK TX)

Regions VII and VIII
911 Walnut Street
Kansas City, MO 64106
(CO IA KS MO MT NE ND SD UT WY)

Regions IX and X
71 Stevenson Street
P.O. Box 193766
San Francisco, CA 94119-3766
(AK AS AZ CA GU HI ID NV OR WA)

Products and Services for
Local Area Analysis

BLS Bulletins

Area Wage Surveys. These bulletins cover office, professional, technical, maintenance, custodial, and material movement jobs in major metropolitan areas. The annual series is available by subscription, $73 per year. Single copies are available while supplies last.

Geographic Profiles of Employment and Unemployment (annual). Annual averages for 50 large metropolitan areas and 17 central cities. Current edition is 1991 (Bulletin 2410), $11 (est.)

Industry Wage Surveys. These studies include results from the latest BLS surveys of wages and employee benefits, with detailed occupational data for the Nation, regions, and selected areas (where available). Sample: *Banking, 1989* (Bulletin 2371, 77 pages, $4.25).

References

BLS Handbook of Methods. The 1992 edition replaces the 1988 edition.

Periodicals

CPI Detailed Report. This monthly publication provides a comprehensive report on price movements for the month, plus statistical tables, charts and technical notes. Annual subscription, $21; single copies, $7.

Employment and Earnings. This monthly report covers employment and unemployment developments, plus statistical tables on national, State, and area employment, hours, and earnings. (Statistics are derived from the Census Bureau's Current Population Survey and the Local Area Unemployment Statistics program.)

Monthly Labor Review. Each issue includes analytical articles, 53 pages of current statistics, reports on industrial relations, book reviews, and other features. Annual subscription, $24; single copies, $5.50.

Occupational Outlook Quarterly. Monitors changing career opportunities. Annual subscription, $6.50; single copies $2.50.

Press Releases
(partial listing)

"Annual Pay in States and Metropolitan Areas"

"The Consumer Price Index" — U.S. city average indexes for two populations—All Urban Consumers (CPI-U) and Urban Wage Earners and Clerical Workers (CPI-W).

"The Employment Situation" — Latest monthly figures on employment and unemployment (subsequently reported in the periodical *Employment and Earnings*).

"State and Metropolitan Area Employment and Unemployment"

Data Services

BLS News Releases Online — Economic indicators from BLS are available electronically at the time of their release, through a commercial contractor. There is no charge for the data. Users pay for the computer time used, at a rate of about $10 per hour for local access and about $25 per hour anywhere in the country. More than 100 releases a year are available online. They include monthly releases on consumer and producer prices, earnings, and employment and unemployment and quarterly releases on productivity, employment costs, colelctive bargaining, and import and export price indexes.

BLS Telephone Hotline: 202/523-1221 — Timely recorded messages from the Bureau's latest news releases including The Consumer Price Index, Producer Price Indexes, The Employment Situation, and The Employment Cost Index.

Data Files on Tape — BLS major data series are available on magnetic tape. Request the pamphlet "BLS Data Files on Tape" for a listing. In addition to the listed files, BLS makes available some microdata tapes (usually unpublished series) and also prepares customized data files on a cost-of-service basis. Sample: *Local Area Unemployment Statistics*, $125; *Industry Employment, Hours, and Earnings: States and Areas*, $120.

Data Diskettes — Selected BLS series, including *Local Area Unemployment Statistics*, are available on diskettes for use with IBM-compatible microcomputers. Request the pamphlet "BLS Data Diskettes" for a listing. Single diskettes, $38.

Microfiche — *Unemployment in States and Local Areas*, a subscription service, provides monthly estimates of the labor force, employment, and unemployment in States, labor market areas, counties, county equivalents, and cities of 25,000 or more. Annual subscription, $50. Order from Superintendent of Documents, U.S. Government Printing Office, Washington, D.C. 20402.

APPENDIX C

STANDARD INDUSTRIAL CLASSIFICATION SYSTEM

- 1987 SIC Codes and Titles (1- to 3-digit)

- SIC Code Changes: 1972 to 1987 Crosswalk

- "1987 Standard Industrial Classification Revision" (OMB explanation of changes), *Federal Register*, October 1, 1986.

AGRICULTURE, FORESTRY, AND FISHING

07   Agricultural Services
071   Soil Preparation Services
072   Crop Services
074   Veterinary Services
075   Animal Services, except Veterinary
076   Farm Labor and Management Services
078   Landscape and Horticultural Services

08   Forestry

09   Fishing, Hunting, and Trapping
098/   Ag, For, & Fish Administrative and Auxiliary

MINING

10   Metal Mining
101   Iron Ores
102   Copper Ores
103   Lead and Zinc Ores
104   Gold and Silver Ores
106   Ferroalloy Ores, except Vanadium
108   Metal Mining Services
109   Miscellaneous Metal Ores

12   Coal Mining
122   Bituminous Coal and Lignite Mining
123   Anthracite Mining
124   Coal Mining Services

13   Oil and Gas Extraction
131   Crude Petroleum and Natural Gas
132   Natural Gas Liquids
138   Oil and Gas Field Services

14   Nonmetallic Minerals, except Fuels
141   Dimension Stone
142   Crushed and Broken Stone
144   Sand and Gravel
145   Clay, Ceramic, & Refractory Minerals
147   Chemical and Fertilizer Minerals
148   Nonmetallic Minerals Services
149   Miscellaneous Nonmetallic Minerals
149/   Mining Administrative and auxiliary

CONSTRUCTION

15   General Contractors and Operative Builders
151   General Building Contractors
153   Operative Builders

16   Heavy Construction, exc. Building
161   Highway and Street Construction
162   Heavy Construction, except Highway

17   Special Trade Contractors
171   Plumbing, Heating, Air-conditioning
172   Painting and Paper Hanging
173   Electrical Work
174   Masonry, Stonework, and Plastering
175   Carpentry and Floor Work
176   Roofing, Siding, and Sheet Metal Work
177   Concrete Work
178   Water Well Drilling
179   Misc. Special Trade Contractors
179/   Construction Administrative and Auxiliary

MANUFACTURING

20   Food and Kindred Products
201   Meat Products
202   Dairy Products
203   Preserved Fruits and Vegetables
204   Grain Mill Products
205   Bakery Products
206   Sugar and Confectionery Products
207   Fats and Oils
208   Beverages
209   Misc. Food and Kindred Products

21   Tobacco Products
211   Cigarettes
212   Cigars
213   Chewing and Smoking Tobacco
214   Tobacco Stemming and Redrying

22   Textile Mill Products
221   Broadwoven Fabric Mills, Cotton
222   Broadwoven Fabric Mills, Manmade
223   Broadwoven Fabric Mills, Wool
224   Narrow Fabric Mills
225   Knitting Mills
226   Textile Finishing, except Wool
227   Carpets and Rugs
228   Yarn and Thread Mills
229   Miscellaneous Textile Gods

23   Apparel and Other Textile Products
231   Men's and Boys' Suits and Coats
232   Men's and Boys' Furnishings
233   Women's and Misses' Outerwear
234   Women's and Children's Undergarments
235   Hats, Caps, and Millinery
236   Girls' and Children's Outerwear
237   Fur Goods
238   Miscellaneous Apparel and accessories
239   Misc. Fabricated Textile Products

24   Lumber and Wood Products
241   Logging
242   Sawmills and Planing Mills
243   Millwork, Plywood & Structural Members

384	Medical Instruments and Supplies	492	Gas Production and Distribution
385	Ophthalmic Goods	493	Combination Utility Services
386	Photographic Equipment and Supplies	494	Water Supply
387	Watches, Clocks, Watchcases & Parts	495	Sanitary Services
		496	Steam and Air-Conditioning Supply
39	**Miscellaneous Manufacturing Industries**	497	Irrigation Systems
391	Jewelry, Silverware, and Plated Ware	497/	TCPU Administrative and Auxiliary
393	Musical Instruments		
394	Toys and Sporting Goods		
395	Pens, Pencils, Office, & Art Supplies		**WHOLESALE TRADE**
396	Costume Jewelry and Notions		
399	Miscellaneous Manufactures	**50**	**Wholesale Trade - Durable Goods**
399/	Manufacturing Administrative and auxiliary	501	Motor Vehicles, Parts, and Supplies
		502	Furniture and Homefurnishings
		503	Lumber and Construction Materials
	TRANSPORTATION, COMMUNICATION, AND PUBLIC UTILITIES	504	Professional & Commercial Equipment
		505	Metals and Minerals, except Petroleum
		506	Electrical Goods
41	**Local and Interurban Passenger Transit**	507	Hardware, Plumbing & Heating Equipment
411	Local and Suburban Transportation	508	Machinery, Equipment, and Supplies
412	Taxicabs	509	Miscellaneous Durable Goods
413	Intercity and Rural Bus Transportation		
414	Bus Charter Service	**51**	**Wholesale Trade - Nondurable Goods**
415	School Buses	511	Paper and Paper Produots
417	Bus Terminal and Service Facilities	512	Drugs, Proprietaries, and Sundries
		513	Apparel, Piece Goods, and Notions
42	**Trucking and Warehousing**	514	Groceries and Related Products
421	Trucking & Courier Services, exc. Air	515	Farm-Product Raw Materials
422	Public Warehousing and Storage	516	Chemicals and Allied Products
423	Trucking Terminal Facilities	517	Petroleum and Petroleum Products
		518	Beer, Wine, and Distilled Beverages
44	**Water Transportation**	519	Misc. Nondurable Goods
441	Deep Sea Foreign Trans. of Freight	519/	Wholesale Trade Administrative and Auxiliary
442	Deep Sea Domestic Trans. of Freight		
443	Freight Trans. on the Great Lakes		
444	Water Transportation of Freight, nec		**RETAIL TRADE**
448	Water Transportation of Passengers		
449	Water Transportation Services	**52**	**Building Materials & Garden Supplies**
		521	Lumber and Other Building Materials
45	**Transportation by Air**	523	Paint, Glass, and Wallpaper Stores
451	Air Transportation, Scheduled	525	Hardware Stores
452	Air Transportation, Nonscheduled	526	Retail Nurseries and Garden Stores
458	Airports, Flying Fields, & Services	527	Mobile Home Dealers
46	**Pipelines, except Natural Gas**	**53**	**General Merchandise Stores**
461	Pipelines, except Natural Gas	531	Department Stores
		533	Variety Stores
47	**Transportation services**	539	Misc. General Merchandise Stores
472	Passenger Transportation Arrangement		
473	Freight Transportation Arrangement	**54**	**Food Stores**
474	Rental of Railroad Cars	541	Grocery Stores
478	Miscellaneous Transportation Services	542	Meat and Fish Markets
		543	Fruit and Vegetable Markets
48	**Communications**	544	Candy, Nut, and Confectionery Stores
481	Telephone Communications	545	Dairy Products Stores
482	Telegraph & Other Communications	546	Retail Bakeries
483	Radio and Television Broadcasting	549	Miscellaneous Food Stores
484	Cable and Other Pay TV Services		
489	Communication Services, nec	**55**	**Automotive Dealers & Service Stations**
		551	New and Used Car Dealers
49	**Electric, Gas, and Sanitary Services**	552	Used Car Dealers
491	Electric Services	553	Auto and Home Supply Stores

554	Gasoline Service Stations		64	**Insurance Agents, Brokers, & Service**
555	Boat Dealers			
556	Recreational Vehicle Dealers		65	**Real Estate**
557	Motorcycle Dealers		651	Real Estate Operators and Lessors
559	Automotive Dealers, nec		653	Real Estate Agents and Managers
			654	Title Abstract Offices
56	**Apparel and Accessory Stores**		655	Subdividers and Developers
561	Men's & Boys' Clothing Stores			
562	Women's Clothing Stores		67	**Holding and Other Investment Offices**
563	Women's Accessory & Specialty Stores		671	Holding Offices
564	Children's and Infants' Wear Stores		672	Investment Offices
565	Family Clothing Stores		673	Trusts
566	Shoe Stores		679	Miscellaneous Investing
569	Misc. Apparel & Accessory Stores		679/	FIRE Administrative and auxiliary

57 Furniture and Homefurnishings Stores
571 Furniture and Homefurnishings Stores
572 Household Appliance Stores
573 Radio, Television, & Computer Stores

58 Eating and Drinking Places
581 Eating and Drinking Places

59 Miscellaneous Retail
591 Drug Stores and Proprietary Stores
592 Liquor Stores
593 Used Merchandise Stores
594 Miscellaneous Shopping Goods Stores
596 Nonstore Retailers
598 Fuel Dealers
599 Retail Stores, nec
599/ Retail Trade Administrative and Auxiliary

FINANCE, INSURANCE, AND REAL ESTATE

60 Depository Institutions
601 Central Reserve Depository
602 Commercial Banks
603 Savings Institutions
606 Credit Unions
608 Foreign Bank & Branches & Agencies
609 Functions Closely Related to Banking

61 Nondepository Institutions
611 Federal & Fed.-sponsored Credit
614 Personal Credit Institutions
615 Business Credit Institutions
616 Mortgage Bankers and Brokers

62 Security and Commodity Brokers
621 Security Brokers and Dealers
622 Commodity Contracts Brokers, Dealers
623 Security and Commodity Exchanges
628 Security and Commodity Services

63 Insurance Carriers
631 Life Insurance
632 Medical Service and Health Insurance
633 Fire, Marine, and Casualty Insurance
635 Surety Insurance
636 Title Insurance
637 Pension, Health, and Welfare Funds
639 Insurance Carriers, nec

SERVICES

70 Hotels and Other Lodging Places
701 Hotels and Motels
702 Rooming and Boarding Houses
703 Camps and Recreational Vehicle Parks
704 Membership-Basis Organization Hotels

72 Personal Services
721 Laundry, Cleaning, & Garment Services
722 Photographic Studios, Portrait
723 Beauty Shops
724 Barber Shops
725 Shoe Repair and Shoeshine Parlors
726 Funeral Service and Crematories
729 Miscellaneous Personal Services

73 Business Services
731 Advertising
732 Credit Reporting and Collection
733 Mailing, Reproduction, Stenographic
734 Services to Buildings
735 Misc. Equipment Rental & Leasing
736 Personnel Supply Services
737 Computer and Data Processing Services
738 Miscellaneous Business Services

75 Auto Repair, Services, and Parking
751 Automotive Rentals, no Drivers
752 Automobile Parking
753 Automotive Repair Shops
754 Automotive Services, except Repair

76 Miscellaneous Repair Services
762 Electrical Repair Shops
763 Watch, Clock, and Jewelry Repair
764 Reupholstery and Furniture Repair
769 Miscellaneous Repair Shops

78 Motion Pictures
781 Motion Picture Production & Services
782 Motion Picture Distribution & Services
783 Motion Picture Theaters
784 Video Tape Rental

79 Amusement & Recreation Services
791 Dance Studios, Schools, and Halls
792 Producers, Orchestras, Entertainers

793	Bowling Centers	835	Child Day Care Services
794	Commercial Sports	836	Residential Care
799	Misc. Amusement, Recreation Services	839	Social Services, nec

80	**Health Services**	**84**	**Museums, Botanical, Zoological Gardens**
801	Offices & Clinics of Medical Doctors	841	Museums and Art Galleries
802	Offices and Clinics of Dentists	842	Botanical and Zoological Gardens
803	Offices of Osteopathic Physicians		
804	Offices of Other Health Practitioners	**86**	**Membership Organizations**
805	Nursing and Personal Care Facilities	861	Business Associations
806	Hospitals	862	Professional Organizations
807	Medical and Dental Laboratories	863	Labor Organizations
808	Home Health Care Services	864	Civic and Social Associations
809	Health and Allied Services, nec	865	Political Organizations
		866	Religious Organizations
81	**Legal Services**	869	Membership Organizations, nec

82   Educational Services

87   Engineering & Management Services

821	Elementary and Secondary Schools	871	Engineering & Architectural Services
822	Colleges and Universities	872	Accounting, Auditing, & Bookkeeping
823	Libraries	873	Research and Testing Services
824	Vocational Schools	874	Management and Public Relations
829	Schools & Educational Services, nec		

89   Services, nec

899/   Services Administrative and auxiliary

83   Social Services

| 832 | Individual and Family Services |
| 833 | Job Training and Related Services |

NONCLASSIFIABLE ESTABLISHMENTS

nec - not elsewhere classified

Source: Standard Industrial Classification Manual

**Description of Changes in Industry Classification,
2-Digit SIC Major Groups**

1987 Major Group	1972 Industry Removed from Group--	Added to Group--	Major Group/Industry Description[1]
1200		1100	Coal Mining[2]
			Anthracite Mining
1600			Heavy construction, except building
	1610 pt		Highway and street construction (culverts and curbs)
1700			Special trade contractors
		1620 pt	Highway and street construction (culverts and curbs)
2400			Lumber and wood products
		1660 pt	Building paper and board mills (insulation board)
		3442 pt	Metal doors, sash, and trim (doors, etc. covered in metal)
2600			Paper and allied products
		2660 pt	Building paper and board mills (insulation board)
3000			Rubber and miscellaneous plastics products
	3070 pt		Miscellaneous plastics products (plumbing fixture fittings)
		3293	Gaskets, packing and sealing devices
		3555 pt	Printing trades machinery (printer rolls, covers, etc.)
3200			Stone, clay, and glass products
	3293		Gaskets, packing and sealing devices
		3679 pt	Electronic components, n.e.c. (porcelain electrical supplies)
3400			Fabricated metal products
	3433 pt		Heating equipment, except electric (incinerators)
	3442 pt		Metal doors, sash, and trim (doors, etc. covered in metal)
		3070 pt	Miscellaneous plastics products (plumbing fixture fittings)
		3555 pt	Printing trades machinery (printers mallets)
		3728 pt	Aircraft equipment, n.e.c. (hydraulic valves)
3500			Industrial machinery and equipment
	3555 pt		Printing trades machinery
	3573 pt		Electronic computing equipment (magnetic disks)
		3433 pt	Heating equipment, except electric (incinerators)
		3623	Welding apparatus, electric
		3636 pt	Sewing machines (commercial and industrial)
		3661 pt	Telephone and telegraph apparatus (teletypewriters)
		3699 pt	Electrical equipment and supplies, n.e.c. (comfort heating)
		3728 pt	Aircraft equipment, n.e.c. (fluid power pump, motors)
3600			Electronic and other electronic equipment
	3623		Welding apparatus, electric
	3636 pt		Sewing machines (commercial and industrial)
	3661 pt		Telephone and telegraph apparatus (teletypewriters)
	3662 pt		Radio/TV communication equipment (search, navigation equipment)
	3679 pt		Electronic components, n.e.c. (porcelain electrical supplies)
	3693		X-ray apparatus and tubes
	3699 pt		Electrical equipment and supplies, n.e.c. (comfort heating)
		3573 pt	Electronic computing equipment (magnetic disks)
3700			Transportation equipment
	3728 pt		Aircraft equipment, n.e.c.
3800			Instruments and related products
		3662 pt	Radio/TV communication equipment
		3693 pt	X-ray apparatus and tubes
4400			Water transportation
	4469 pt		Water transportation services, n.e.c. (oil spill cleanup)
4900			Electric, gas, and sanitary services
		4469 pt	Water transportation services, n.e.c. (oil spill cleanup)

1987 Major Group	1972 Industry Removed from Group--	Added to Group--	Major Group/Industry Description[1]
5000			Wholesale trade - durables goods[3]
		5930 pt	Used merchandise stores (automotive parts)
5900			Miscellaneous retail[3]
	5930 pt		Used merchandise stores (automotive parts)
6000			Depository institutions
		6112 pt	Rediscounting, not for agriculture (central reserve)
		6120	Savings and loan associations
		6140 pt	Personal credit institutions
6100			Nondepository institutions
	6112 pt		Rediscounting, not for agriculture (central reserve)
	6120		Savings and loan associations
		6140 pt	Personal credit institutions
		6600 pt	Combined real estate, insurance, etc. (loans; personal, etc.)
6400			Insurance agents, brokers, and service
		6600 pt	Combined real estate, insurance, etc. (insurance)
6500			Real Estate
		6600 pt	Combined real estate, insurance, etc. (real estate)
7200			Personal services
	7290 pt		Miscellaneous personal services (medical equipment rental, health clubs and spas)
7300			Business services
	7369 pt		Personal supply services, n.e.c. (facilities support)
	7391		Research and development laboratories
	7392		Management and public relations
	7394 pt		Equipment rental and leasing (video tape rental)
	7397		Commercial testing laboratories
		7290 pt	Miscellaneous personal services (medical equipment rental)
7800			Motion pictures
		7392 pt	Equipment rental and leasing (video tape rental)
7900			Amusement and recreation services
	7999 pt		Amusement and recreation, n.e.c. (commercial museums, etc.)
		7290 pt	Miscellaneous personal services (health clubs and spas)
8100			Legal services[4]
		6600 pt	Combined real estate, insurance, etc. (law offices)
8400			Museums, botanical, zoological gardens
		7999 pt	Amusement and recreation, n.e.c. (commercial museums, etc.)
8700			Engineering and management services
		7369 pt	Personnel supply services, n.e.c. (facilities support)
		7391	Research and development laboratories
		7392	Management and public relations
		7397	Commercial testing laboratories
		8910	Engineering and architectural services
		8920	Noncommercial research organizations
		8930	Accounting, auditing and bookkeeping
8900			Services, n.e.c.
	8910		Engineering and architectural services
	8920		Noncommercial research organizations
	8930		Accounting, auditing and bookkeeping

[1] Type-of-business also may be shown where only part of an industry was reclassified.
[2] Establishments in PA only.
[3] Note change in trade areas from Retail to Wholesale.
[4] Note change from Finance, Insurance and Real Estate to Services.

Source: Bureau of Economic Analysis

OFFICE OF MANAGEMENT AND BUDGET

1987 Standard Industrial Classification Revision

AGENCY: Office of Management and Budget.

ACTION: Notice of final decisions.

SUMMARY: This notice presents the Office of Management and Budget's final decisions for the 1987 revision of the Standard Industrial Classification (SIC) and information for ordering the new "Standard Industrial Classification Manual 1987." The SIC is revised periodically to reflect the economy's changing industrial composition and organization. Changes in the economy since the last major revision in 1972 require an updating of the standard. The revised SIC provides a more current classification structure with which to collect, disseminate, and analyze data on the industrial makeup of the U.S. economy.

EFFECTIVE DATE: The revision is effective January 1, 1987.

ADDRESSES: Correspondence about the final decisions should be sent to: Paul Bugg, Office of Management and Budget, 3001 New Executive Office Building, Washington, DC 20503. Orders for the new "Standard Industrial Classification Manual 1987" should be sent to the National Technical Information Service, 5285 Port Royal Road, Springfield, VA 22161, (703–487–4650).

FOR FURTHER INFORMATION CONTACT: Paul Bugg, Office of Management and Budget, telephone number 202–395–3093.

SUPPLEMENTARY INFORMATION: The Standard Industrial Classification (SIC) is the statistical classification system underlying all establishment-based Federal economic statistics. The SIC is used to promote the comparability of establishment data describing various facets of the U.S. economy. The SIC's basic classification unit is the establishment, i.e., an economic unit, generally at a single physical location, where business is conducted or where services or industrial operations are performed, such as a farm, mine, factory, store, or hotel. The SIC covers the entire field of economic activities by defining industries in accordance with the composition and structure of the economy. It is revised periodically to reflect the economy,s changing industrial composition and organization. The 1972 SIC Manual, as supplemented in 1977, contains the current

classification of industries.[1] On February 22, 1984, the Office of Management and Budget (OMB) published a **Federal Register** (49 FR 6582) notice of intent to revise the Standard Industrial Classification for 1987, containing the "Principles and Procedures for the Review of the SIC."[2] In response, businesses; trade associations; individuals; and Federal, State, and local government agencies submitted proposals for over 1100 individual changes.

To provide technical advice for the 1987 SIC revision and to make recommendations on the individual proposals, OMB established a multiagency Technical Committee on Industrial Classification (TCIC). The TCIC is chaired by OMB and is composed of senior economists, statisticians, and classification specialists representing 18 of the Federal agencies that use the SIC. To aid in its review, the TCIC established subcommittees for Construction; Manufacturing; Trade (Wholesale and Retail); Communications; Transportation and Public Utilities; Finance, Insurance, and Real Estate; Services; and Computers. The TCIC evaluated each of the submitted changes and recommended approximately 40 percent for acceptance and inclusion in a revised SIC.

In evaluating each proposed change, the TCIC followed the guidelines presented in the published "Principles and Procedures." These guidelines specify how the proposed change should relate to: The structure of the classification; historical continuity of data; economic significance criteria; specialization and coverage ratios; compatibility with international industry and product classification systems; classification stability; the ability of statistical agencies to classify, collect, and publish industry data; disclosure of individual firm data; the cost and reporting burden to respondents; and the cost to the government.

For 1987, the scope of the review for the SIC revision took into account technological changes; institutional changes such as deregulation in the Banking, Communications, and Transportation industries; and the tremendous expansion in the service sector. Also, changes were made that

---

[1] The "Standard Industrial Classification Manual 1972" is available from the Government Printing Office. The stock number and price are 041-001-00066-6 and $15.00, respectively. The "1977 Supplement" is now out of print and is no longer available.

[2] For your information the "Principles and Procedures for the Review of the SIC" are reprinted at the end of this notice.

improved industry detail, coverage, and definitions, or clarified definitions of individual activities and classification concepts.

The primary reasons why the TCIC accepted proposals to establish new industries are: (1) Proposed industries meet the minimum criteria for economic significance, (2) proposed industries meet required specialization and coverage ratios, (3) proposed industries present no significant difficulties or costs in collecting the information needed to make a correct classification of establishments, and (4) improvement in statistical information is large relative to the costs of the proposed change. Similarly, the TCIC generally recommended accepting proposals to combine an existing industry with a compatible category if the existing industry no longer meets the economic significance, specialization, or coverage criteria.

Special consideration was given to new industries and industry changes that meet the above criteria and also increase the capability of assessing the impact of international trade on domestic industries. In the course of U.S. participation in developing the new Harmonized Commodity Description and Coding System for international trade classification, comparisons were made between trade classification detail and the SIC. Problems and inconsistencies were identified in the SIC, in some cases confirming difficulties that had already been encountered in SIC data collection. Examples of such difficulties currently exist in Industries 3662, 3811, 3829, and 3832 covering the manufacture of communications equipment and certain instruments. To resolve such inconsistencies, changes and new industries have been accepted that meet basic SIC criteria and recognize products that are important in international trade.

After the TCIC completed its initial review, each accepted change was examined in terms of expected benefits relative to costs of implementation. During this process some changes that the TCIC had found technically feasible were rejected because the expected benefits did not balance the substantial costs involved. Once this process was finished, the TCIC recommendations were published in the **Federal Register** (51 FR 5640, February 14, 1986) with a 60-day comment period ending April 15, 1986.

OMB's Final Decisions

Taking into consideration benefits and costs, comments submitted in response to the February 14, 1986, **Federal Register** notice, and other factors, including the operating budgets of the Federal agencies that must implement the revised SIC, OMB has made the final determination of the scope and substance of the 1987 revision. In general, OMB accepted the TCIC recommendations. However, in response to public comment, OMB made several changes to improve the usefulness and administration of the classification, avoid unnecessary industry code number changes, and reduce the number of detailed industry distinctions. For example, in the depository banking area there are far fewer industries than were recommended by the TCIC. Instead, distinctions based on the type of charter—Federally chartered or not Federally chartered, are retained, but those related to regulatory body or insurance are dropped. A separate industry for bank holding companies is established. Two new industries are created for courier services in Motor Freight Transportation and Air Transportation. New industries, divided between freight and passengers, are created in Water Transportation to facilitate analyses of these components. The production of prepackaged computer software is recognized as a separate industry in Services (Division I) instead of Manufacturing. In Retail Trade a new industry is created for opticians stores.

Implementation

The revision is effective January 1, 1987. In some programs, data based on the new SIC may be available beginning in 1988. However, for most programs, such data will be introduced over several years. Data series for these programs may not always be revised for years prior to the programs' implementation of the new SIC.

Highlights of the 1987 SIC Revision

The 1987 SIC revision has resulted in a net increase of 19 industries for Services (Division I), 8 for Wholesale Trade, and 7 for Manufacturing, with a net decrease of 34 for the other SIC Divisions. Deleted industries are merged into other industries and new industries are created by subdividing or restructuring existing industries. Various industries are also changed by transfers of individual activities, primarily to increase data classification accuracy, consistency, and usefulness, or by renumbering to change the existing three-digit structure.

Most of the industries that are deleted no longer meet the economic significance criteria for continued

recognition as a separate industry. However, a few are dropped because the number of companies represented by the establishments classified in the industry is now so small as to cause disclosure problems in publishing data or because the distinctions required cause difficulties in classification.

As a supplement to other proposals submitted, the revision process included a comprehensive review of Transportation (Major Groups 40–47), Communications (Major Group 48), and Finance (Major Groups 60–62, and 67) to identify revisions needed due to changes in technology and government regulation. As mentioned above, basic revisions occur in Water Transportation and in the structure an ' detail of Banking and Other Credit Agencies (Major Groups 60–61), in particular to recognize changes in depository regulations. In addition, the decisions include the recognition of new industries for Cable and Other Pay Television (from 4833 and 4899) and Radiotelephone Communications Services (from 4811).

The growth of computer-related activities has resulted in a number of new industries. Several new industries are recognized for computers and computer peripheral equipment in Manufacturing (from 3573). There are industries for the sale of Computers and Computer Peripheral Equipment and Software in Wholesale Trade (from 5081) and Retail Trade (from 5732). Computer establishments are classified in Wholesale Trade if they sell primarily for business or government use and in Retail Trade if they sell primarily for household use. Additional detail is also added for computer services within current Group 737, including a separate industry for Prepackaged Computer Software.

The 1987 revision places considerable emphasis on improved detail for Services (Division I). There is a new Major Group 87 for selected professional and technical services, comprising elements of the current Business Services (Major Group 73) and Miscellaneous Services (Major Group 89). Industry 7392, Management, Consulting, and Public Relations, is subdivided into five new industries, and 8911, Engineering, Architectural, and Surveying Services, is subdivided into three. A number of changes are incorporated for Major Group 80, Health Services, to improve detail and data accuracy for this area of rapid growth. Other changes include the recognition of industries for Physical Fitness Facilities (from 7299, 7997, and 7999). Tax Return Preparation Services (from 7299) and

Video Tape Rental (from 7394). Various other industries are also subdivided (e.g., 7321, 7393, and 7539).

There are subdivisions of some of the largest and fastest growing current industries in Manufacturing, including Miscellaneous Plastics Products (3079), Radio and Television Communications Equipment (3662), and Electronic Components, NEC (3679). Recognition of a distinct operating technology is extended to fluid power (from 3494, 3561, 3566, 3569, 3599, and 3728) and of a different fabrication technology to the distinction between die casting and other casting (from 336). Existing problems in data collection and accuracy are corrected by grouping together all relays (from 3613, 3622 and 3679) and all packaging equipment (from 3551 and 3569) and by moving or combining instruments and instrumentation systems currently covered by 3662, 3811, 3829, and 3832.

Notable changes in other SIC Divisions include the recognition of Animal Aquaculture (from 0279); the separation of surface and underground bituminous coal mining (from 1211); the separation of freight and passenger transport in Water Transportation (from Major Group 44) and the recognition of surface and air courier services (from 4211, 4213, 4511, and 4521); the recognition in Wholesale Trade of Medical and Hospital Equipment and of Opthalmic Goods (from 5086); and the separation in Retail Trade of Record and Prerecorded Tape Stores (from 5733), and Opticians Stores (from 5999). Establishments selling used automobile parts at wholesale or retail are placed together in a new industry in Wholesale Trade, because of difficulties in determining whether individual units sell primarily to households or to businesses.

1987 SIC Manual Ordering Information

Clothbound copies of the "Standard Industrial Classification Manual 1987" may be ordered now from the National Technical Information Service, 5285 Port Royal Road, Springfield, VA 22161. The Accession Number for the clothbound manual is PB 87-100012. The prepublication price is $24.00; for orders received after December 31, 1986, the price is $30.00. Orders (including prepublication orders) of five (5) or more copies receive a 25 percent discount. It is expected that the 1987 SIC Manual will be available for shipping in early Spring 1987. The "Standard Industrial Classification Manual 1987" will be available on computer tape (9-track 1600 bpi or 6250 bpi) for $175.00, including documentation. The Accession Number for the tape is PB 87–100020. The "SIC Manual 1987" will also be available on diskettes upon request. A shipping and handling fee of $3.00 must accompany each order for either books or tapes. Telephone orders may be placed using an NTIS Deposit Account or an American Express, Master Card, or Visa credit card by calling (703) 487–4650. Payment must accompany all mail orders.

Description of the List of Changes

The attached list of changes shows only substantive modifications in content, detail, or structure to the current 1972/1977 Standard Industrial Classification. In addition, the new "Standard Industrial Classification Manual 1987" will update and clarify many industry titles and descriptions and add numerous new example items to the indexes to reflect new activities.

The current 1972/1977 industries that are changed are listed in the left-hand column with the corresponding 1987 industries directly opposite in the right-hand column. Where two or more current industries are combined into one, a brace indicates which industries are to be combined.

Instances in which new industries are created or an existing industry changed are indicated by: (1) Specifying each changed 1972/1977 industry code and title in the left-hand column, (2) listing short descriptions of the activities involved in any multiple changes to an industry beneath the industry title, and (3) listing in the right-hand column the corresponding 1987 industry code and title for each listed change. A 1987 industry having a code without an asterisk includes only those activities now covered by the industry code in the left-hand column. A 1987 industry having a code preceded by an asterisk includes the corresponding activities described in the left-hand column plus activities from one or more other 1972/1977 industries; the other activities are included in the 1972/1977 industries

specified in the parenthetical note. For example, current Industry 2065 is changed by moving certain nut processing to new Industry 2068 (which also includes activities from current Industries 2034 and 2099) and establishing a new Industry 2064 (which includes only the remaining activities from current Industry 2065).

Note that only industry (i.e., four-digit) changes are listed. Changes at the two-digit and three-digit levels are only implied. For instance, Major Groups 11 and 66 are deleted since all their industries are deleted and Industry Group 738 is added because of the four-digit industry changes.

Please note that the abbreviation "nec" used in the attached list stands for Not Elsewhere Classified.

Authority: 31 U.S.C. 1104(d), 44 U.S.C. 3504(d).

Wendy L. Gramm,
Administrator for Information and Regulatory Affairs.

BILLING CODE 3110-01-M

APPENDIX D

TWO-DAY TRAINING SEMINAR FORMAT

The techniques that are presented in this manual do not require an extensive background in statistics or sophisticated data management skills. They can be accomplished using a personal computer and widely available business planning software. Individuals familiar with basic techniques of social science research or business planning should be able to master them with little difficulty. Examples illustrating the use of various techniques are drawn from the work of the authors. However, workshop sponsors are encouraged to supplement the examples provided with additional localized examples that may be available.

This appendix begins with an outline of a suggested seminar format for presenting the material covered in this book, followed by a chapter-by-chapter summary of key points.

DAY 1

PART I: INTRODUCTION

Session 1
(1 hour)
Introduction to Economic Development Planning
(Handbook Chapter 1)
- Strategic planning for economic development and the role of economic analysis
- Course overview

Session 2

(1 hour)

(1 hour)
Structuring the Analysis: Concepts and Issues
(Handbook Chapter 2 and Appendices A, B, C)
- Preliminary considerations (unit of analysis, selecting a time period for analysis, selecting variables and data elements, establishing a comparative framework)
- Working with data (data availability issues, data series and their pros and cons, estimating missing data, key data sources for local economic analysis)

PART II: AUDITING THE LOCAL ECONOMY

Session 3
(1 hour)
Assessing Economic Performance and Condition
(Handbook Chapter 3)
- Comparative analysis of levels and trends using five variables that provide broad indicators of local economic vitality (total employment, unemployment rates, earnings per worker, area personal income, population)

Session 4
(1.5 hours)
Analyzing Industrial Structure
(Handbook Chapter 4)
- Analyzing the distribution of employment and earnings by sector to identify 1) the industrial composition of the local economy and how it may be changing and 2) industry growth patterns that underlie economic performance and condition
- Using location quotient analysis to identify basic sectors of the local economy and local industry specializations
- Using shift-share analysis to assess the growth performance of local industries

DAY 2

Session 5   **Evaluating Local Growth Prospects**
(2 hours)   (Handbook Chapter 5)
- Introduction to target industry analysis (using location quotient analysis and shift-share analysis to assess local industry competitiveness)
- Examining the existing business base (data and techniques for assessing attributes of the local business base that affect the competitiveness and growth prospects of firms and industries)
- Analyzing economic geography (evaluating development opportunities and constraints related to population-serving economic functions)

PART III: AUDITING LOCAL RESOURCES

Session 6   **Evaluating Local Human Resources**
(1.5 hours)   (Handbook Chapter 6)
- Analyzing labor availability (labor force participation rates, discouraged workers, labor force composition by demographic group)
- Assessing labor force quality (analyzing local occupational mix, educational attainment, worker productivity and motivation)
- Assessing labor costs (conducting pay-per-worker comparisons)

Session 7   **Evaluating Non-Labor Resources**
(1 hour)   (Handbook Chapter 7)
- Location theory and considerations in assessing local strengths and weaknesses with respect to nonlabor location factors (physical resources, capital resources, knowledge resources, infrastructure, civic culture)

PART IV: THE ACTION PLAN

Session 8   **Strategy Development: Linking Analysis and Planning**
(1 hour)   (Handbook Chapter 8)
- Participants and sequencing of activities
- External and internal evaluations to identify "actionable" issues and potential response options
- Defining goals and objectives and strategies to achieve them
- Developing and implementing an action plan

Chapter 1
Overview of Strategic Planning

Points to Cover

- Definition of strategic planning

- Role of economic analysis in strategic planning

- Unit overview and introduction to analytical framework

Summary

The first unit introduces the concept of strategic planning and identifies the types of economic analysis that are useful in supporting that process. The benefits of developing local capacity to conduct this type of analysis should be noted, including the value of local input and insights in directing the analysis and the advantages of being able to monitor and evaluate the local economy on an ongoing basis. The text includes a summary of the types of questions addressed by the analytical techniques presented in subsequent units.

Resources/Examples

Figure 1.1 depicts the strategic planning process and the types of economic analysis that support different phases of the process. Steps 1-6, identified in the figure, represent a framework for the analytical component of strategic planning. Each step is treated in a separate handbook unit beginning with Chapter 3 and following sequentially (refer to "Chapter Overview" in Chapter 1).

Chapter 2
Structuring the Analysis:
Concepts and Issues

Points to Cover

- Selecting a unit of analysis

- Selecting a time period for analysis

- Selecting variables and data elements

- Establishing a frame of reference for interpreting data

- Working with data

Summary

This unit outlines the preliminary considerations for undertaking local economic analysis, including conceptual issues that will shape the analysis as well as practical considerations related to locating, acquiring, and using data.

Resources/Examples

- The handbook recommends using county-based geographic units—such as counties, metropolitan statistical areas (MSAs) or labor market areas (LMAs)—for much of the data analysis. Appendix A provides 1) a list of federally-defined U.S. metropolitan areas and 2) federal standards for defining metropolitan areas that will apply in the 1990s. This list can be used as a reference for identifying an appropriate study area and potential comparison areas. The instructor may wish to supplement this list with a list of labor market areas (LMAs) within the state or region.

- Figure 2.1 illustrates business cycles throughout U.S. history, for use in discussing trend analysis.

- Figures 2.2 and 2.3 illustrate long-term employment trends in a sample locality, overall and for a dominant industry, to illustrate the problem of distinguishing cyclical and secular change.

•   Table 2.1 summarizes data availability at the sub-county level, illustrating the data constraints that inhibit analysis at the sub-county level.

•   Figure 2.1 depicts the federal Standard Industrial Classification (SIC) code system that is used for reporting data by industry. Further information on the SIC system, including a list of industries at the 3-digit level of detail, is provided in Appendix C.

•   The box, "Estimating Undisclosed Data," provides a step-by-step method for overcoming the problem of nondisclosure of data due to privacy requirements, which often arises in working with industrially detailed federal data.

•   Use of comparison areas is suggested as a way to establish a frame of reference for data interpretation. The box, "Identifying Comparison Areas for Flint, Michigan," provides an example of how to select comparison areas.

•   References to major federal sources of data for local area analysis are provided in Appendix B, including references to reports and release dates for the 1990 Census. The instructor may wish to supplement this information with references to state-specific sources of data.

Chapter 3
Assessing Economic Performance and Condition

Points to Cover

•   Selecting variables useful for comparing "economic performance" (e.g., trends over time) and "economic condition" (e.g., levels at particular points in time).

•   Developing indicators to measure economic performance and condition (deriving annual rates of growth, adjusting for inflation)

•   Arraying and analyzing the data (with reference to examples)

Summary

       This unit introduces concepts and techniques for analyzing broad indicators of local economic vitality. After distinguishing between levels and trends for purposes of analysis, the unit introduces five variables that are routinely covered by published data sources and that are especially useful for initiating analysis: employment, unemployment, earnings, area personal income, and population. The unit concludes with examples of how each of these variables can be used in comparative analysis.

Resources/Examples

•   Separate boxes illustrate techniques for assuring data comparability by 1) annualizing and averaging to derive annual growth rates and 2) adjusting for inflation.

•   Tables 3.1 - 3.4 illustrate techniques for comparative analysis of total employment, unemployment rates, earnings, and area income and population.

Chapter 4
Analyzing the Structure and Dynamics
of a Local Economy

Points to Cover

•   Analyzing local industrial structure (examining the distribution of employment and earnings at the one-digit level of industrial detail, including shifts over time and in relation to other areas)

•   Analyzing industry growth patterns (examining rates of change in industry employment and earnings over time and in comparison to other areas)

•   Using location quotient analysis to identify local industry specializations

•   Using shift-share analysis to assess local industry growth performance

Summary

This unit presents techniques for analyzing the industrial structure of the local economy and underlying factors contributing to the economy's overall performance and condition. The unit begins with examples of the use of industry data at the one-digit level to analyze industrial structure and growth patterns. Attention then turns to more advanced techniques that can be used with data at the two-digit or three-digit level to assess local industry strengths and weaknesses. The accompanying discussion introduces relevant concepts from economic base theory.

Resources/Examples

•   A separate box compares the major federal sources of data for analyzing local industrial structure

•   Tables 4.1 and 4.2 illustrate the use of employment and earnings data at the one-digit level for comparative analysis of local industrial structure and industry growth patterns

•   Table 4.3 illustrates the use of employment and establishments data at the two-digit level to refine the analysis of industry growth patterns

•   A separate box provides a "Service Industry Classification Framework" to aid in categorizing service industries for meaningful analysis

•   Table 4.4 provides an example of location quotient analysis using industry data at the two-digit level

•   Supplementing discussion in the text, a separate box provides a simplified, step-by-step example of how to perform shift-share analysis

Chapter 5
Evaluating Local Growth Prospects

Points to Cover

• Using location quotient analysis and shift-share analysis for a "target industry analysis" that assesses local industry competitiveness

• Examining characteristics of the existing business base that may affect growth prospects, such as the nature of industry clusters, market and product development activities of area firms, and local entrepreneurship

• Examining aspects of local economic geography as they relate to site-specific development opportunities or prospects for development in non-basic, population-serving sectors

Summary

This broad-ranging unit presents a variety of techniques that can be used to highlight a local area's specific development opportunities and constraints. The unit begins by showing how location quotient analysis and shift-share analysis can be combined to categorize local industries for purposes of development planning. The next section presents techniques for analyzing attributes of industry operations in a local area that may influence competitiveness. The unit closes by introducing considerations related to an area's economic geography, or the geographic, population, and market characteristics that define a local economy's position in a regional economy.

At the conclusion of this stage of the analysis, there should be sufficient information to enable strategic planning participants to define critical issues and establish directions for subsequent analysis of local resources and response options.

Resources/Examples

• Figure 5.1 is a "decision tree" illustrating the use of location quotient analysis and shift-share analysis to assess industry competitiveness in order to target industries for development attention.

• The box, "Stimulating Service Sector Development," considers issues for development strategy that are raised by the shift to services.

•   Table 5.1 provides an example of shift-share analysis using industry data at the two-digit and three-digit level.

•   Table 5.2 draws upon the location analysis example in Table 4.4 and the shift-share example in Table 5.1 to illustrate the approach to industry targeting outlined in Figure 5.1.

•   Figure 5.2 presents a model of the determinants of industry competitive advantage, which has been adopted here as a useful framework for structuring the analysis of the local business base.

•   Table 5.3 illustrates data available for input-output analysis of local industry clusters.

•   Tables 5.4—5.7 illustrate uses of data available on business establishments.

•   Table 5.8 illustrates comparative analysis of components of population change.

•   Figure 5.3 illustrates use of a "population tree" to analyze and compare local demographic characteristics, as a way to derive insight on local markets for particular goods and services.

Chapter 6
Profiling Local Human Resources

Points to Cover

• Assessing labor availability (size of the potential labor force and numbers employed and unemployed, labor force participation rates overall and by demographic group)

• Assessing labor force quality (occupational mix, educational attainment, perceptions of workers and education and training institutions)

• Labor force costs

Summary

This unit and the next focus on the "supply" side of the economic development equation. Chapter 6 considers the role of human resources and how they can be evaluated. Techniques are introduced for evaluating 1) trends in the size and composition of the labor force, 2) labor force quality as revealed by the area's occupational mix and other available measures, and 3) labor force costs as indicated by payroll data.

Resources/Examples

• Table 6.1 provides an example of analysis of labor force data to understand the significance of the reported unemployment rate in terms of changes in the size of the labor force and the numbers employed and unemployed.

• Tables 6.2 and 6.3 illustrate the use of labor force participation data to assess the extent of discouraged workers or to identify labor force segments that are underutilized.

• Table 6.4 illustrates analysis of employment patterns by demographic group, which may clarify labor force implications of employment shifts.

• Table 6.5 provides the most recent industry-occupational matrix for the U.S. (1986), which can be used to estimate occupational employment from industry data when up-to-date occupational data are not available.

•   Tables 6.6 and 6.7 illustrate analysis of occupational employment data.

•   Table 6.8 compares unemployment rates and educational attainment among Michigan MSAs, showing an inverse relationship between unemployment levels and education levels.

•   Figure 6.1 summarizes questions appropriate for a structured interview with area employers about their growth prospects and requirements, including issues related to labor force availability, quality, and cost.

•   Tables 6.9 and 6.10 illustrate uses of payroll data for comparative analysis of labor force costs.

Chapter 7
Evaluating Nonlabor Resources

Points to Cover

•   Current perspectives on factors that support industry location and development in a particular area

•   Evaluating nonlabor attributes that comprise the local environment for business growth and industrial development (physical resources, knowledge resources, capital resources, infrastructure, civic culture)

Summary

This unit reviews current perspectives on location theory and determinants of industry competitive advantage, highlighting factors other than input costs that are increasingly coming into play in advanced economies like the U.S. Five major categories of nonlabor factors are identified and discussed in terms of analyzing their implications for local development strategy.

Resources/Examples

•   A separate box, "Investing in Information Capital," discusses the challenges facing those who hope to stimulate capital investment in an era when investment needs have changed dramatically.

Chapter 8
Linking Analysis and Planning:
Strategy Development

Points to Cover

•   Undertaking a systematic review of "external" trends and "internal" community attributes (business base characteristics, location factors, civic culture) to identify options for capitalizing on development opportunities or overcoming constraints.

•   Using the results of the external and internal evaluations to define goals and objectives and strategies to achieve them.

•   Developing an action plan to pursue the agreed-upon strategies that reflects community consensus, identifies resources, and assigns responsibility for implementation.

•   Providing for monitoring and adjusting the plan as needed.

Summary

This chapter discusses how to integrate the results of the data analysis into the larger planning process. It presents a framework for systematically reviewing the information that has been generated to identify steps the community can take to enhance prospects for economic growth. It also describes the process for using the results of this review to define goals and objectives leading to the adoption of strategies that comprise a plan of action.

Resources

•   Figure 8.1 is a matrix that lists the local business base characteristics and location factors discussed throughout the handbook, which can be used to aid community deliberations on possible response options.

•   The box "Strategic Development Goals," provides an example of goal statements based on strategic planning in Flint, Michigan.

•   The box, "Strategy Selection Criteria," provides an example of criteria that can be used to evaluate proposed development strategies for inclusion in an action plan.

INDEX